THE ITALIAN AMERICANS

Above: A group of *contadini* (peasants) in front of a house in Sensano (Siena), Tuscany, about 1892, photograph by Mario Nunes Vais/Credit: Gabinetto

THE ITALIAN AMERICANS

ALLON SCHOENER

COMMENTARY BY A. BARTLETT GIAMATTI

Bibliography by Remigio U. Pane

Macmillan Publishing Company
New York

Macmillan Publishing Company
866 Third Avenue, New York, NY 10022
Collier Macmillan Canada, Inc.

Library of Congress Cataloging-in-Publication Data

Schoener, Allon.
   The Italian Americans.

   Bibliography: p.
   Includes index.
   1. Italian Americans—History. I. Title.
E184.I8S44   1987   973'.00451   87-11040
ISBN 0-02-607180-0

Macmillan books are available at special discounts for bulk purchase for sales promotions, premiums, fund raising, or educational use. For details contact Special Sales Director, Macmillan Publishing Company, 866 Third Avenue, New York, NY 10022.

10 9 8 7 6 5 4 3 2 1

Printed in Singapore

TEXT PERMISSIONS

The author gratefully acknowledges permission to publish the following:

"Discovery of the New World" by Christopher Columbus, from *The Four Voyages of Christopher Columbus*, edited and translated by J. M. Cohen, copyright © 1969. Reprinted by permission of J. M. Cohen. "The Introduction of Italian Opera" from *Memoirs of Lorenzo Da Ponte*. Reprinted by permission of Elisabeth Abbott. "The Italians of California" by Marius J. Spinello, from *Sunset*, January 1905. Reprinted by permission of Lane Publishing Company. "Emigrating in the 1920s" by Luigi Barzini from *O America: When You and I Were Young* by Luigi Barzini, copyright © 1977 by Luigi Barzini. Reprinted by permission of Harper & Row, Publishers, Inc. "The Giannini Success Story" from *The New York Times*, October 30, 1927, copyright © 1927 by The New York Times Company. "A Second-Generation View," from "Memoir of My Mother" by Angelo P. Bertocci, copyright © 1937 by *Harper's Magazine*. All rights reserved. Reprinted from the June 1937 issue by special permission. " 'Breaking Away' " from *Mount Allegro: A Memoir of Italian American Life* by Jerre Mangione, published by Columbia University Press, copyright © 1942, 1981 by Jerre Mangione. Reprinted by permission of the author. "Emigrating in 1939" by Riccardo Massoni, from *American Mosaic: The Immigrant Experience in the Words of Those Who Lived It* by Joan Morrison and Charlotte Fox Zabusky, copyright © 1980 by Joan Morrison and Charlotte Fox Zabusky. Reprinted by permission of the publisher, E. P. Dutton, a division of NAL Penguin Inc. "Italian Americans, Fascism and the War" by Constantine Panunzio, from *The Yale Review*, 1941–1942, copyright © by Yale University. "600,000 Italians No Longer Regarded as Enemy Aliens" by Carlo Sforza and Gaetano Salvemini, from *The Nation*, November 7, 1942, copyright © 1942 by The Nation Magazine/The Nation Company. "Second-Generation Teenagers" by Francis A. J. Ianni, in volume 338 of *The Annals of The American Academy of Political and Social Science*, copyright © 1961 by The American Academy of Political and Social Science. " 'I Am Another Italian Success Story' " from "Hell's Kitchen" by Mario Puzo, from *The Immigrant Experience*, edited by Thomas G. Wheeler, copyright © 1971 by Dial Press. Reprinted by permission of Doubleday & Co., Inc. "A Recent Immigrant" by Mario Lucci, from *American Mosaic: The Immigrant Experience in the Words of Those Who Lived It* by Joan Morrison and Charlotte Fox Zabusky, copyright © 1980 by Joan Morrison and Charlotte Fox Zabusky. Reprinted by permission of the publisher, E. P. Dutton, a division of NAL Penguin Inc. "Mafia Myths and Mafia Facts" from "The Big Lie About Organized Crime: An *Attenzione* Magazine Symposium," copyright © 1980 by *Attenzione* Magazine. Reprinted by permission. "Coming Into Their Own" by Stephen S. Hall, from *The New York Times Sunday Magazine*, May 15, 1983. Copyright © 1983 by The New York Times Company. Reprinted by permission.

Other books by Allon Schoener

Portal to America: The Lower East Side (1967)
Harlem on My Mind: Cultural Capital of Black America (1969)
The American Jewish Album (1983)

Front endpaper: Emigrants in the port of Naples, about 1900/
Credit: Fototeca Touring Club Italiano

Back endpaper: The annual reunion of the Troiano family, representing three generations, Wyckoff, New Jersey, 1984/
Credit: Orazio Troiano

FOREWORD

Allon Schoener

Growing up in Cleveland, an urban-industrial center studded with Afro-American, Czech, German, Greek, Hungarian; Irish, Italian, Jewish, Polish, Rumanian, Russian and Slovak enclaves, it was impossible not to think "ethnic." I was exposed on daily trips by automobile, streetcar or bus to a multitude of languages and foods representing the map of Europe, all within a territory of one hundred square miles. As a teenager I worked in a relative's store in the heart of a remnant of Cleveland's initial Italian American immigrant neighborhood, and this was my first contact with either Italian or Italian American culture.

Although the language was not comprehensible, I learned to count and make change in Italian. When making deliveries to wholesale grocers, I savored imported Italian olives and peppers by reaching into the numerous open crocks which lined the aisles of these vast stores. Occasionally, I had lunch at the original Chef Boiardi's (later Chef Boy-ar-dee) restaurant, where Hector Boiardi, in his pristine white apron and chef's hat, stood behind the counter in an open kitchen, concocting incredible pastas and his special marinara sauce, which he sold in mason jars to his dedicated customers. Through my visits to homes in the area, I experienced the warmth, tenderness and affection characteristic of Italian families. I learned how much the combination of zesty food and wine could add to everyday life. Clearly, I became an Italian Americanophile (if there is such a thing) at an early age!

Later, at Yale, my second-generation Italian American roommate provided me with a first-hand opportunity to learn more about his group experience. When we often discussed our families, we realized there were both similarities and differences between the experience of Italian Americans and Jewish Americans. As representatives of our generation, we wanted to take advantage of new opportunities and become part of mainstream American society—in short, to break away from some of the constraints that had dominated our parents' lives.

Studying Italian Renaissance art history at London's Courtauld Institute led to frequent trips to Italy; I visited cities, churches and museums where I saw art and architecture representing the great monuments of Italian achievement. Not only was I exposed to the glories of historical Italian culture, and the beauty of the countryside and towns; I came to admire contemporary Italy, a nation with an illustrious past which managed to bring some of that same sensitivity into the present-day world. When the train reached the Swiss border at the end of my first trip to Italy, I wept for fear that I would never return. In addition to becoming an Italian Americanophile, I also became an Italophile!

And so I approached this book with affection and passion. It represents my strong desire to create a record of the lives and experiences of those representatives of one of the world's richest cultures who have chosen to settle in the United States. I am pleased that this will be the first book to present a comprehensive view of the experiences of Italian Americans from the time of Columbus to the present day. Although the public heroes are well represented, essentially this book focuses on the experiences of ordinary people. This is in keeping with my selection of visual

Processing tomatoes, Bensonhurst, Brooklyn, 1986, photograph by Ethel Wolvovitz. From left to right: Carmine Lupo, Allon Schoener, Nicola Lupo, Maria Lupo and Caterina Lupo.

and text documents which, as a cultural historian, I have edited. It is not my intention to rewrite history only through my own interpretation of data; I prefer to let visual and text documents speak for themselves. I hope readers will immerse themselves in the visual and verbal information I have assembled and in the scholarly and highly personal commentary by A. Bartlett Giamatti, and that they will create their own patterns of reading and viewing and come to their own conclusions. By making such decisions, the reader becomes an active agent in determining the effectiveness of this book.

TABLE OF CONTENTS

COMMENTARY
    A. Bartlett Giamatti   *Page 9*

CHAPTER ONE
ITALIAN CULTURE IN AMERICA/1492-1880
    Discovery of the New World, Christopher Columbus   *Page 25*
    An Appraisal of Columbus's Discovery, Girolamo Benzoni   *Page 28*
    "On the Principles of the American Revolution," Philip Mazzei   *Page 31*
    The Introduction of Italian Opera, Lorenzo Da Ponte   *Page 32*
    Garibaldi on Staten Island   *Page 34*
    Controversy About Brumidi's Frescoes in the Capitol,
        The New York Daily Tribune   *Page 37*

CHAPTER TWO
THE OLD COUNTRY/TURN-OF-THE-CENTURY ITALY
    "Everybody works. There is poverty," Pascal D'Angelo   *Page 41*
    The Italian Attitude Toward Emigration, Antonio Mangano   *Page 46*
    Against the Supposed Concern of the Bourgeoisie for the Emigrants,
        La Plebe   *Page 53*
    Letter from *Contadini* of Northern Italy to the Minister of the Interior, *La Plebe*   *Page 54*
    Serious Riots in the Streets of Milan, *Corriere della Sera*   *Page 54*

CHAPTER THREE
NEW LIVES IN THE NEW WORLD/1881-1914
    The Trauma of Departing from a Sicilian Village, Angelo Mosso   *Page 57*
    The Emigrants' Lament in Song   *Page 60*
    Conditions Endured by Emigrants Aboard Ship, Edmondo De Amicis   *Page 62*
    The Italians of New York, Jacob Riis   *Page 68*
    Arriving in Boston, Constantine Panunzio   *Page 70*
    A Son Writes to His Parents in Siena, G. Battista Turchi   *Page 74*
    Miserable Working Conditions, *Forum*   *Page 88*
    The Italians of California, Marius J. Spinello   *Page 112*

CHAPTER FOUR

SUCCESSES AND DISAPPOINTMENTS/1915-1929

Emigrating in the 1920s, Luigi Barzini   *Page 143*

Returning Home, Constantine Panunzio   *Page 150*

The Giannini Success Story, *The New York Times*   *Page 154*

Caruso's Silver Jubilee, *The World*   *Page 158*

The Last Statement of Bartolomeo Vanzetti   *Page 165*

CHAPTER FIVE

IMMIGRANTS AND THEIR CHILDREN/1930-1945

A Second-Generation View, Angelo P. Bertocci   *Page 167*

"Breaking Away," Jerre Mangione   *Page 169*

Emigrating in 1939, Riccardo Massoni   *Page 172*

Italian Americans, Fascism and the War, Constantine Panunzio   *Page 188*

600,000 Italians No Longer Regarded as Enemy Aliens,

    Carlo Sforza and Gaetano Salvemini   *Page 190*

CHAPTER SIX

FROM LITTLE ITALY TO FRONT PAGE/SINCE 1946

Second-Generation Teenagers, Francis A. J. Ianni   *Page 197*

"I Am Another Italian Success Story," Mario Puzo   *Page 207*

A Recent Immigrant, Mario Lucci   *Page 216*

Mafia Myths and Mafia Facts, *Attenzione*   *Page 224*

Coming Into Their Own, Stephen S. Hall   *Page 229*

EPILOGUE

Lee Iacocca   *Page 245*

BIBLIOGRAPHY   *Page 246*

Remigio U. Pane

ACKNOWLEDGMENTS   *Page 251*

PICTURE SOURCES   *Page 252*

TEXT SOURCES   *Page 252*

INDEX   *Page 253*

COMMENTARY
A. Bartlett Giamatti

Who is the Italian American? This volume, rich in documents and images, offers a many-textured answer. Or rather, it provides the reader with a wealth of materials with which to fashion his own answer. Any answer will be, however, necessarily cumulative. The experience of being Italian American is the result of individual family histories, and memories, as well as Italian traditions (cultural, social and political), all filtered through when a family arrived in America, where it settled, who has joined the family since and whether Italy continues to play a role in the individual's or family's life.

This experience is less a culture, I believe, than a shared sensibility, an awareness of similar roots, of common myths and of a pride whose chief ingredient is filial piety. By filial piety I mean that fierce delight in being descended from a culture that created or transmitted many of the core values, secular and religious, of Western civilization. For those who refer to themselves as Italian Americans or (less frequently now) as Italo-American or (more frequently in this age of ethnic differentiation) as Italian, the term "filial piety" may also point to one of the sustaining ideals of the Italian American, the family.

In what follows we will see the powerful image of the Italian family, intimate and extended, reiterated over and over again, each iteration reinforcing the image until the family, its sanctity and durability, becomes a part of our mythology. The myth of the Italian family is now an indispensable component of the Italian American family's genuine closeness and enduring strength.

Myths are not falsehoods; they are unifying fables that tell essential truths. The Italian, and Italian American, family is strong, its strength derived from many sources in addition to the constant attention the idea of the family receives from its members. Through almost fifteen centuries of domination by numerous foreign conquerors, and across almost a millennium of factional strife and division and political upheaval, the Italian family emerged as one of the few institutions on the peninsula to survive intact. And when the great wave of emigration began to roll toward America about one hundred years ago, and the Italian family became the Italian American family, its tensile strength was tested

A. Bartlett Giamatti in his office as President of Yale University, 1984, photograph by T. Charles Erickson/Credit: Yale University Office of Public Information

as the family stretched across the Atlantic and finally to the Pacific.

As husbands left wives and children behind, often to return and bring the whole family back to America; as young men left Italy only to go back to marry and then return to start American families; as families came over together and spread out, now part of the family of a village or a region often settled wholesale in the New World; or as Italian families simply remained apart for decades or more, the Italian American family tested itself. While it was at times unmended, it was almost always unbroken. The primacy of those for whom one worked, those whom one trusted and those whom one cherished remained constant despite separation and struggle. In an imperfect world, it is the family, where one does not have to be on guard, where one finds support, that reinforced and today reinforces the central place of the family in Italian American consciousness, and in this book as well.

The freedom from constant wariness, the freedom to assume support and nurture rather than external oppression or casual duplicity, is part of any strong family's strength. And freedom, in these terms and others, is also a constant in this book: the surge to freedom, freedom to find room to breathe, to find work, to find a way to break the ceaseless monotony of centuries of brutal sameness, is a chord, played in variations, over and over.

A visceral devotion to the ideals of republicanism and of liberty, as old as the Roman Republic, revived again in Renaissance Florence and spread throughout Europe by humanist learning and teaching, is reflected here in the passionate principles of Philip Mazzei (in language we would describe as Jeffersonian); in the deeds (inspired in part by Mazzini's egalitarian principles) of Giuseppe Garibaldi; in the academic yet memorable frescoes by Constantino Brumidi in the nation's Capitol. Despite the fact that the idea of Italy was as old as Virgil, Italy itself long lacked political coherence or civil stability. Yet the ideals of civic unity, liberty of individual choice and freedom from foreign oppression were, from Dante on, constantly articulated, and the core of these values, drawing on Roman principles, would be car-

World map, by Battista Agnese, 1544/Credit: John Carter Brown Library. Agnese, a Genoese mapmaker who worked in Venice in the mid-sixteenth century, was recognized as one of the most prolific cartographers of the period. He was noted for his great skill as a draftsman and for the beauty of his embellishments. This world map represents re-

cent geographical discoveries and shows in black the route of Ferdinand Magellan's voyage around the world. The route from Spain to America is shown in gold. Also indicated is a narrow strip of land on the coast of North America, reflecting Giovanni da Verrazzano's voyage from North Carolina to New York and to Newfoundland in 1524-1525.

ried at various levels of consciousness by early travelers and later immigrants to the New World. There, it was thought in a thousand different ways, ancient promises might be kept. In important ways, though not in every way, those promises were kept.

Almost nothing, however, comes without its opposite somewhere in attendance. And so it would be with this hunger for personal liberty and yearning for freedom from exploitation. The very perception of a world unchanging in its harshness or hostility bred into the family its strength, including its strength to resist all outsiders; and bred into the individual Italian, particularly the poor, as well a reticence and an instinct for independence. In its cultural manifestations, this outlook showed itself as an Italian hauteur concerning cultures and peoples from over the Alps, whence since Hannibal had come foreign oppressors. In its individual manifestations, this wariness showed (and shows) itself in an anarchic strain in the Italian soul, a strain that holds no faith in any kind of institutional continuity or institutionally inspired coherence but which lauds itself for independence and a belief that only the single self can be trusted. (The family is thus an extension of self.)

This darker hue, a mistrustful, self-absorbed streak that refuses to acknowledge any authority or rule except the code of the individual, was translated to America's shores as well. It came with a people, many of whom long poor and oppressed, who had become accustomed to believing that anyone outside the immediate self or family circle could only wish one ill.

Beneath whatever came or comes to be the experience of being Italian American lies the dynamic culture of an ever-changing Italy. While it is obvious how much Italian culture has contributed to Western culture, and thus in myriad ways to American culture, the Italian American of the second or third or fourth generation may often no longer know where to locate the older culture within, or to assess what the older culture gives to native American culture and experience. Yet if the Italian American wishes to begin to answer the question posed at the outset of this essay—who is the Italian American?—he cannot do it either in ignorance of the culture of his forebears as it existed or exists today, or in reliance solely upon some comfortable but vague notion that Italian Americans exist in America as a unitary group, separate unto themselves and largely without a defining earlier history. Indeed, to the extent that Italian Americans believe they are a people without defining roots in an older European culture, they are quintessentially American. For it is above all Americans who tend to ignore history in their pursuit of "self-reliance."

Nor in arguing for a definition of Italian Americans as Americans focused with pride upon changing Italian culture do I presume to deny that Italian Americans share experiences unconnected to Italy or to Italian culture. Certainly for Italian Americans there are shared assumptions—the primacy of the family being one of them, the inevitability of work (very different from a Protestant "work ethic") being another. But after two or three generations in this country, these Americans share assumptions based mostly on handed-down memories—or rather handed-down assumptions based on memories—about the first arrivals who founded the family in America, about language perhaps, about food certainly, about how to behave and where to go on holidays, about perceived or painfully real instances of discrimination, about why perhaps it is not necessary to be totally absorbed by the (or any) Church. In many cases, these memories are living ones, that is, experiences for good or ill

which repeat themselves. As such, they add to the faded pictures and old postcards and albums and to family or community oral traditions and serve to freeze those memories in time, with a renewed clarity.

If there is, therefore, a distinctively American experience of being Italian American, as opposed to a changing relationship with Italian culture seen proudly by American eyes, it is that sense of the moment frozen, the shared memory of steerage or Ellis Island or early struggles that few now, if any, are old enough to hold first-hand, but which millions remember as a version of someone else's memory. That interior life lived by remote control is not invalid and it is not illegitimate; it is, however, increasingly second-hand (and third-hand and fourth-hand). This memory of someone's earlier memories must be cherished but should not be allowed, in my opinion at least, to be a substitute for the primary experience of direct contact with the history, language, literature, customs, politics, institutions, leisure, food—culture—of Italy: Italy as it was when first one's forebears left it, and Italy as it is today.

In the children of first immigrants there was often ambivalence: ambivalence about whether one was completely American or only transplanted Italian. This was the generation that grew up in households whose life was a displaced, frozen version of Old Country ways, as would be true in any immigrant family anywhere in the world. It was also the generation that first went to American schools, American military service, American jobs, and first knew American forms of nativistic contempt and prejudice. For that generation, the deepest ambivalence consisted in not being certain how to cherish the older generation and its ways and also to accommodate the culture, so palpable in the family, that the older generation had by definition rejected by coming to America. That generation, however, can now look upon its American children, its grandchildren, perhaps its great-grandchildren. It can feel a fit in a country which, while never perfect, is always good and is now completely its own.

Arma virumque cano, Troiae qui primus ab oris
Italiam fato profugus Laviniaque venit
litora—

I sing of arms and the man
who exiled by fate first came
from the coasts of Troy
To Italy and the Lavinian shores—

So Virgil opens *The Aeneid*, the poem of those who would become the Italic people, singing of the weapons of war and the man who first came from Troy to Italy and Lavinian shores, *fato profugus*, propelled or exiled by fate. The phrase will resonate through the history of the peninsula, and will mark a people who saw themselves as constantly conquered. Theirs would be a history streaked by fatalism, an attitude of melancholy acquiescence in the conviction that a nameless destiny controls all and all is passing. As a result, they would be a people perceived by foreigners, friendly or hostile, as attached only to the moment, to the sun and song and flesh of today, to the here and now.

Virgil's great poem is about many things but it is at bottom a poem about burden: about the labor of making a new city out of the memory of a city in flames, about the pain of turning individual needs into institutional certainties, about how long striving to build a future only finds the past repeated, the old patterns too desirable to deny. It is a poem about work, and loss—loss of parent, loss of home, loss of love, loss of the ability (if one is dutiful) to lay down burdens. No poem of our culture is so driven by the past, so respectful of the past, so instinctively retrospective as it inexorably progresses. The closer we come to founding Rome, to reaching home, the clearer it is how much has been lost in the effort, how shot through any future will be with the past, how heavy is the burden of being conscious of what went before.

Fato profugus: driven by fate. Europe is founded by those who go west. The western lands are discovered and colonized by the losers, the exiles, those who flee toward where the sun sets, where the light fails. Only those driven away from home to find a new home go west. As they go, they are condemned to remember a time, now past, when one did not live burdened by remembering the past.

Fato profugus: fate is the constant companion. Not an abstraction, not some disembodied force, like History or the Spirit of the Time, or a proposition, like All Men Are Created Equal. Fate is a familiar spirit, in constant attendance, a household presence. Not a god to be worshiped or feared, not a guest to be served or resented. It is a whisper in the blood, an assumption that is so old and accepted that it is unspoken. Fate is like the smell of cooking, the sound of rain on the roof, the first memory of the first beloved. It is part of what explains who we are. It is at the beginning—*fato profugus*—the uncontroversial cause for how we came to be the way we are.

Virgil's poem in ways profound and subversive shaped Western culture from the Empire through the Age of Expansion. The poem was primer to the schoolchild, moral allegory to the faithful, storehouse of style for the learned, and it seeped into the Christian West as only those expressions of genius that set a language and a perspective on history can. Nowhere did this Virgilian sentiment seep more deeply than into the culture of his countrymen. For more than a thousand years, Virgil's sweet bitterness, about gain and loss, about law proving stronger than love, about how no one is free of what was, about fate as the prime source of all, found its way into every crevice of Italic consciousness.

What does Virgil have to do with immigrants? Nothing and everything. The unlettered or barely literate who crowded the docks and decks, waiting to leave, would not have known *The Aeneid* and would not have believed they were affected by Roman culture. They would have understood completely, however, what *fato profugus* meant. And they would have immediately grasped the rightness, the fitness, of the phrase, and all it meant, to explain their lives and why they too were going west.

In Chapter Two, the faces of those fateful people stare out at us. They are faces accustomed to sameness—the same sun, the same work, the same land, the same responsibilities, the same hunger, the same sense of sameness that had been experienced by all who came before. They are faces for whom nothing is unfamiliar. Whether at work, or pausing for a photo that will change nothing, or waiting to leave home, *fato profugus*—whether urban or rural, northern or southern, goaded by Socialism, stirred by rebellion, or seemingly innocent of ideology—the faces that look out are not curious faces. They are faces that know they will see nothing new. They are not unhappy; they are not happy. Neither pleasure nor pain, neither joy nor despair is available—such emotions do not enter. Those are mere words, not serious considerations. These are faces

without illusions and, in those past puberty, without the desire to entertain or generate illusions. They are faces at peace with burden, comfortable with ceaseless work, occasionally—as they pose—amused, not so much at the novelty of the camera as at the failure of novelty to enthrall. They are sophisticated faces, endlessly wise in the futility of thinking wisdom will make anything better.

Work is everywhere. Work is life. Who said it would be otherwise? Work is the great given—work with the hands, the back, the legs, the head. Work is a part of nature, and seems inexhaustible. It is neither dignified nor undignified—any more than the sun or drought or the pain of childbirth or a constant measure of hunger is dignified or undignified. Work is no more to be sentimentalized than fate is, or than any other fact of nature should be. These people do not know some would see them as "picturesque" or noble or—to quote the part of the poem on the Statue of Liberty that is usually omitted in our pageants—as "the wretched refuse of your teeming shore."

Work is breathing. For work one needs space. Without space to work there is no space to breathe. The decision to leave, to go west, to emigrate, therefore, is not a romantic decision—involving dreams of adventure or high principle; it is not often a rebellious decision—involving deep ideological convictions. It is a difficult and momentous decision, involving great risks, and it is a brutally simple decision, involving a choice to submit to be driven by fate. It is the decision to find work. It is the decision to seek the freedom to labor, to fulfill an instinct.

Not to find gold in the streets, though the simple said that is why they went and why they are bitter about how it came out; not primarily to find political equality, though, in a way no one could ever have imagined, they did. They now encountered a

Above: A group of farm workers, Alto Adige, about 1900/Credit: Gabinetto

Above: Miniature portrait of Philip Mazzei, attributed to Pierre-Alexandre Tardieu, about 1790/Credit: Biblioteca Nazionale di Firenze. Philip Mazzei was born in 1730 near Florence. At the urging of Benjamin Franklin, whom he met in London, Mazzei emigrated to Virginia in 1773, where he established an experimental agricultural colony. He was elected to local office in Albemarle County and, at the suggestion of Thomas Jefferson, Mazzei prepared a series of articles which presented a philosophical justification for the American Revolution against England. *Below:* Portrait of Giuseppe Garibaldi, chromolithograph, about 1870/Credit: Garibaldi Meucci Museum. Giuseppe Garibaldi, the liberator of Italy, arrived in New York as a political refugee and lived on Staten Island with Antonio Meucci, whose disputed invention of the telephone was never fully resolved. This was a particularly discouraging period in Garibaldi's life because he found himself unable secure the command of a merchant vessel in this country. *Opposite page: George Washington in Consultation with Thomas Jefferson and Alexander Hamilton,* U.S. Capitol fresco by Constantino Brumidi in Senate Reception Room, 1870–1873/Credit: National Geographic Photographer Courtesy U.S. Capitol Historical Society. Called "Michelangelo of the United States Capitol," Brumidi became an American citizen in 1857. During the terms of six presidents, he prepared wall and ceiling frescoes throughout the building, culminating with the dome of the Capitol in 1865.

country, America, that was not built by fate but was dedicated to a proposition. It was a country conceived not as a statue to be shaped by centuries of labor but as a great, green, wild Eden where you shaped yourself first.

They went to find room to breathe work. I often have thought of what an act of extraordinary courage it is to emigrate in a time of peace, to give up land and language, to shuck off precisely what is familiar, even if endlessly so. To go when only hope for betterment or the belief that it cannot be worse over there impels one, must be an extraordinary act of courage, I thought. In some cases perhaps it is. But in most of the cases glimpsed at in this book, I believe now that such an overlay as I once projected would have been treated by those involved as a sentimental fiction.

To decide to leave because you cannot breathe, cannot find work, cannot see a future that is anything but a long, long past is not an act of great courage or moral assertion. It is an act of common sense. It is an act of survival. And like all acts of survival, it involves overcoming real fear, and gauging high risks, and then—doing it. Not talking about it, or worrying it, or beating it "to airy thinness": But simply, momentously, doing it.

And so over five million—about eighty percent from the Kingdom of the Two Sicilies and about twenty percent from northern Italy—did it. Many returned—bitter or broke or desperately homesick or, relatively speaking, well-to-do—permanently to Italy, but the great majority did not return. They went to America, for the freedom to breathe and the room to work, and they settled. Even when these new Americans went back to visit Italy, they were changed. They were different. They had ridden their fate to another shore, and seen things unseen before. Whatever in their heart of hearts they thought of America—and for many the experience was very mixed—they told great tales of the New World, fables and fibs and truths and fictions, thereby justifying their exile by calling America home. They made up an America that did not exist but which took on a reality, not only in the Italian village or neighborhood but also in the head of the temporarily returned immigrant. When back there, the meanness and narrowness of that life now appeared obvious—as a childhood room suddenly seems too small to the adult who returns to visit. America now in the telling became more spacious, more free, more abundant in the goods of the world. The creature comforts even of tenement life were somehow more creaturely than the stone or thatched or mud dwellings that had baked forever in the sun. The temporarily returned immigrant became more and more American, focused attention on America, identified with America in his moments of explanation and realized how American he had become. Never more so than when back there.

Once immigrants had seen America, they were spoiled forever for the old life because now they knew a fantastic, open secret: life—even life tough and demanding in a strange land—can change. Change is possible. Change is America. Change can happen in the space to change. America was a place which was not like Italy, the Italy that was ever the same, shaped by fate, burdened by history. America was different, and Americans were all different. And anyone, by work, could become an American, could change or make up or refashion oneself into this new, different and (everyone in America said) better creature.

In America there was the chance for change. That story went back, and millions came. The American dream began with the dream of a land of change. It was the first dream not

fated-to-be that anyone could remember. It was itself, like America, a new thing.

In the new century, they continued to come, now not driven by fate so much as drawn by the dream.

In 1910, Pascal D'Angelo said it most clearly:

Our people have to emigrate. It is a matter of too much boundless life and too little space. We feel tied up there. Every bit of cultivable soil is owned by those fortunate few who lord over us.

There is the motivation of the vast majority—the desire to breathe, the desire to seek the space to work. There also is the tone of resentment that would never leave many who came over (and would impel not a few to return)—the anger of having been denied one's homeland, one's very soil, by the fortunate few who controlled the land and therefore the means to life.

Not all who came beginning a hundred years ago were the southern Italian poor. There were also the young, the adventurous, the middle class, the educated, the professionally trained. They too came, and not only from central or northern Italy; nor were all those from the north or the central region well-off or well-educated or better situated by fate or circumstance than the southerner. Let us remember at all times that generalizations about "everyone" are false. The peculiarly American desire to espouse humble origins—most people in the world would have you believe they derive from noble antecedents; our culture exalts Horatio Alger, not the ruined aristocrat—should not gloss over those who in fact came in relative comfort and prospered relatively early. But the vast majority were poor; and their experience, caught in Chapters Three and Four, shows the face of struggle.

Where there was indeed more space, and a climate similar to Italy, the Italian immigrant—in California—shook off the grimness and the ghettoized existence quicker. In the eastern cities, in Chicago, it remained the predominant experience that those who sought space lived in crowded tenements, bursting streets, laundry-festooned alleys. Those who had never been more than ten miles from a small village now became quintessentially urban—adding to the sounds, smells, street cries, religious traditions, festivals, crime and swirling polyglot life of some of the world's fastest-growing, most distinctive cities. Whenever Italian immigrants settled in the East or Midwest, their urban life was a version of New York's life, the dominant port, first place of entry, unique collection pool for the streams flowing to America from the Ukraine to Ulster, Piraeus to Oslo. A. P. Giannini, a genius and pioneer in his profession, might have emerged anywhere, but in retrospect at least, San Francisco seems the most plausible soil. Remembering a Giannini or Luigi Barzini, remembering all the mixtures implicit in the millions who came, we must also remember that the predominant experience, the experience of the mass, as it was recorded in pictures and words and popular stereotypes, becomes the screen through which virtually all immigrant experience, including that of immigrants who did not share the mass experience, is seen.

If, for instance, a male founder of a family in this country came at the turn of the century from Sicily and possessed a law degree and quickly prospered in the New World, living surrounded by non-Italians, assimilating with his family more quickly to America because less impeded by any number of factors but above all by any sense of insecurity, then all that family history, distinctive, atypical, burnished by retelling, will remain alive in the family. It will animate subsequent generations. But it will rarely be told or recorded, because it will not be "typical" to many other Italian Americans and therefore will be viewed in a curious way as less "American." *No great struggle, no great pride in achievement* runs the axiom of the third generation.

Unless it is too overwhelming, too strong to be hidden or rounded into shape, the atypical experience is often, in the telling, bypassed because it does not conform to what the mass of Italian Americans wish to believe—for whatever reason—about themselves. Not only is any immigrant group always conceived by the dominant majority of people not in the group as being composed of people who are all alike, but each immigrant group has its own versions of what all its members went through. The anomalous background of experience in America is not accepted by the rest of the group as "representative" or by other (nongroup) Americans as "typical." (Sephardic Jews in America, for example, have not had the same life here as the mass of Jews from Eastern Europe; most accounts of Jewish immigrant life composed by Jews ignore the Sephardic experience almost entirely; most non-Jews in America would not understand the differences in rite, education, language, memory or status or think them worth remarking.) All this is asserted so that when trying to assimilate the rich variety of text and image about Italian immigrants and their Italian American descendants after 1880 and until today, we may be mindful of the nuances that are lost, and the differences that are collapsed as we try to reassemble what this life may have been like.

Take language. That was the first barrier to the Italian immigrant. Work was easy. If one could find it. Work for men in mines, on railroads, as stone or marble cutters; digging canals or tunnels, building buildings, paving or cleaning streets, serving in shops or restaurants, working in factories—to find work might be hard, but working was no barrier in itself.

For women, sewing or washing or piecing or picking or ironing or weaving or carrying—work was natural, once obtained. Singing, teaching, baking; priest, nun, lawyer, doctor. Work is part of life, like bread or wine, if it is available.

Language was a barrier. Not for the Irish, who spoke English; not for the Scandinavian, nor the German, who spoke Germanic languages (as English is) and for whom learning another was not a great barrier. But for any Italian, English is very difficult. It is not simply that certain sounds in English do not exist at all in Italian (like *th*) or that certain letters in the alphabet in English would never have been seen by Italian eyes (certainly *k*; perhaps *j* or *y*). Italian is a language in which every consonant or vowel in every word is pronounced, and English is not. To learn to speak, read and write English is for most people not born to it a very difficult task.

Jacob Riis, Danish immigrant, patron-saint observer of immigrants, sums up the language problem while observing the *padrone*, or middleman, the broker of life, liberty and pursuit of happiness in the New World. Of the Italian immigrant, says Riis:

> *His ignorance and unconquerable suspicion of strangers dig the pit into which he falls. He not only knows no word of English, but he does not know enough to learn. Rarely only can he write his own language. . . . Even his boy, born here, often speaks his native tongue indifferently. He is forced, therefore, to have constant recourse to the middle-man who makes him pay handsomely at every turn.*

I am not sure how to read Riis's comment—"he does not know enough to learn." Does he mean the Italian is too ignorant to learn English, does not even know it is in his self-interest to learn? Or does Riis mean that learning a foreign language is like making money—if you wish to acquire a great deal, it helps to begin with some—and the Italian immigrant did not have enough English capital even to get started properly?

Riis probably intended the former meaning. I think he overestimates the immigrants' ignorance or indifference and underestimates the difficulty of the language itself. The ambiguity remaining in his own prose may make my point about the difficulty of mastering English as he asserts his. No matter. Many Italian immigrants were barely literate, if literate at all, in

Above: "Pietro learning to write," Jersey Street, New York, photograph by Jacob Riis, about 1890/Credit: MCNY

their own language. To learn to read and write English if one could barely read and write at all was, in addition to learning spoken English ("by ear," as it were, in the streets), another barrier. And then—beneath the difficulty of learning to speak English, or to read or write any language, much less English—there is a basic question: What was the language of the Italian immigrant?

In most or at least the majority of cases, the first language of the immigrant was not Italian. That is, it was not the Italian descended from the grammar, syntax and vocabulary of Tuscan, which, since Dante's *Commedia*, had evolved into the standard Italian of Italy. The first language of a majority of early immigrants was a dialect, often, as in the case of those from Lombardy or Piedmont or Sicily, virtually a separate language; in other cases, as with those from the Abruzzi or the peninsula south of Naples, the language had a style and vocabulary and pronunciation virtually impenetrable to other Italians. Dialects, or at least regional accents and styles, were ubiquitous, often distinguishable as slightly different from village to village. The differences from major city to major city (Genoa to Venice, for instance) or from region to region, even when they were proximate, much less from north to south, were vast. Late-nineteenth-century Italy was unified in name and perhaps by ancient dream. But the differences, tiny and large, among her people were deep and extensive, and nowhere were they more pronounced than in language. Even those immigrants who spoke and read and wrote "Italian" often spoke a dialect or a regional or local speech as well. This was true also of those from Tuscany; there was, after all, and is today a form of pronunciation whereby the hard *c* sound is aspirated, and a syntactic style (and a linguistic snobbery) among Florentines that makes their discourse, while not strictly speaking dialectal, at the very least unsusceptible of easy (or at times any) comprehension by the uninitiated. They say they cannot help it.

After the Second World War, the power of radio and then television brought to all Italians, including those in the more remote reaches or rural parts, the sound of standard Italian on a consistent basis. The ability to speak a dialect, or to speak with a marked regional accent, was overlaid by the capacity, if not always by the disposition, to speak Italian. Regional differences of accent and style, however, have no more disappeared in Italy today than they have in the United States. And as in America, so in Italy—an accent, a regional inflection, a syntactic style or the use of local vocabulary brings with it to the ears of the general population a host of biases, assumptions, stereotypical reactions, smiles.

Today's reactions are built upon an Italy which, a hundred years ago, was truly divided by how one spoke, by how one spoke when binding oneself into an extended family braced against the world. A Sicilian or Neapolitan aristocrat in 1880 could (and would) spend the morning reading an English novel or corresponding in French with a friend in Paris, in Italian with a friend in Milan, and then could (and would) turn to his footman and ask, in the purest Neapolitan or Sicilian, to see the steward of his estates for a report on the health of his holdings. He would then converse with the steward in the same dialect or a variant of it, depending on how far the steward lived from the city. The language the aristocrat, the footman, the steward, and by extension the artisan or peasant, spoke between or among themselves did not obliterate the distinctions of class and education between and among them. Those distinctions remained firmly intact. But they remained intact within a common

world, a world completely, comfortably, impenetrably defined by the common, local language. Was that language technically a variant of Italian? Technically, yes. It was also a shield against outsiders (beginning with all other Italians) who did not speak it.

When Riis refers to the "ignorance and unconquerable suspicion of strangers" as the tools that dig the Italian a pit, a pit out of which he cannot climb by learning English, Riis is correct to associate suspicion with language. He sees, however, only half the picture, the Italian who cannot learn English, the Italian sealed off from the rest of America. He does not see how secure the Italian immigrant was, how happily sealed in, in a dialect or quasi-dialect, a way of speech only technically Italian, a language precious, familiar, dear. A language that at home in Italy had shaped a stable—if difficult or claustrophobic—world and which here, in America, was the only instrument available to shape coherent space in the vastness. It was a tool not to dig a pit but to build a house; it was a tool to build a place to live, one in which you know not only where you are but who you are.

Language was a barrier. Because spoken English was difficult. Because language written, language read—any language—was unknown territory, a new world to which no passage was available. And because the native language one spoke—whatever language it was, whatever they might be—was so necessary to retain, as shield, as security blanket, as proof of identity.

The barrier of language broke, however, as time passed. English became the language of the first generation born here. For a child growing up hearing his parents' native language at home, English was encountered first at school. What the child heard at home, and spoke to his parents then and perhaps for years to come, was in most instances another language entirely. It was not Italian, and it was no longer the Italian dialect the original immigrants came with. It was, over time, a language that had absorbed English, lost its ties to the Old Country, evolved into a tongue neither Italian in any sense of the word (no one in the old village would recognize it) nor English. It was a tongue spoken in the family, on the block, to the relatives, in the neighborhood. English words had acquired vowels to fill lacunae in the original dialect (*car* became *carro*) and the immigrant language, spoken only in America to others whose lives were passed here, evolved.

The evolution was not unlike the evolution of Italian names in America—some names lost vowels or consonants (Giammattei became Giamatti), some were anglicized (Benedetto became Bennett), some were translated (Vinciguerra became Winwar). The evolution of names, or of dialects, was usually a function of adaptation or convenience, rarely of planning. Names were changed by immigration officials or school administrators to suit themselves; language changed to suit new circumstances. In the Old Country cellars were unheard of; there was no word in any dialect, or within reach in Italian, for the English *basement*. Thus, in the New World the word *basciamento* (or, pronounced southern Italian–style, *basciament'*) was born. One can claim the original immigrants who remained in America were often people without a language; they had forgotten their native dialect, they never mastered English, they often could speak only the third thing—whatever their native tongue (whatever it was) had turned into after thirty or forty years in America.

Such a view, however, is true for some but unfair to many. In fact, comprehension of English often became total, while the ability to pronounce clearly lagged. Often the old tongue remained fully serviceable, even if changed. The changes, after all, were sensible, comprehensible and fully in accord with the essential flexibility any living language possesses in order to remain the miraculous thing a language is—a common medium for human exchange. If there are those who suffered from never really being at home in the house of a language, it is or was many in the generation of the original immigrants' children. Despite being American, speaking English and making their way with often remarkable success in the world, there lingered for many of the second generation an insecurity, a hesitancy, a diffidence rarely glimpsed but always there. And this ambivalence about how well one fit, about how far one might go, about how at ease at some profound inner level one might dare to be, stemmed not from speaking the old/new tongue of parents that one first heard and spoke, but from finally speaking and reading and writing English first encountered in a public school where others were native speakers. For many in the second generation, their native tongue would always be somewhere down deep a second language. Their children, the original immigrants' grandchildren, would be free. They would be at home, in one language. In college many of them would study Italian.

But that would be later. At the beginning of emigration, language was a barrier. Constantine Panunzio, in 1902, says it all:

> In the homes and on the streets no English language was spoken save by the children; on the newsstands a paper in English could scarcely be found; here were scores if not hundreds of societies, national, provincial, local and sub-local, in which English was not usually spoken and in which other than American interests were largely represented.

Panunzio is resentful of those who used language as a barrier, a barrier to keep out America, and the English language. He will have none of it. Would he have approved of the self-help book of Professor Augusto Bassetti, with its three columns of language designed to help the immigrant learn English—the first column a "polite" and incredibly stilted English; the second a strange, phonetic-like transcription which, when read aloud, sounds like a parody of broken English; and the third column an artificial, textbook Italian never spoken anywhere? This pedagogical tool would have been useless to the illiterate; it could have been only minimally useful to the semiliterate, for whom the "Italian" would be as baffling as the English. Perhaps to the hardworking, dialect-speaking immigrant such a book was useful to pick out how to mispronounce English and simultaneously help create the Italglish that evolved in every community. Let Professor Bassetti's manual stand for all the middlemen who translated, brokered, mediated in the New World. (Many *padroni*, however, were not as well intentioned as Augusto Bassetti.)

Panunzio's annoyance at Italian used to avoid America is understandable, but so is the immigrant who clings to his old language in a world where even his own could not be trusted. In this, America was no different from Italy. One had to beware of everyone.

Constantine Panunzio touches on another crucial point as he comments on the tenacity of the Italian language in the immigrant community. He notes the plethora of associations: clubs, sodalities, societies—for mutual assistance, for insur-

ance, to provide burial, to promote Italian nationalism, or sport or culture or fellowship or regionally defined (Old Country–style) solidarity. The Italian is an instinctively gregarious creature, comfortable in extended families, crowds, markets, piazzas—in song, debate, commerce. The Italian has for centuries cherished the primary aggregation of the human family and all the versions of the family he could find, in his work, his village, his quarter, his region. And the Italian in America was no different.

The Italian becoming an American had come to a country that was also, from 1870 on, recovering from a savage Civil War. Reconstruction in America was a time when, among other things, the surge to fraternal organizations quickened, some ugly and nativistic, but most of them part of a decent desire to heal the wounds and mend the divisions made by the war. The immigrants who came to the country after mid-century brought their own associations, formed others of the types noted above for mutual support and comfort in the New World, and caught the fraternal current flowing in post-Bellum America, and in their way but for different reasons swelled that stream. (The mere presence of new immigrants, particularly those from Catholic Europe, particularly those with swarthy skins, also hastened the formation of societies like the Ku Klux Klan, devoted to hate.)

Not all the societies clung to or cherished by the immigrants had American roots. Some were brought with the immigrants. Among all the societies or associations brought over to or created in nineteenth-century America, the most infamous, most mythologized and most onerous for Italian Americans then and now is whatever is meant by "the Mafia."

More nonsense continues to be written about this alleged secret society than about any other group. Immense anguish has been caused to millions of upright and honorable Americans with Italian heritage and surnames by the myths, stereotypes and assumptions concerning the Mafia and "organized crime." Otherwise sensible and savvy Americans with Italian surnames have allowed themselves to look foolish denying the existence of American gangsters with Italian surnames (they exist) or denying that criminal organizations exist, among others, that are dominated or controlled by such gangsters. It is finally as foolish to deny the existence of Italian American gangsters and criminal combines of various kinds as it is bigoted to believe that the Mafia (or Cosa Nostra or any other media-sanctified name) is all-pervasive or that in America only Italian Americans are gangsters or, worst, that because one has an Italian surname, one may or must be "connected" in some sinister way. Much of the bigotry felt by Italian Americans throughout this century has its origins in fear and prejudice arising out of ignorant assumptions about the mysterious and malevolent Mafia.

On the other hand, for all the pain and human anguish the Mafia and all its myths have caused for generations of innumerable Italian Americans of probity and decency, it has also been Italian Americans (among others) who insist on romanticizing the Mob, in popular novels, on television and in films. It is also some Italian Americans who continue to urge the band at their daughters' weddings to play the so-called "Love Theme" from the film *The Godfather*, and who in other ways—if the truth be told—take a perverse kind of pleasure in mythologizing mobsters and in romanticizing people and (a largely fictional) way of life that causes such destruction to American society and so much shame to honest American citizens who proudly bear Italian names. Bigots will learn quicker that it is sheer, brute prejudice to associate only Italian names with criminality or criminal groups when some portion of the Italian American community, currently motivated by inner insecurity or desire for commercial gain, ceases making folk heroes out of thugs and ceases peddling the stereotypes bigots love to hate.

Much more a sensibility than a structure, an attitude rather than a society, the term "Mafia" and its variants have a Sicilian set of origins that are both mysterious and well researched. Because popular accounts, even those purporting to be serious, ignore or are ignorant of the large body of research on the phenomenon in nineteenth-century Sicily, I offer a brief account, in no way original but drawn from readily available nineteenth- and twentieth-century Italian sources, for the two-fold purpose of laying to rest some egregious fictions and of providing a basis for assessing the origins of what would, in America, change into a criminal class. That criminal element in the Italian American community, flourishing under Prohibition with other ethnically cohesive criminal groups against whom it competed, was never and is not now as organizationally coherent or structured as FBI Tables of Organization of Crime Families would lead anyone to believe. In fact, the relations among criminal groups (whether defined as ethnically cohesive or not) are more tribal than corporate, more the relation of clans through chiefs than a set of interlocking directorates sanctioned by some Satanic SEC.

In the case of groups of Italian Americans engaged in crime, the very family values which are so real and valuable in Italian and Italian American culture provide material for parody or inversion. The mythical Italian American crime families or sets of families are an image playing off the authentic devotion of Italian Americans to family values, just as the allegedly "organized" nature of criminal groups—complete with charts and boardrooms—is an image playing off the fact that criminal enterprise does provide a ghastly parody of legitimate free enterprise in some ways and the fact that groups—of whatever racial or ethnic background—compete, collude, collide and occasionally connect in ways that invert the principles and procedures of legitimate corporate life. In short, stereotypes contain grains of authentic reality, distorted and bloated into caricatures and parodistic images.

In nineteenth-century Sicily, what was *mafia*, and what was *mafioso*? First an adjective in Sicilian dialect for *pretty* or *potent*, and then the title of a play.

The word *mafia*, a noun used to describe a quality, and its principal variant, *mafioso* or *mafiusu*, used either as a noun (to describe a type of person) or as an adjective, existed in Sicilian dialect in the nineteenth century, particularly (according to Pitré, see below) in that section of Palermo, virtually a world unto itself, known as the Borgo. The words were known in speech but not in print before 1860. *Mafia* and *mafiusu* do not appear, for instance, in the first edition of the *Dizionario siciliano-italiano* published in Palermo in 1838.

There is evidence for the existence and meaning of the words *mafia* and *mafiusu*, and this evidence is found in the extraordinary work of the pioneer and founder of the study of folklore in Italy, Giuseppe Pitré. Pitré (b. Palermo, 1840 – d. Palermo, 1916) was trained as a physician and spent his life, as a professor and writer, studying all facets of the life of his fellow Sicilians. His prodigious scholarly efforts are collected in many volumes, including the twenty-five volume *Biblioteca delle tradizioni popolari siciliane (Library of Sicilian Popular*

Traditions or *Library of the Traditions of the Ordinary Life of the Sicilian People*). In his two-volume work entitled *Usi e costumi, credenze e pregiudizi del popolo siciliano (Habits and Customs, Beliefs and Prejudices of the Sicilian People)*, published in Palermo in 1889, Pitré devotes a substantial essay to the meaning of *mafia* and allied concepts including *omertà*, the code of secrecy and self-reliance that bound the poor together in their common abhorrence of civil authority.

Pitré's remarkable essay opens by mocking the false derivations even then current to explain the origins of the word (a subject to which we will return) and notes the notoriety already attendant upon the term. He notes that the word *mafia* first appears in a dictionary in 1868 (in Traina's *Nuovo vocabolario*) and that the subject had been treated by as distant a journal as *Lippincott's Magazine* (of Philadelphia) in 1879. He points out that the word existed in the spoken dialect of the Borgo in Palermo and then he offers this striking passage on the meaning of the word *mafia* in Sicilian dialect. It meant, he says:

> *Beauty, graciousness, perfection, excellence of its kind. A pretty girl, who appears to know she is good-looking, who is well-proportioned, and at the same time has about herself a certain quality of superiority and elevated bearing, has* mafia *and is* mafiusa, mafiusedda. *A simple person's small house, well-ordered, clean, neat, which is pleasant, is a house* mafiusedda, ammafiata. . . . *A domestic object, of such quality that it strikes the eye, is* mafiusu; *and how many times have we heard the cries in the streets [selling] fruit or housewares* mafiusi, *and even [the cries] for brooms:* Haju scupi d' á mafia! Haju chiddi mafiusi veru! . . . *[I have beautiful brooms! I have those really beautiful ones!]*

(Pitré, *Opere complete*, 1889, vol. 2; Florence, 1939, vol. 15, pp. 289–290)

The word that meant an innate superiority, a special quality of excellence that struck the eye as beauty, came to denote the quality, particularly in men, of comporting oneself with assurance, strength, faith in one's own ability to handle deftly any situation. The word meant a "style" as well as an inner quality, a way of comporting oneself with panache, as well as consummate faith in one's "manliness." In this sense, *mafia* was an unsophisticated or primitive version of what in the sixteenth century Baldassare Castiglione in *The Courtier* called *sprezzatura*, the courtier's capacity to conduct all phases of life—intellectual, amorous, artistic, social, political—with an effortless grace that concealed rather than emphasized the courtier's mastery of all demands, disciplines and situations. In a different way, the concept of *mafia* is—as has been remarked by others—also somewhat akin to the idea of *virtù* as propounded by Machiavelli in *The Prince*. *Virtù*, derived from Latin *vir*, "man," can be translated as "virtue" only if we forget connotations of moral qualities and remember that virtue has an older meaning, closer to "attractive power" or "valency," the ability to exercise force. Machiavelli's *virtù*, chief attribute of the successful prince, is best translated as "potency," and indeed some of that meaning resides in *mafia*. By adducing the sixteenth-century concepts of *sprezzatura* or *virtù*, I certainly do not intend to imply an influence on the formation of the nineteenth-century concept of *mafia*. None of the three terms is even remotely synonymous or connected (though the two sixteenth-century terms are complementary, both representing different ideals for successful courts), but they do all occur in a larger, self-conscious culture where questions of *bella figura*, of "face," of one's effectiveness as a function of how one appears, are important. And the terms all inhabit a common zone, where elegance, forcefulness and self-assertion (in various proportions) come together.

So *mafia* is at its origins a sensibility, a style of comportment, a masculine quality in a patriarchal world. Even in the nineteenth century, *mafia* or being *mafioso*—being, as it was said, *Cristianu* or *omu d'onuri* ("Christian" or "man of honor," in short, a real man)—was described as a kind of abased chivalric value, the romanticizing of *mafia* being part of its nineteenth-century (Romantic) origins. What was meant by conceiving *mafia* as the value of a primitive chivalry was that the term became connected to a code—the so-called code of silence, or *omertà*. *Omertà*, derived from *omu*, or "man," meant, like *mafia*, manliness or self-reliance.[1] But whereas *mafia* meant radical self-assertion and self-reliance in a hostile world, *omertà* meant a negative—silence, not speech; not having recourse in a hostile world to civil (or spiritual) authority; not assisting civil or spiritual authority in its work. *Omertà* meant trusting no one but oneself and therefore being one who could be trusted by family and friends to trust no one who was not family or friend. *Mafia* and *omertà* became intertwined; each word retained its own specific meaning, but they shaded into each other. To be one was to apprehend the other. So when in his essay Pitré could say the following about the meaning of *mafia*, we can see (as he does) the link to *omertà*. "La mafia," says Pitré, "is the consciousness of one's essential being, the exaggerated concept of individual force 'as the sole and only judge of every conflict, of every clash of interests and ideas' " (p. 292).

So far there is no identification of *mafia* (or indeed of *omertà*) with criminality. The exaggerated sense of the individual and his force as being alone sufficient to manage all human affairs and contingencies certainly implies a world bristling with hostility and oppression. It implies a sensibility deeply suspicious of authority, of law, of rule. It certainly exalts force over reason or mediation, and glorifies the heroic individual as the source of right and justice rather than any communal or commonly held religious ethic. It bespeaks a way of life, perhaps even a code of behavior, that is extralegal—so deeply are established authorities distrusted and feared—but which is not necessarily an illegal way of life. Because one hates policemen or priests does not necessarily mean that one is a criminal. One may be antisocial, or anarchic, or even in some basic sense uncivilized. But such a cult of radical individualism is not yet a criminal act per se, nor does such a sensibility necessarily create a criminal organization. Such a cult of radical individualism, built on centuries of suspicion and oppression, however, creates a fertile soil for criminality. Out of the deep, unrecorded Sicilian past emerged this cult of the man of strength, the swaggerer, the bully (the definition of *mafioso* in the 1888 edition of the *Dizionario siciliano-italiano*).

The word *mafia* has obscure roots. No one agrees on its derivation. Is it from Tuscan *maffia* ("misery") or a corruption of French *mauvais* ("bad")? Most probably not. Does it come from the initial letters of a purported nineteenth-century revolutionary slogan—"*Mazzini autorizza furti, incendi, avvelenamenti*"? Hardly likely. Even less likely, indeed the least likely of all on grounds of language, politics and common sense (and the derivation most often encountered today in popular accounts of the Mafia) is that the word *mafia* is formed of the first letters of a cry uttered during the Sicilian Vespers, a revolt against French

rule in the thirteenth century—"*Morte ai Francesi, Italia anela.*" This is perhaps the cry in history least likely to have been cried. I do not believe acronyms existed in the nineteenth, much less the thirteenth, century.

Some Italian scholars think the origins of the word may be Arabic. One source that has been proposed is *Ma^cafir*, the name of a clan in Sicily during the Arab domination; a second is *mahfil*, referring to a meeting place or place of gathering; a third is *ma'is*, "swaggering," "bragging." The last is the one most recently proposed (in the *Grande dizionario della lingua italiana*, ed. Salvatore Battaglia, UTET, Torino, 1975, vol. 9) but there is no certainty about the etymology. The mystery of the word's origins has always been part of the mystique of the Mafia.

There is no mystery, however, about when the word first appeared in print. It was in 1863, in Palermo, in the title of a play, *I Mafiusi di' li Vicaria*, by Giuseppe Rizzotto. Here the word, which meant a quality of personal self-assertion (and would continue to mean it), became the term for a type of dandy cum bully, embodying swagger, bravado and force.[2] The word became clearly and forever linked with criminals and, ultimately, with criminality.

Rizzotto (b. Palermo, 1828 – d. Trapani, 1895) participated in the revolutionary uprising of 1848 in Italy. An actor in various theatrical companies, he wished to create a Sicilian dialect theater. He wrote a trilogy, *I Mafiusi*, the first play of which was a hit, not only in Sicily but on the mainland; the subsequent plays were much less successful. The first, *I Mafiusi di' li Vicaria*, is about (and can be translated as) *The Tough Guys of the Big House*, the Vicaria being Palermo's prison. This play about prison life took, as a recent critic has noted, the model of the Neapolitan *camorra*, a criminal consortium, and applied it to a Sicilian setting, using the term *mafioso* from the general dialect and prison slang, and blending in elements from folklore and from earlier, popular literature that had romanticized bandits and brigandage (though *not* necessarily mafiosi) as part of the romantic, anti-Bourbon, revolutionary and nationalistic trends of the times.[3]

The impulses, local, national, even international, conspired to create a success for Rizzotto's play, and so a word indicating a sensibility, and a type, became indissolubly linked to a criminal class, to figures—urban or rural—who broke the law instead of merely distrusting legal authority. Whether in fact the city toughs, now given local habitation and a name—that is, circumstantiality and currency—by a literary work, came before or simultaneous with or after their rural cousins who are usually credited with creating a secret criminal class is not clear. Usually one reads that the stewards of vast, feudal-like

---

[1] Pitré, p. 294, derives *omertà* from *omu* and in a note adduces an analogy to "*virtus* in the basic Latin sense, that is, ruler of oneself and of that which pertains to a man."

[2] The same type in Naples, with perhaps less force and more flash, was called in Neapolitan a *guappo*, or, pronounced in a Neapolitan accent, a *guapp'*. The prevalence of the type, and his visibility in America as a neighborhood cult figure in the Little Italys of American cities, meant that the flashy, assertive, dandified *guapp'* became the stereotypical "wop."

[3] Pietro Mazzamuto gives an interesting account from before Rizzotto down to our day, with an anthology of relevant excerpts, in *La Mafia nella letteratura* (Palermo, 1970).

estates (*latifondi*), owned by absentee landlords in Palermo and other big cities, exploited their position as overseers and extorted from the peasants, terrorized the peasants, and thus—loosely organized into *cosche* or *famiglie*—created what would be known as the *mafia*, a secret criminal consortium. One can also read that the peasants, in order to protect themselves from corrupt stewards on the *latifondi*, organized themselves into a loosely linked series of groups, collectively known as the *mafia*, and that from these associations for mutual aid eventually grew a criminal code and "organization."

The basic problem with the pastoral theory of the Mafia—that is, the notion of rural roots for a criminal group—is that there is very little, if any, hard evidence for it. Like all pastoral visions, this theory of rural origins probably has city sources in various senses. It is most probably a product of urban-based authorities (prefects, police chiefs, professors) reading back into the countryside a concept, a terminology and even a set of types they had encountered first-hand in the cities. I do not doubt there were stewards of the vast estates who brutally took advantage of the peasants. I do not doubt peasants were forced together in bonds of suffering, silence and a hunger—sometimes satisfied—for retribution. Nor do I doubt the harsh, primitive life of western Sicily was particularly rich in oppression and resentment. Before one rushes, as some popular accounts I have read in English do, to a rural organization of criminals whose tight lines of organization stretch back to the structure of the Roman legions (!), one might pause to ask some simple questions—such as: In an incredibly impoverished countryside, upon whom did these highly organized rural "families" prey? What could they conceivably have garnered? One might also distinguish between a hatred, born of bitter experience, for any authority, and an active, organized criminal class. And one might note, finally, the urban-based data—philological, folkloristic, literary—which is available, and proceed from there.

In the earliest accounts of the word or concept of *mafia*, there is a romantic strain, just as at the time the word and concept appeared there was a romantic (and revolutionary) environment. It is very difficult, given the silences in history, the mystery of the word's origins, the conflicting (sometimes contradictory) contemporary accounts, the literary visibility of a notion supposedly strongest among the illiterate or barely literate, to come to any definitive views on when the term for a sensibility became a social type and, perhaps, an (anti-)social structure. As Americans, we might remember one of our own cherished, animating social fables—for we also were and still are enthralled by a lone, laconic figure, self-reliant, intensely male, source of violence and his own justice, a chivalric figure arising in the period after 1860 and the Civil War, a figure glamorous, independent, forceful, given to acts not words—the Cowboy. The urban mafioso, as Pitré describes him, and the Cowboy are not—*mutatis mutandis*—so very different. Each sums up how a people grappling for control (of crowded lives; of a vast, untamed West) distilled their hero, the man who was in control.

And how much of the legend of the range-riding, gun-toting Cowboy in fact derives, in the last decades of the nineteenth century, from Wild West shows playing mostly in cities and towns of the East, from vast quantities of (contemporary) pulp fiction and journalism produced by and for urban readers, from popular stage plays and from the movies? How much of what we believe about heroic self-assertion in primi-tive, rural circumstances, about nobility in savage settings in fact derives from the literate imaginations and longings of city-dwellers? A great deal. Pastoral visions, myths of noble savages are always created by urban sophisticates. As this process has been true in its peculiarly American context for the Cowboy, so also for the mafioso. In Sergio Leone's so-called spaghetti Westerns starring Clint Eastwood, the two types may actually have come together—Billy The Kid meets *Omertà*. The result is a sublime parody of two already exaggerated types—and a compelling composite image that, in its strange way, is loyal to each type's original.

Fables prove more durable than facts, and for many they are easier to manage. Whatever *mafia* was in the nineteenth century, it has evolved into a code word for crime, for criminal conspiracy and indeed—as one now hears in everyday conversation—for any mysterious combine or exclusive in-group. "He belongs to that country-club Mafia," one hears, or "There's a Mafia of bond dealers in city X." This kind of comment, sprinkled across the media, in conversations, in jests, in classrooms, on talk shows, in locker rooms and boardrooms and places of business, wounds without intending to hurt the Italian American who knows how deep go the roots of any prejudice that is so ubiquitous in casual discourse. For the associations clustered around the word are not "ordinary" but ugly, and the very presence of the term in all kinds of contexts only reinforces for many Americans of Italian heritage an awareness of how they are not free of the potential backlash and prejudice the word, and its associations, can engender.

Is the Italian American ultrasensitive on the subject? Probably. Can he or she be blamed for such sensitivity? Only by those who have never felt the sting of prejudice. Anyone who has not felt a phone call or a casual meeting change its atmosphere upon hearing a name or an inflection (or seeing a skin color); who has not caught a subtle (or not so subtle) alteration in the manner or approach of others; who has not heard epithets hurled or seen them written, or had children baffled or angry by a sudden encounter with a rebuff based on prejudice; or who has not experienced advancement denied or barriers increased, will assume the Italian American is ultrasensitive, is complaining unduly, is carrying on "emotionally" about ethnic slur or prejudice. Anyone who has felt the range of reaction suggested above will be less sure that the Italian American is overreacting.

In fact, since the late nineteenth century there has been discrimination about or prejudice against the Italian American, some subtle, some not so subtle. In fact, today there are television advertisements for products associated with Italians (spaghetti, spaghetti sauce, pizza) that are astonishingly tasteless in their exploitation of physical and cultural stereotypes. One sees the same stereotypes in television series, in films, in books. Whether in advertisements or extended presentations, there are images of "Italians" projected that, were they stereotypes of Black or Jewish Americans, could never and should never be projected or shown. So also with jokes: since it became taboo in "polite" or "liberal" or "educated" discourse and circles to tell racist or anti-Semitic stories or jokes or to make clearly bigoted or racist remarks about Blacks or Jews, the so-called Italian (or Polish) joke has filled the void.

Let there be no mistake: ancient and not-so-ancient forms and expressions of discrimination or bigotry about Black and Jewish Americans have by no means disappeared; America is not at all free of racism or prejudice. But there occur moments when some reprehensible forms of expression and behavior are viewed by a culture as less reprehensible than others. Any Italian American who has achieved more prominence in public life or private endeavors than many in the non–Italian American majority would have thought "believable" or "expected" can tell, often with bafflement or sorrowful dismay, of how anomalously his or her background is regarded, of how patronizing otherwise sensible acquaintances suddenly become, of how often mail, reporters' questions, introductions to speak and strangers' comments will contain slighting or painfully self-conscious or indeed slurring references to an Italian heritage. American politicians of Italian heritage, in particular, think long and hard before venturing "too far," for the press, always a mirror of society's attitudes, has not yet become accustomed to the emergence of this ethnic group from a private life of comfortable assimilation into roles of public trust and public service. There still lingers the assumption that the whole story needs to be dug out, that there is more likely something sinister in the background that needs to be ferreted out.

And yet the burdens of misshapen assumption or bigotry that must be borne not uniquely by Italian Americans cannot discolor the portrait of a group of Americans who have given to and received from America tremendous blessings. No more than the individual lives of most Americans of Italian heritage is more than passingly marred by prejudice when compared to the satisfactions and fullness of most of those lives.

On the whole, Italian Americans have flourished and prospered in America, and the darker hues of portions of history or the shadows of bigotry emphasized in the last few pages should not be read as obscuring the brightness and highlights of the overall experience. Perspective must be maintained. As this century has unfolded, Italian Americans have brought their special blends of individualism, loyalty, energy and passion for experience to America and have been taken into every corner of her life.

As one looks through the final chapters of this volume, one sees the chronicle of assimilation. The painful episode of Sacco and Vanzetti, redolent with injustice and suspicion and, at bottom, mutual bafflement, gives way to images of work and achievement, to the flight of antifascists and Italian Jews in the thirties and the subsequent enrichment of America's intellectual and cultural life, to a gallery of portraits of distinguished Americans in the arts, sport, industry, science, law, commerce of all kinds. By the end of the Second World War, which served both to introduce a whole generation of Italian American GIs to the Italy of their parents or grandparents, and to introduce Italy to a generation of Americans derived from her shores, now serving as liberators and conquerors and prodigal sons all at once, the Italian American had moved out of the city toward the suburbs. College was the goal of the second or third generation, law and medicine favored above all other professions, while the energies of other Italian Americans were directed to making a father's craft or a grandfather's trade into a bigger, more diverse family business.

In the last thirty or forty years, the Italian American has become thoroughly Americanized, regarded as a block only by political pollsters and survey takers (though not a very predictable one—registering as Democrats, voting like Republicans), regarded as a somewhat maverick element in the view of a "traditional" American Catholic Church. Because of intermarriage, particularly to fellow Catholics of Polish or Irish heritage and to Jews, in larger numbers than the oft-proclaimed self-consciousness as *Italian* Americans might have led one to believe, the question after mid-century—who is the Italian American?—begins to have a myriad of answers.

Is the Italian American the young stockbroker with an Italian surname, a paternal grandfather from Italy and no other connection to or awareness of things Italian? Is it the young student named Murphy or Edelmann or Stepniak whose mother had one (or two) pairs of Italian grandparents? Is it the doctor whose parents were both Italian American, who grew up in an urban community where "ethnic" consciousness ran high, and who now finds herself married to a man named Johnson and living in Phoenix? Or is it the successful advertising executive who grew up with an Italian name in Georgia and had no idea he was "Italian" and what it was supposed to mean (he knew only in the late thirties and forties that he was white) until he arrived in Chicago? Is it the "professional" ethnic, the insurance man or politician or car dealer or accountant who belongs to Italian American clubs and lives a life in which the clientele or constituency depends on being constantly reminded of "Italian" affiliations, assumptions and issues? Or is it, finally, the Italians who have come to America since Italy became a major industrial nation—restaurateurs, fashion executives, opera singers, theoretical physicists, engineers, bankers, consultants, designers—of scenery, clothes, automobiles, furniture, buildings? The answer can only be that the Italian American is all of these people and, in complex ways beyond my capacity to imagine, millions of others as well. Italian Americans retain to varying degrees a sense of identity with other Italian Americans, differing in intensity and self-consciousness depending on the duration, locale and history of the family. It is also fair to say, however, that rarely if ever is there no sense of heritage, even if attenuated; rarely is one innocent of the memory of someone's memory, completely without any sense of a past defined by family and a certain pride. Most often there is far more—a sense of identification, if not of separate identity, identification with certain traditions and family histories, identification with "success stories" in the general society by those with identifiable Italian names. No matter how dispersed, no matter where assimilated, there is still and will be the instinct to keep track of how "we" are doing, to know when there is the chance that the common bond (even if hidden by a different name) will be recognized and acknowledged. Everyone has seen it—two people, both with Italian surnames, meet in a roomful of people named Smith, and there is a flicker, a moment of pause, as introductions are exchanged. There is communication neither sinister nor cerebral; it is simply a look, as old as blood.

When an Italian American emerged as the leader of the American Cardinals of the Roman Catholic Church, the first female candidate of a major party for the Vice-Presidency of the United States, a leading and visible corporate CEO and automobile manufacturer, the Governor of New York State, the President of Yale, the President of NOW (the National Organization for Women), an Associate Justice of the Supreme Court, the winner of the Nobel Prize for Economics, the Secretary of HEW (as it was then called), the Attorney General of the United States, the junior Senator from New York, all within about ten years, one suddenly began to hear that it was "in" or "chic" to be Italian, as the media kept score and added these names and others to prominent figures in the arts, sports, entertainment and commerce and then decided that Italian Americans had made it. Implicit, indeed in some accounts explicit, was less the belief that Italian Americans had risen above their station (though there was a touch of that) than the disconcerting query—why has it taken so long? Why have these people, who have been here in great numbers since the nineteenth century, who have not suffered the racism Blacks or others of color still suffer, who have never felt the lash of bigotry and discrimination as the Jews have, why has it taken the Italian Americans so long?

The question was not inappropriate or, at heart, necessarily unfriendly. The stigma, unfair to all Italian Americans but a tiny number, attaching to the Mafia; the nervous bigotry noted previously notwithstanding, the energy and efforts of the Italian American had long been noticed and appreciated. Not simply the virtues of devotion to family and a willingness to work, but also the virtues of a people dedicated to traditional moral values—qualities rightly recognized within and outside the Italian American community as marking so many members of that community. These virtues were seen not as the exclusive possession of Italian Americans, for millions of Americans of all backgrounds shared those qualities (though Italian Americans were and are less abashed in this and in other areas to sing those virtues and their genuine attachment to them). The American people had also had ample opportunity to see other virtues as well—again, none as the exclusive property of Italian Americans but theirs all the same—to see an individualism, a feistiness, occasionally at variance, in an anarchic direction, with "American" traditions of individualism but most often enriching and expanding native American traditions of standing up for what one believes, following one's own convictions, willingly taking an unpopular course or view. All Americans had also seen in Italian Americans an energy that is a desire to give of oneself without stint or meanness of measure, a spirit willing to immerse oneself to solve a problem, right a wrong, work hard, paint a picture, sing an aria, build a building, visit the sick—an energy that is an instinct for life, a capacity to embrace, to absorb, to enter in the common stream of existence, and to love it; an energy that is gregarious, social, communal—that hungers to build, whether an argument, a market, a mall, a role, a scene, a highrise, a victory, a team, a symphony. And in the Italian American all Americans had recognized a capacity for loyalty—to family and to forebears, to community and to country, and a capacity for an equal measure of pride in whatever is worthy of that unstinting loyalty.

These and other strengths, in general recognized and admired, sometimes envied at the neighborhood or family level, force the question: Why has it taken the Italian American, energetic and talented, longer than one might have thought to play his or her part on the larger American stage? Success in material terms came early and often. After all, comfortable lives were attained and fortunes, even great fortunes, were accumulated by Italian Americans through hard work, imagination, a belief in the land of opportunity. With this material success, however, a tradition of philanthropy, so important to America in general, has been far slower to develop within the Italian American community—either materially to assist or to promote Italian culture in America or to assist each other. While philanthropic individuals exist, the Italian American impulse is not to share the wealth beyond the family. Did the absence of philanthropic tradition mean that self-promotion lagged, and that public emergence was therefore seen as slower?

Perhaps the slowness, the reticence (one might say, if it did not sound odd about such a verbal if not vociferous group) of Italian Americans to play a larger public role sooner is attributable to a weakness of a basic strength, that is, to the necessary, universal trade-off for their being so strong for family. For all their public gifts—of performance, of love of a crowd, for friendship, in the political arts—the Italian American's basic arena or stage was for generations the essentially private realm of the family. Whereas others said to their young, "Get an education," the early, not especially lettered generations of Italian Americans often said to their young, "Get a job." Of course there were exceptions, many of them. And of course poverty or hard times dictated work over education. Though as soon as one says that, one must add that millions were poor when they arrived in America from around the world. Italian Americans were not the only ones to work or to have to work.

Without a tradition, millennia long, of a culture whose apogee was a scholar/official class and whose base was a unifying, written language, like the Chinese; without a history of dispersal whose agonies were salved by an ancient sacred language and by religious texts and commentaries, like the Jews, the mass of Italian immigrants respected education but had little of it; they knew work and trusted it. The new Italian American family would be sustained by work, by all its members; work would produce, in time, the goods of the world, in order to secure the family in the New World. The family, mother-dominated at home (like the Roman family; like the Italian vision of the Holy Family) but patriarchal in values and structure beyond the front door, as it were, was loath to let its young go too far, too far away to college, too far away to Church, too far to work—too far from the village of the family. Italian American girls and young women were encouraged (in many cases that is too weak a word) not to go too far away but rather to marry and commence building a family. A son in the second or third generation would be sent to college; a daughter got married, another version of work. If there is a European ethnic group of American women whose talents beyond the home were for several generations stunted or ignored, it is strong, intelligent, energetic Italian American women. It is a loss to the country (and to themselves), if a gain for traditional values and a traditional family model, that Italian American women were until fairly recently so little encouraged to educate themselves with their American peers.

By being less inclined to leave home, as it were, in so many ways the Italian American was slower to gain the recognition for talents that were otherwise—at home, as it were—so manifest. Thus assimilation by Italian Americans has struck many, including many Italian Americans, as correspondingly slow. But to press such a view very far is finally to equate assimilation with visibility, and that is not necessarily an appropriate or logical equation. Rather, assimilation comes when fundamental values, inherited from forebears and borne with pride, irradiate into the new culture, adapting without losing their essence, absorbing without losing their form the strengths and values of the new place. If assimilation is a two-way process, of giving and receiving, of becoming American while adding to America what is enduring in the energy, history and devotion to life in being Italian, if assimilation is this reciprocity of response, as I believe it to be, then Americans of Italian heritage have much to be proud of and have millions of successes to celebrate.

Above: Portrait of Christopher Columbus, undated, by Sebastiano del Piombo/Credit: MMA. *Right:* Portrait of Amerigo Vespucci, undated, by an unknown artist/Credit: Uffizi/ Alinari. Vespucci, a Florentine navigator for whom South and North America were named, as the result of two voyages in the service of Spain and Portugal in which he explored the Atlantic coast of South America as far south as the River Plate, became convinced that the newly discovered lands were a New World: *Mundus Novus.*

CHAPTER ONE

ITALIAN CULTURE IN AMERICA

1492-1880

Discovery of the New World

1492. Christopher Columbus's voyages and discovery of the New World were recorded in letters and dispatches written by him and his officers. The sixteenth-century historian Bartolomé de Las Casas prepared a digest from Columbus's logbook, which is quoted here in part. When the narrative is in the first person, Las Casas is using the admiral's words; when in the third person, it is his own interpretation.

I departed from the city of Granada on Saturday, 12 May, and went to the seaport of Palos, where I prepared three ships very suitable for such a voyage and set out from that port well supplied both with provisions and seamen. Half an hour before sunrise on Friday, 3 August, I departed on a course for the Canary Islands, from which possession of your Highnesses I intended to set out and sail until I reached the Indies, there to deliver your Highnesses' letters to their princes and to fulfill your other commands. I decided therefore to make this careful daily report of my voyage and of everything I should do, see or experience. In addition to a report of the day's events recorded each night, and of the night's sailing recorded each morning, I decided to make a new chart for navigation, giving the correct disposition according to their bearings of the land and water in the ocean sea. I intended also to compile a book which would contain everything mapped by latitude measured from the Equator and by longitude from the west. Though all these things will be a great labor it is essential that I should neglect sleep and carefully watch my course.

THURSDAY, 11 OCTOBER. He sailed west-southwest. They ran into rougher seas than any they had met with on the voyage. They saw petrels and a green reed near the ship. The men of the *Pinta* saw a cane and a stick and picked up another small stick, apparently shaped with an iron tool; also a piece of cane and some land grasses and a small board. Those on the caravel *Niña* saw other indications of land and a stick covered with barnacles. At these signs, all breathed again and were rejoiced. That day they went twenty-seven leagues before sunset and after sunset he resumed his original western course. They made twelve miles an hour and up to two hours before midnight had gone ninety miles, which are twenty-two leagues and a half. The caravel *Pinta*, being swifter and sailing ahead of the Admiral, now sighted land and gave the signals which the Admiral had commanded.

The first man to sight land was a sailor called Rodrigo, from Triana, who afterward vainly claimed the reward, which was pocketed by Columbus. The Admiral, however, when on the sterncastle at ten o'clock in the night, had seen a light, though it was so indistinct he would not affirm that it was land. He called Pero Gutierrez, butler of the King's table, and told him that there seemed to be a light and asked him to look. He did so and saw it. He said the same to Rodrigo Sanchez of Segovia, whom the King and Queen had sent in the fleet as accountant, and he saw nothing because he was not in a position from which anything could be seen. After the Admiral spoke, this light was seen once or twice and it was like a wax candle that went up and down. Very few thought that this was a sign of land, but the Admiral was quite certain that they were near land. Accordingly, after the recitation of the *Salve* in the usual manner by the assembled sailors, the Admiral most seriously urged them to keep a good lookout from the forecastle and to watch carefully for land. He promised to give a silk doublet to the first sailor who should report it. And he would be entitled also to the reward promised by the sovereigns, which was an annual payment of ten thousand maravedis.

Two hours after midnight land appeared, some two leagues away. They took in all sail, leaving only the mainsail, which is the great sail without bonnets, and lay close-hauled waiting for day. This was Friday, on which they reached a small island of the Lucayos, called in the Indian language Guanahani. Immediately some naked people appeared and the Admiral went ashore in the armed boat, as did Martin Alonso Pinzón and Vicente Yanez his brother, captain of the *Niña*. The Admiral raised the royal standard and the captains carried two banners with the green cross which

AMERICVS VESPVCCI

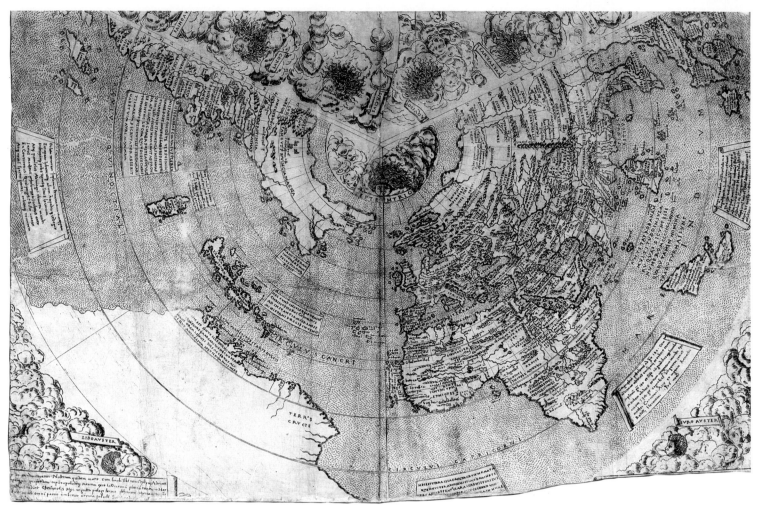

were flown by the Admiral on all his ships. On each side of the cross was a crown surmounting the letters F and [I] (for Ferdinand and Isabella). On landing they saw very green trees and much water and fruit of various kinds. The Admiral called the two captains and the others who had landed and Rodrigo Escobedo, recorder of the whole fleet, and Rodrigo Sanchez of Segovia, and demanded that they should bear faithful witness that he had taken possession of the island—which he did—for his sovereigns and masters the King and Queen. He further made the required declarations, which are recorded at greater length in the evidence there set down in writing. Soon many people of the island came up to them. What follows are the Admiral's actual words in his account of his first voyage and the discovery of these Indies.

"In order to win their friendship, since I knew they were a people to be converted and won to our holy faith by love and friendship rather than by force, I gave some of them red caps and glass beads which they hung round their necks, also many other trifles. These things pleased them greatly and they became marvelously friendly to us. They afterward swam out to the ship's boats in which we were sitting, bringing us parrots and balls of cotton thread and spears and many other things, which they exchanged with us for such objects as glass beads, hawks and bells. In fact, they very willingly traded everything they had. But they seemed to me a people very short of everything. They all go naked as their mothers bore them, including the women, although I saw only one very young girl.

"All the men I saw were young. I did not see one over the age of thirty. They were very well built with fine bodies and handsome faces. Their hair is coarse, almost like that of a horse's tail, and short; they wear it down over their eyebrows except for a few strands at the back, which they wear long and never cut. They are the color of the Canary Islanders (neither black nor white). Some of them paint themselves black, others white or any color they can find. Some paint their faces, some their whole bodies, some only the eyes, some only the nose. They do not carry arms or know them. For when I showed them swords, they took them by the edge and cut themselves out of ignorance. They have no iron. Their spears are made of cane. Some instead of an iron tip have a fish's tooth and others have points of different kinds. They are fairly tall on the whole, with fine limbs and good proportions. I saw some who had wound scars on their bodies and I asked them by signs how they got these and they indicated to me that people came from other islands nearby who tried to capture them and they defended themselves. I supposed and still suppose that they come from the mainland to capture them for slaves. They should be good servants and very intelligent, for I have observed that they soon repeat anything that is said to them, and I believe that they would easily be made Christians, for they appeared to me to have no religion. God willing, when I make my departure I will bring half a dozen of them back to their Majesties, so that they can learn to speak. I saw no animals of any kind on this island except parrots." These are the Admiral's own words.

Above: World map by Matteo Contarini, engraved by Francesco Roselli, 1506/Credit: BL. This is the first map to illustrate the newly discovered coasts of North and South America. *Right:* Portrait of Giovanni da Verrazzano, drawn by G. Zocchi and engraved by F. Allegrini, 1767/Credit: PML. In the employ of Francis I of France, Verrazzano was the first European explorer to enter and describe New York harbor and the Hudson River.

GIOVANNI DI PIER ANDREA DI   BERNARDO DA VERRAZZANO

PATRIZIO FIOR. GRAN CAPIT.^{NO}   COMANDANTE IN MARE PER

IL RÈ CRISTIANISSIMO   FRANCESCO PRIMO,

DISCOPRITORE   DELLA NUOVA FRANCIA.

nato circa il MCDLXXV.   morto nel MDXXV.

Dedicato al merito sing.^{re} dell' Illmo e Rev.^{mo} Sig.^{re} Lodovico da Verrazzano

Patrizio, e Canonico Fiorentino Agnato del Med.^o

Preso dal Quadro Originale in Tela esistente presso la sud.^a Nobil. Famiglia

LA HISTORIA DEL MONDO NVOVO

DI M. GIROLAMO BENZONI MILANESE.

LAQVAL TRATTA DELL'ISOLE,
& Mari nuouamente ritrouati, & delle nuoue
Città da lui proprio vedute, per acqua
& per terra in quattordeci anni.

Con Priuilegio della Illuftrifsima Signoria di Venetia, Per anni XX.

Above from left to right: Title page and illustrations from Girolamo Benzoni's *History of the New World*, published in Venice in 1565/Credit: LC. A native of Milan, Benzoni described his experiences in the Americas over a fourteen-year period; his work was later translated into Latin, French, German and Flemish. The illustrations of native people in the Americas served as a model for T. de Bry's *America*, published in 1595, which is often considered to be the first printed book with pictorial images of the New World.

An Appraisal of Columbus's Discovery

1565. Girolamo Benzoni, a Milanese who joined Spanish expeditions in the Americas, describes both his attitude and that of Spaniards toward the significance of Columbus's discoveries.

It will not be out of place to relate what I heard happened in Spain to Columbus, after he had discovered the Indies; although it had been done in ancient times in other ways, but was new then. Columbus being at a party with many noble Spaniards, where, as was customary, the subject of conversation was the Indies: one of them undertook to say: "Mr. Christopher, even if you had not found the Indies, we should not have been devoid of a man who would have attempted the same that you did, here in our own country of Spain, as it is full of great men clever in cosmography and literature." Columbus said nothing in answer to these words, but having desired an egg to be brought to him, he placed it on the table, saying: "Gentlemen, I will lay a wager with any of you, that you will not make this egg stand up as I will, naked and without anything at all." They all tried, and no one succeeded in making it stand up. When the egg came round to the hands of Columbus, by beating it down on the table he fixed it, having thus crushed a little of one end; wherefore all remained confused, understanding what he would have said: that after the deed is done, everybody knows how to do it; that they ought first to have sought for the Indies, and not laugh at him who had sought for it first, while they for some time had been laughing, and wondered at it as an impossibility.

Now let us return to our first subject, of the searching for and the discovery of the Indies. Columbus seeing that the Genoese would not help him in so worthy an enterprise, he determined to go to the west, considering that there were some very rich and very powerful princes, in the hope that someone of them would give him every requisite to find the country by him so much wished for. Thus he went to Portugal, and sent his brother, Bartholomew, to Henry VII, king of England, to ask him for ships and favor to find the Indies, promising him that in a short time he would bring him very great treasures from those unknown parts. But he had to return without any conclusion, so that he betook himself to treat with King Alfonso V of Portugal, supplicating his highness to be willing to grant him some ships with provisions, and he would oblige himself to go westward to seek for some abundant countries, rich in gold, and in various other precious articles of value. But if Columbus was held as fabulous by the Genoese, he was thought ludicrous by the English—*da gl' Inglesi risibile*—and by the Portuguese he was mocked as a dreamer; for there being men in Portugal who professed to know everything connected with cosmography, they, with haughty and proud talk, asserted to the king that this man was quite bewildered, and that he should on no account

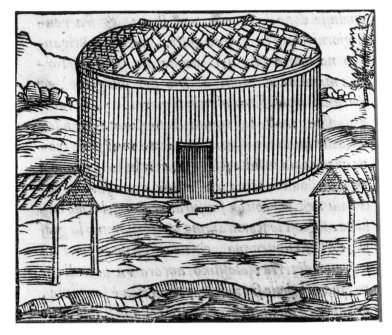

give credence to the words of Columbus. They asserted that in no way could there be in the west any of the things he said, neither gold nor riches, and that the country, from its extreme heat, was uninhabitable; insomuch that anyone passing under the equinoctial line would be burnt up by the sun, from its having more power there than in any other part of the sphere, in consequence of its being constantly between the two tropics, Cancer and Capricorn.

Columbus, thus seeing that in Portugal everyone laughed and scoffed at his words, deemed it useless to remain; so he went to Castile, to the court of King Don Fernando and Queen Donna Isabella, and submitted the same project that he had proposed to everybody else, in the best way that he could; giving the most efficacious reasons, together with the best authorities, examples, and information. It seemed that he was still on those principles derided almost as if he promised impossibilities. Yet, after consuming several years at court, and always remaining constant in his assertions and persevering in his reasons, strengthening the hopes with very rational examples, at the intercession of some grandees of Spain, he obtained time and opportunity to speak familiarly with Queen Donna Isabella; and so well did he persuade her with his good and very strong arguments, that he induced her to believe his assertions so far as to promise to speak to the king, and make every endeavor that he should be enabled to go and perform this enterprise. Wherefore in a short time, first by the divine grace, and then through the intercession of the magnanimous queen, the king, Don Fernando, armed a ship and two caravels for Christopher Columbus. Thus, in company with his brother Bartholomew, in the beginning of August 1492, he sailed from Cadiz, and touched at Gomera, which is one of the seven islands of the Canaries, and there he remained some days, taking in water and other necessaries. He then sailed, following his western voyage, and having navigated several days without seeing land, the soldiers began to murmur against Columbus; but he quieted them and sailed on during thirty-five days, still without seeing any signs of land, whereupon they began to use menaces and to give him bad language, calling him a Genoese impostor and trickster, who did not know where he wanted to arrive or to go, and that he was leading them to death. Here Columbus as much as possible urged his reasons, and begged and supplicated them to have patience, for in a short time, with the help of God, he hoped to see a new land. Thus quieted they navigated for some days more, but not seeing land, they betook themselves again to murmur, telling him that he must turn back or they would throw him overboard; affirming that if they sailed on any farther their provisions would fail, especially their water, as they would still require some for their return to Spain. Finally the dispute was reduced to these conditions, that if in three days they did not discover land he would turn back, showing them that by only putting themselves on allowance, not only would there be sufficient provisions to return to Spain, but also to go farther on. And thus happily continuing their course, the next day he ordered the sails to be lowered, and it was believed that when Columbus uttered these words he felt near land, that he knew it by the atmosphere and the clouds, which are observed on the horizon at sunset; or, indeed, through some inspiration of his unconquerable soul. And, in fact, the next evening a sailor named La Leppe, having gone aloft, began to cry out with a loud voice, *"I see fire,"* and immediately a youth added, "It is not long since Mr. Columbus told me the same thing." The sailor, much delighted and pleased, thought that, on his return to Spain, there was no doubt but he should receive from his majesty the king some remuneration; but not receiving any reward or favor, he went over to Barbary in such an ill humor, that he became a renegade from the faith. Now, how great the pleasure of each man was at having discovered the new country, it is not possible to relate in words; for rejoicing, no one could satisfy himself in looking at the new land. Some could not restrain their tears in embracing Columbus, others reverently kissed his hands, those who had offended him asked pardon for their ignorance, and all offered themselves as servants and humble slaves to his great courage. Columbus had the boat lowered and leaped on shore; they cut down a tree and made it into a cross, erecting it on the spot in the name of Jesus Christ crucified. He thus took possession of the Indies and the New World for the sacred Catholic kings. In this way did Columbus discover the Indies, through his own valor and glorious genius.

THE AUTHOR.

In his Days when among the Indians.

See Vol. 2. Page 180 181.

A
PILGRIMAGE
IN
EUROPE AND AMERICA,
LEADING TO
THE DISCOVERY
OF
THE SOURCES OF THE MISSISSIPPI
AND BLOODY RIVER;
WITH A DESCRIPTION OF
THE WHOLE COURSE OF THE FORMER,
AND OF
THE OHIO.

By J. C. BELTRAMI, Esq.
FORMERLY JUDGE OF A ROYAL COURT IN THE EX-KINGDOM OF ITALY.

IN TWO VOLUMES.
VOL. I.

LONDON:
PRINTED FOR HUNT AND CLARKE,
YORK STREET, COVENT GARDEN.
1828.

Above: The first letter patent granted by Henry VII to John Cabot and his sons to seek out, subdue and occupy at their own charges any regions which before had been "unknown to all Christians," 1496/Credit: PRO. John Cabot (Giovanni Caboto), an Italian navigator and naturalized Venetian citizen living in Bristol, England, by his two voyages exploring the coast of Nova Scotia and Newfoundland, gave the British reason to claim Canada. His son Sebastian Cabot made significant discoveries and explorations in the service of England and Spain. *Left:* Title page of J.C. Beltrami's *A Pilgrimage in Europe and America*, 1828/Credit: NYPL. *Opposite page:* George Washington's letter of July 1, 1779, to Philip Mazzei/Credit: LC

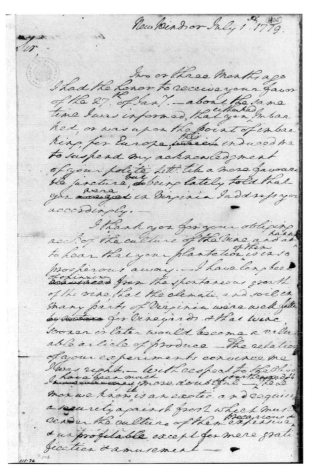

"On the Principles of the American Revolution"

1774–1775. Philip Mazzei was born in 1730 near Florence. At the urging of Benjamin Franklin, whom he met in London, Mazzei emigrated to Virginia in 1773, where he established an experimental agricultural colony. He was elected to local office in Albemarle County, and at the suggestion of Thomas Jefferson, Mazzei prepared a series of articles which presented a philosophical justification for the American Revolution against England.

In order to achieve our end, my dear fellow citizens, we must discuss man's natural rights and the grounds of a free government. Such a discussion will clearly show us that the British government has never been free at the peak of its perfection, and that our own was nothing more than a bad copy of it, with in addition such handicaps as to render it barely above a state of slavery.

Later we shall examine how a government must be formed in order to be impartial and enduring.

This matter has been so amply treated by several prestigious writers that I seek no other merit than that of treating it in familiar and simple forms in order to be easily understood.

Practitioners of fine writing will forgive me. They need no one to write for them. I write for people who, endowed with good sense, did not acquire book learning. I desire to adapt my writing to their capacity. I know indeed that high-flown language has often attracted the consensus of men, alas, only too prone to admire what they do not understand. But the time has finally come to change ways: our duty is to try to understand so that we may judge for ourselves.

All men are by nature equally free and independent. Their equality is necessary in order to set up a free government. Every man must be the equal of any other in natural rights. Class distinction has always been and will always be an effective obstacle and for a very plain reason. When in a nation you have several classes of men, each class must have its share in the government, otherwise one class will tyrannize over the others. But shares cannot be made perfectly equal. Were it possible, the course of human events shows that they would not keep in balance. No matter how little one outweighs the others, the structure must collapse.

That is the reason why all ancient republics were short-lived. When they were founded, the people were divided into classes and always in competition, each class trying to have a greater share in the government. As a consequence, the lawmakers had to give in to established prejudices, to the conflicting claims of the parties, and the best they were able to accomplish was a grotesque mixture of freedom and tyranny.

The imperfections in their constitutions gave rise to many riots, which lately have been depicted in the most terrible colors by evil-intentioned persons in order to set the people against republican governments. Some persons of good faith have done the same thing because, having paid no attention to the good principles of government, they were prevented from realizing that the republics they were depicting the faults of had nothing of a republic but the name.

I repeat that a true republican government cannot endure except where men, from the richest to the poorest, are perfectly equal in their natural rights. Fortunately we are so on this continent. But in other countries where an attempt was made to introduce such a government, the inhabitants were (according to what we learn from history) divided into ranks, as we said. And when in a country there is a class enjoying privileges not enjoyed by another, it is in vain to hope to establish a free and enduring government unless the privileged class gives up its privileges and is incorporated on perfectly equal terms into the other, for class distinctions inevitably create envy and discontent. There will always be attempts to predominate, freedom will always be wavering and fall in the end.

We shall make some observations on the Roman Republic not so much because it is historically the most famous as because the English use it as a term of comparison in order to exalt the alleged perfection of their own government.

The Roman state was initially a monarchy since it was ruled by one man. When the kings were banished, it became an aristocracy since the rule was taken over by a class of people called *patricians*, a word corresponding to what in England is meant by *lords* or *noblemen*, and all the other inhabitants, called *populace*, were excluded. After much struggle the populace was allowed to take part in the government. Then, taking advantage of circumstances to improve its position, it was granted an allegedly equal share in it. The government thus became a mixture of aristocracy and democracy.

The nobles resenting equality with the populace and the populace being opposed to the nobles' superiority, the two parties were kept in almost continuous dissension until a usurper working his way between them attained the throne.

Thus in less than five centuries was that great and powerful republic brought to an end. Sentiments of patriotism and heroism which seemed hereditary in almost all Romans proved insufficient to preserve freedom since the government had not been founded on grounds of equality. If the patricians had given up their hereditary privileges and allowed themselves to be incorporated on a footing of equality with the others, the government would then have been perfectly democratic, stable, and would perhaps be in existence in our days.

Democracy—I mean representative democracy—comprising every individual in a simple body without any distinction whatsoever, is surely the only government under which true and lasting freedom can be enjoyed. Unfortunately for humankind, such a government has never existed. Tumultuous governments, built on a wrong or very weak foundation and full of errors, have made abusive use of that sacred name.

The lowest class of the common people has never held the reins of government except when it has forcibly wrested them from the hands of the powerful, whose insolence and tyranny had caused the uprising. The populace has never been the aggressor and has never rebelled before its oppressor had gone to such extremes as to try the most submissive patience. Can we not therefore be shocked by the confusion and disorders springing from the spirit of vengeance of a reckless multitude so unjustly provoked? Indeed, it is a wonder that there are people so blinded by prejudice as to dare qualify as democratic such a disorganized and confused state of affairs, and to fear, or pretend to fear, the same evils in order to inculcate maxims injurious to the rights of the lowest class of the people, whereas the evils were always a consequence of its being deprived of its rights.

The government of England, from the time of recorded history, to the death of Queen Elizabeth, was either a despotic monarchy or an intolerable aristocracy, or a mixture of both, the nobles possessing more or lesser power in relation to the greater or lesser ability of their monarch.

The history of the irregularities, cruelties, and tyrannical acts of those barbarous centuries is not our concern, nor is the rise of the commons and how long they continued to be insignificant. Our only concern is to examine that government at its peak of perfection.

The Introduction of Italian Opera

1825–1826. Lorenzo Da Ponte, Mozart's librettist for The Marriage of Figaro, Don Giovanni *and* Così Fan Tutte, *settled in New York in 1805. He was appointed the first professor of Italian at Columbia College in 1805. Through his efforts the first Italian opera companies were imported to this country.*

Though, to my joy, I could see the interest in Italian letters increasing daily in both New York and other cities of the Union, I still thought there was another way of making them both more widely spread and more highly esteemed; but, to tell the truth, I did not dare to hope for such a thing. What, therefore, was my delight, when a number of persons assured me that the famous Garzia, with his incomparable daughter and several other Italian singers, was coming from London to America, and in fact to New York, to establish the Italian opera there—the desideratum of my greatest zeal?

He came, in truth, and the effect was prodigious. Unimaginable the enthusiasm in the cultivated portions of the public aroused by our music when executed by singers of most perfect taste and highest merit. The *Barbiere di Siviglia* of the universally admired and praised Rossini was the opera fortunate enough to plant the first root of the great tree of Italian music in New York [November 29, 1825, premiere].

A short time before our singers were to arrive, a young American, a youth of much talent, and a great lover of the noble art of music, was talking of it with friends of his one day in my presence, and as it were ex cathedra. Finding his notions erroneous, I remarked in jest:

"Silence, King Solomon! You know nothing of music yet!"

That excellent young man felt a flash of anger, but I begged him to be calm and promised soon to convince him. Sometime later Garzia arrived. *The Barber of Seville* of the Rossini mentioned was announced for the opening night. I took him to the fifth performance, with others of my pupils, and that admirable music caught them up, along with the rest of the audience, into a sort of ecstatic spell. Having observed from

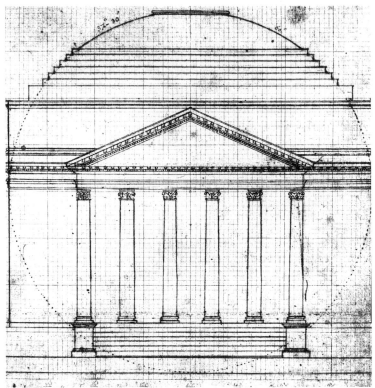

their perfect silence, the expressions on their faces and in their eyes, and their constant clapping of hands, the marvelous effect that music had had on them, I approached my skeptic when the performance was over, and asked him what he thought of it: "Mr. Da Ponte," he said generously, "you are right. I confess with real pleasure that I did not know an iota about music." Not far different the impressions of the first performance on all those who did not have their ears lined with that sheepskin of which drums are made, or some particular interest in speaking ill of it (a newspaper critic of the dishonest tribe honored Italian music with the name of "monstrous"), whether to give the palm to the music of other countries, or to praise to the stars the clucking of some amorous hen. But despite such prattling, the delight in our music in New York was so constant, that few were the evenings when the theatre was not filled with a large and select audience; and that happened, when it happened, I believe, through lack of poise in the Spanish conductor.

How great an interest I took in the continuance and success of such an enterprise is too easy to imagine to require words of mine. I clearly foresaw the many enormous advantages our literature would derive from it and how it would tend to propagate our language through the attractiveness of the Italian Opera which, in the eyes of every cultivated nation of the world, is the noblest and most pleasurable of all the many spectacles the human intelligence ever invented, and to the perfecting of which the noblest arts have vied with one another in contributing.

But however beautiful, however esteemed the operas set to music by Rossini might be, it seemed to me that to give fewer performances of them and alternate them with those of other composers would be a most profitable thing, both for the reputation of the excellent Rossini and for the treasury of the

producers. A good fowl is certainly an appetizing dish; but it was served often enough by the Marchioness of Montferrat at the dinners which she gave the King of France, to prompt that Majesty to inquire whether hens were all one could find in that country. I mentioned the point to Garzia; he liked it; and at my suggesting to him my *Don Giovanni* set to music by the immortal Mozart, he uttered another cry of joy and said nothing but this:

"If we have enough actors to give *Don Giovanni,* let us give it soon. It's the best opera in the world!"

I was as happy as could be at such an answer, both because I hoped for an excellent success, and from a keen desire, natural enough in me, to see some drama of mine presented on the stage in America. But looking over the field, we discovered that the company lacked a singer capable of playing the part of Don Ottavio. I undertook to find him myself, and I did find him; and then when the manager of the Opera refused to incur additional expense, between me, my pupils and my friends, we provided the money to pay him; and *Don Giovanni* appeared on the stage [May 23, 1826, premiere].

I was not disappointed in my hopes. Everything pleased, everything was admired and praised—words, music, actors, performance; and the beautiful, brilliant and amiable daughter was as distinguished, and shone as brilliantly, in the part of Zerlinetta as her father seemed incomparable in the part of Don Giovanni. Varying, in truth, were opinions in the audience as to the transcendent merit of those two rare portents in the realm of harmony. Some preferred Rossini, some the German, nor could I say with assurance which had the more partisans, *Il Barbiere di Siviglia* or *Don Giovanni.* It should be observed, however, that Mozart, either because he is no more or because he was not an Italian, not only has no enemies, but is exalted to the heights for his supreme merit by impartial judges and connoisseurs; whereas Rossini has a very goodly part of enemies, some because they are envious of his renown, others through malice inborn and an accursed instinct to criticize and to depreciate anything remarkable that Italy produces.

Above: Portrait of Giuseppe Garibaldi, engraving, undated/Credit: LC. *Below:* Antonio Meucci, photograph, undated/Credit: SIHS. Meucci is considered by some historians of science to be the actual inventor of the telephone. *Right:* The Garibaldi Guard, engraving, 1861/Credit: LC. Although offered a commission as lieutenant general in the Union army, Garibaldi refused. This group of volunteers fought with the Union army in the Civil War.

Garibaldi on Staten Island

1850–1851. Giuseppe Garibaldi, the liberator of Italy, arrived in New York as a political refugee and lived on Staten Island with Antonio Meucci, whose disputed invention of the telephone was never fully settled. This was a particularly discouraging period in Garibaldi's life because he found himself unable to make a living in the United States.

About June 1850, I embarked for Gibraltar, proceeding thence to Liverpool, and from Liverpool to New York. During the crossing I was assailed by rheumatic pains, which lasted through a great part of the voyage, and was at last carried ashore like a bale of goods at Staten Island, New York.

These pains continued for a couple of months, which I passed partly in Staten Island and partly in New York City, at the house of my dear and valued friend Michele Pastacaldi, where I enjoyed the charming society of the illustrious Foresti, one of the martyrs of the Spielberg.

Carpanetto's plan could not, however, be carried into effect for want of contributors. He had got three shares, of 10,000 francs each, taken up by Piazzoni and the brothers Camozzi of Bergamo; but what ship could be bought in America for 30,000 francs? Nothing larger than a small coasting-vessel; and, not being an American citizen, I should have been obliged to engage a captain of that nation, which did not suit me.

At last it became necessary to do something. An honest man of my acquaintance, Antonio Meucci of Florence, who had determined to establish a candle factory, offered me a place as his assistant. No sooner said than done. I could not take a share in the business for want of funds, as the 30,000 francs above mentioned, being insufficient for the purchase of a ship, had remained in Italy; but joined on condition of giving my services as far as I could.

I worked for some months under Meucci, who treated me, not as one of his factory hands, but as a member of the family, and with great kindness.

One day, however, tired of making candles, and perhaps driven by natural and habitual restlessness, I left the house with the intention of changing my trade. I remembered that I had been a sailor. I knew some words of English, and made my way to the shore of the island, where I perceived a number of coasting craft, busy loading and unloading goods. Reaching the first, I expressed my wish to come on board as a sailor. The men I saw on deck scarcely took any notice of me, and went on with their work. Approaching a second vessel, I made another trial, with the same result. At last I passed on to a third, which was just being unloaded, and, asking whether I might be allowed to help in the work, was told that no more hands were required. "But I do not ask for wages," I insisted. No reply. "I want to work to warm myself." In fact, there was snow on the ground. No one paid any heed to me, and I was overwhelmed with mortification.

My thoughts went back to the times when I had the honor of commanding the Montevidean fleet—not to speak of the gallant and immortal army of that Republic. What was the use of all that? No one wanted me. At last I swallowed my vexation, and returned to work at the tallow. It was fortunate that I had not told the excellent Meucci of my resolution, and therefore my chagrin, being concentrated in myself, was easier to bear. I must confess, besides, that my good employer's behavior to me had not been the cause of my unseasonable resolve; he was

always kindness itself, and so was Signora Ester, his wife. My position in his house, then, was in nowise deserving of pity, and it was only an attack of melancholy that had driven me to leave it. I was perfectly at liberty there; could work if I wished (and naturally I preferred useful work to any other occupation); or go shooting whenever I felt inclined; and often accompanied Meucci himself and various other friends from Staten Island and New York, who frequently favored us with their visits, on fishing expeditions. Though there was no luxury in his house, there was no want of comfort as regards either food or lodging.

I must now mention Major Bovi, the same who lost his arm at the defense of Rome, my comrade in several campaigns. He had joined me at Tangier, at Signor Carpanetto's house, toward the close of my stay in that place of refuge; and when I decided on crossing to America, my means not allowing me to take all my friends with me, I left Leggiero and Coccelli behind, with good recommendations, and chose Bovi to accompany me, as, wanting his right hand, he was unable to work.

Coccelli! Why should I not record a brief recollection of this comrade of mine, so young, brave, and handsome? Coccelli entered the Montevideo legion as a mere boy, and, having great musical gifts, played the key-bugle in the fine band belonging to the legion, and was our trumpeter in the famous charges by which that gallant corps made the name of Italian respected in America. Coccelli followed the legion through all its campaigns, and took part in our Italian expedition of 1848. As an officer he bore an honored part in the Lombard and Rome campaigns, and accompanied me when, proscribed by the Sardinian Government of 1849, I repaired to Tangier. When I quitted Tangier for America, I left my gun and other hunting appliances with Coccelli. He died very young, of a sunstroke.

My hound Castore also had to be left at Tangier with my friend Mr. Murray, and this faithful companion died of grief at our separation.

At last Francesco Carpanetto came to New York himself, having initiated at Genoa a commercial undertaking on a large scale, to be carried out in Central America. The *San Giorgio*, a vessel belonging to him, had left Genoa with part of the cargo, while he himself went to England to prepare the remainder and send it to Gibraltar, where the vessel was to pick it up. It being decided that I should accompany him to Central America, we at once made preparations for starting, and in 1851, I set out for Chagres with Carpanetto, on board an American steamer commanded by Captain Johnson.

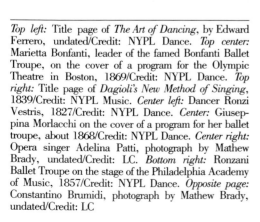

Top left: Title page of *The Art of Dancing*, by Edward Ferrero, undated/Credit: NYPL Dance. *Top center:* Marietta Bonfanti, leader of the famed Bonfanti Ballet Troupe, on the cover of a program for the Olympic Theatre in Boston, 1869/Credit: NYPL Dance. *Top right:* Title page of *Dagioli's New Method of Singing*, 1839/Credit: NYPL Music. *Center left:* Dancer Ronzi Vestris, 1827/Credit: NYPL Dance. *Center:* Giuseppina Morlacchi on the cover of a program for her ballet troupe, about 1868/Credit: NYPL Dance. *Center right:* Opera singer Adelina Patti, photograph by Mathew Brady, undated/Credit: LC. *Bottom right:* Ronzani Ballet Troupe on the stage of the Philadelphia Academy of Music, 1857/Credit: NYPL Dance. *Opposite page:* Constantino Brumidi, photograph by Mathew Brady, undated/Credit: LC

Controversy About Brumidi's Frescoes in the Capitol

1858. In a letter to the editor of The New York Daily Tribune *on May 31, Gugliemo Gajani, a New York resident, replied to naive and nationalistic criticism of Constantino Brumidi's recently completed frescoes in the United States Capitol in Washington.*

I have lately been at Washington and derived much pleasure from visiting the national capital and its splendid buildings and works of art. I admired them, and was much pleased with the frescoes and decorations of my fellow citizen Signor Constantino Brumidi. But on my return to New York my attention was directed to a correspondence of the *Tribune* (May 17) and to other attacks made against that artist and his works at the Capitol. I knew him in Rome, where he was much esteemed and has left excellent specimens of his artistic skill. I can hardly believe that ten years of exile could have so entirely destroyed his capacity or impaired my judgment. Had the attack been confined to the ground that artists or workmen of foreign birth, who are satisfied with a small compensation, should be excluded from the Capitol in order to have the work done exclusively by natives well paid, I would have nothing to say, for I keep off entirely from your administrative questions and politics. But on the ground of art and taste a Roman might be allowed to express an opinion quite different from that of your own correspondent and his friends. Fresco painting represents in art what improvisation is in poetry. The artist must execute his work upon a fresh wall, tracing the outlines by a steel point, and using mineral colors, which are instantly absorbed, and do not show their effect, until the wall dries. The artist therefore must work with great rapidity, and has no opportunity for corrections. It does not require a greater capacity than the ordinary painting with oil or water colors on a dry wall, but the artist must have a peculiar disposition, and this the Italians possess in a greater degree than others. A good French painter generally does not attempt to make frescoes. Mediocre artists often use water colors prepared with glue on a dry wall, like whitewashing, a style called "distemper," quite easy, but of short duration and bad effect. Michael Angelo had never practiced fresco painting when Bramante procured him the commission to paint the ceiling of the Sistine Chapel, with a view to ruin his reputation. Michael Angelo called from Florence his former schoolmate, Granacci, and other fresco painters, to teach him the art. He was much perplexed at the beginning, but afterward declared it the best style of painting. I believe that your best painters, by exerting themselves and gaining experience, might have succeeded in doing the work accomplished by Brumidi. But it would have required a long time and an enormous expenditure. A nice piece of velvet might be manufactured in New York as well as Genoa, but it would require an extraordinary patriotism to buy it at fifty dollars a yard, while a better article imported from Genoa can be had at five dollars— *"non omnia fert omnis tellus"*—and your manufacturers wisely direct their energy and skill to other objects in which they excel.

A national and historical gallery, as your own correspondent suggests, should be the object of the ambition of your artists, and there probably they would earn much glory— *"vestigia Graeca ausi deserere et celebrare domestica facta."* Historical truth and severity of taste should be adopted for that gallery, no doubt. But in decorating the volume of a large building it would be absurd from a point of view of art to comply with the insinuation of your correspondent. He would reduce everything to a matter of fact, doing away with the traditional rules of art, the example of the great masters and the free imagination of the artist.

It is a fact that in France, in England, in Belgium, in Italy, and everywhere public buildings have been decorated by competent artists, you meet the same style and symbols, allegories and classical memories occasionally adopted by Signor Brumidi. Before condemning him, you must find fault with all the best painters who preceded him, and especially with Michael Angelo and Raphael, who introduced that style of fresco in the Vatican itself. It is in vain to say that "these absurdities of the old world" should be corrected in America, for no reform has yet been attempted, and all the best American artists have derived their style from "the old world," and I do not know of any American school of art founded on different theory and taste.

It is absurd, therefore, to despise the works of Signor Brumidi because "they look foreign and betray the Italian element," that is to say, because they are classical in the subject and artistic in the execution. A good American artist would have equally offended the taste of your correspondent on this point. I do not believe, besides, that in the fine arts it will be possible to do entirely away with classical memories and symbols having a general acceptance. Classical drapery also cannot be given up for the ever changing and often absurd fashion of the modern dresses.

Canova, requested by Napoleon to cut a statue representing him in his full military costume, utterly refused, saying, "It would be impossible to make it a work of art." I have seen at the eastern entrance to the Capitol at Washington a large statue of the goddess Peace, cut by an Italian in a classical, foreign, Italian style. He could have made it most national by a Quaker's

bonnet, and most modern by the addition of hoops and crinoline, and yet I preferred it "in the absurd style of the old world."

The fine arts are not a matter of fact. We must have feeling in order to appreciate them, and an educated taste in order to judge of their merit. There is life in them, but it cannot be discovered by mechanical observation no more than in our body by the anatomical knife. It must be felt.

A cardinal who, together with Pope Paul III, visited the great fresco of Michael Angelo, *The Last Judgment,* before it was finished, declared himself scandalized, for there were many nude figures. Michael Angelo immediately represented the figure of that cardinal in hell, and said, "A man of such base mind and profligate feelings, who could see nothing but nude figures in my composition, deserves that place." The German writer Kotzebue, who despised "the absurdities of the old world," was requested by a friend to suspend his judgment till he had been in Italy. Kotzebue, from Florence, wrote to his friend, "I have seen the famous Venus de' Medici, but I confess that a chambermaid of Berlin in the same costume pleased me more." He was not a good man, and nature had deprived him of a great source of pleasure, the taste for music and the fine arts.

I confess that my national feelings were a little wounded when I saw vituperated to some extent in Washington an artist much esteemed in Rome. Music and the fine arts are all that remain of our former greatness, and we are naturally jealous of this glory. Besides, I am convinced that Signor Brumidi is a good artist and an excellent fresco painter. He has studied long in Rome, even from his boyhood, and visited for instruction all the most important schools of art in Italy. Baron Camucini was his master in painting, and the great Thorwaldsen taught him sculpture. In both arts Signor Brumidi has left several specimens of his skill in Rome. For instance, he was employed during eleven years in making frescoes and decorations of the villa and of the palace of Prince Torlonia in Rome. These works are admired by visitors. Should an American admire the works of Signor Brumidi at home and despise them at Washington?

Signor Brumidi was also employed by the Government in Rome, together with other distinguished artists, to prepare the chronology of the Popes, in the new Basilica of St. Paul, and was allowed to finish his work after the revolution, notwithstanding that he was persecuted for the part which he took in that movement. The Republican Government of Rome honored Signor Brumidi with an important commission, as he was much esteemed for his talent and personal qualities. I am glad, myself, that he has already executed some works at the Capitol. They speak for themselves to those who have taste for the fine arts.

I admired myself the room decorated with imitations from the frescoes of Pompeii, so hateful to your correspondent. I would challenge any man of sound judgment to enter the room of the Agricultural Committee without being struck by the good choice of the subject and the excellent execution. The Roman Cincinnatus at the plow stands on one side, and opposite to it there is Gen. Putnam, a true American Cincinnatus, also at the plow. Your correspondent himself finds nothing to say against these pictures except that their "tone is Italian (artistic), though the artist has done his best to make the thing American." But as the artist means to offer the example of Gen. Putnam as a counterpart of that of Cincinnatus, the merit of the picture does not consist in their being the best possible portrait of the revolutionary hero, but in conveying the moral idea of its meaning.

Above: Typical street scene in an impoverished Sicilian village, Taormina, about 1900/Credit: LC. *Right:* A group of urban poor assembled in the streets of Naples, one of the most densely populated cities in Europe, about 1900/Credit: LC

CHAPTER TWO

THE OLD COUNTRY
TURN-OF-THE-CENTURY ITALY

"Everybody works. There is poverty."

1910. Pascal D'Angelo came to this country from the Abruzzi at the age of sixteen with his father. Self-taught, he became a poet and writer, living in New York. In his autobiography he described the dire economic conditions endured by his family of typical peasants, which compelled him and his father reluctantly to emigrate to the United States.

The hamlet where I was born on January 20, 1894, is comprised of a small group of stone houses near Introdacqua and not very far from the old walled city of Sulmona. Introdacqua nestles at the head of a beautiful valley whose soft green is walled in by the great blue barrens of Monte Majella. The mother mountain looms to the east of us and receives the full splendor of the dawn. We are proud to call ourselves the sons of the majestic Majella. And our race, the ancient Samnites, is said to have sprung from those sunny altitudes and spread their power over all Italy, making even Rome tremble.

Few roads run to this quiet land and the old traditions have never entirely died out there. Below the town is the garden of Ovid with wild roses and cool springs, and above is an ancient castle that in summer is fantastically crowned with mingling flights of wild pigeons that take care of their younglings on its towered heights. In the valley beyond are finely cultivated fields dotted with the ruins of Italica, the capital of fierce Samnium. . . .

Everybody works. There is poverty. Often there is not enough to eat. There are among us many women whose husbands have gone to alien lands. Sometimes money does not come from across the sea. Perhaps the father is out of work, perhaps he has been hurt in an accident or even killed. These women do not waste much time in crying. They take up the task of keeping the household going with as little expense as possible. Everyone in their family must help, down to the children barely able to walk. Everyone works. The mother will probably hire a small piece of land and cultivate it. If she has a baby it is placed under the shade of the nearest tree. And the strong mother tills and finally harvests the products of their collective toil. . . .

She sighed deeply and whispered, "Your father has decided to go away."

Alarmed, I exclaimed, "Where to?"

"To America."

I felt a wild pain, for I dearly love my father. To America! I had heard much of that strange place into which people we knew had vanished and had never returned. Had never returned! And my own father! After all, I was a young boy, and I could not keep back the tears.

My mother put her arms around me and pressed her toil-marked face in my hair. And she kissed me, begging me not to cry. I looked up into her beautiful eyes and I was calmed.

Sighing deeply, she murmured, "I cannot blame him. He works so hard. And we never seem to get any better. I must bend myself to what has to be."

Still I sobbed at the thought that my father would go away. But she, with a mother's divine art, softly calmed me. And smiling into my eyes, she begged me to go to gentle dreams. So, slowly, together we went up the ladder into our unlit bedroom.

Our people have to emigrate. It is a matter of too much boundless life and too little space. We feel tied up there. Every bit of cultivable soil is owned by those fortunate few who lord over us. Before spring comes into our valley all the obtainable land is rented out or given to the peasants for a season under usurious conditions, namely, for three-fourths, one-half or one-fourth of the crops, the conditions depending upon the necessity either of the owner or of the peasant who is seeking land. Up to a few years ago some peasants had to take land even on the one-fifth basis; that is, the man who worked the land and bought even seeds and manure would only get one-fifth of the harvest, while the owner who merely allowed him to use the land would receive four-fifths. This was possible up to a short while ago. But today such a thing is absolutely impossible since no peasant would agree to it unless his head were not functioning normally. And what is it that saves the man and keeps him from being ground under the hard power of necessity? The New World!

Previously, there was no escape; but now there is. In the old days men from our highlands did go down into the marshes of Latium to harvest and earn some extra money. And there

they sickened with malaria and came back ghosts of their former selves. But now there was escape from the rich landowners, from the terrors of drought, from the specter of starvation, in the boundless Americas out of which at times people returned with fabulous tales and thousands of liras—riches unheard of before among peasants.

The year before, my father had been trying to better our conditions. He had hired two large pieces of arable ground on which he had toiled almost every minute of daylight during that whole season. Having no money to make the first payment on the land, he had to borrow some at a very high rate of interest. At the end of that season, after selling the crops, he found that he had just barely enough money to pay the rest of the rent and to pay back the loan with the enormous interest. It is the landowners and the moneylenders who are the real vampires among us—not pitiable, demented old women.

That season of excessive toil made my father much older. His tall strong body was beginning to bend. He had become a little clumsy and slower. And the results of his futile attempt made him moody and silent. He would sit on our doorstep in the evenings and gaze out at the living darkness of our valley. At times, when one talked to him he would answer very absently as if his thoughts were far away.

And finally, the inevitable decision came into his mind and he was not to be moved from it.

Above left: Flower sellers on the Street of Steps, Gradoni de Chioja, Naples, 1902/Credit: LC. *Above right:* In the Roman countryside shepherds and the homeless lived in thatched huts like this. The housewife depicted here raised free roaming chickens, about 1900, photograph by Giuseppe Primoli/Credit: Primoli. *Below right:* Hauling slabs of marble from a sawmill to the railroad station, Carrara, 1902/Credit: LC

Above left: Straw weavers in Sensano (Siena), Tuscany, about 1892, photograph by Mario Nunes Vais/Credit: Gabinetto. *Above right:* Two people carrying firewood from the forest to their home, Tuscany, about 1900/Credit: Alinari. *Below left:* Farm worker, about 1900/Credit: Sforzesco. *Below center:* A group of farm workers, Alto Adige, about 1900/Credit: Gabinetto. *Below right:* A group of women washing clothes at the communal laundry, Genzano (Rome), about 1895, photograph by Giuseppe Primoli/Credit: Primoli

The Italian Attitude Toward Emigration

1907. Antonio Mangano, a Protestant clergyman and a native of Calabria, returned to the land of his birth to examine the attitudes of Italians toward the effects of emigration on their country.

Emigration and its results is a live topic of conversation among all classes of society in Italy. I have witnessed many a hot discussion in the town secretary's office when I was gleaning statistics. Several men always followed the stranger into the office and stood by, interested listeners until appealed to for their opinions. I was surprised to discover how well posted nine out of every ten are, with definite, well-thought-out convictions, favorable or unfavorable to the movement according to their social position. A southern landlord in the province of Molise told me, with bristling mustache and keen flashing eyes, that every year he is finding it more difficult to secure laborers to raise his wheat, and he is compelled to pay such as are available three times as much as he ever did before.

"Why, my dear sir," said he, "we have simply come to the utmost limit in these parts. We cannot go on in this way any longer. The government must help us, and that very soon. We poor landholders are at the mercy of the few able-bodied men who remain. But [with a deprecatory shrug] we cannot expect anything from the government at Rome. They do not think of us; they are engrossed too much in the interests of northern Italy."

I turned to Pietro, a brawny workman, who stood listening and smiling to himself, with his hands in his pockets.

"Well, and what do you think of this emigration to America?" I asked.

He straightened involuntarily, the hands came out of his pockets to assist his rapid gesticulatory Italian.

"Ah! Signor, emigration is one great blessing to our country. What would all of these people do here, except to live more wretchedly, if that were possible, while the *latifondisti* [landowners] are fattening upon their lifeblood! The fact is, if it hadn't been for emigration, we must have ended by eating one another up. Once there was no money in this town. Now we all have a little and we poor *contadini* don't have to go to the *padrone* and beg a loan and pay him fifty per cent on it. No! No! No one can doubt that emigration is a great blessing!"

These answers are from opposite points of view, but each voiced the feeling of his class, I found upon making similar inquiry in all the forty or fifty towns I visited. Once I did find an affable *civile* who looked at the subject apart from his own personal interests. The usual discussion was waxing hot, when he ended it by this impartial remark: "Emigration is indeed a blessing for the one who emigrates, for he can earn more money and his family can live more comfortably. But for the country, it is an evil, for we are fast losing our working population."

The belated introduction of machinery in farm work is directly due to emigration. Progressive landowners who study the situation are beginning to realize that to work their soil with profit, or even at all, the machines must take the place of departed laborers, and so throughout the province of Molise and elsewhere are found here and there modern reapers, thrashers, ploughs and cultivators, objects of wonder to the entire country-

side. This use of modern implements is still too new to see any great changes in agriculture, and their cost makes such tools too expensive for the small landowner or peasant proprietor. . . .

Another point of interest to me was to discover what change, if any, had been made in the life and manners of the returned emigrant; how he is regarded by those who knew him before and after, so to speak. The consensus of opinion seemed to be that the returned emigrant dresses and carries himself much better than formerly, that he is intellectually awakened, has more cleanly habits, more life and spirit, and that he will not, as a rule, be willing to put his neck under the yoke again and be content with his former life. His visit to his native land is of short duration, usually during the dull winter season, and he returns to America in the spring though there are those who remain two or three years. . . .

I believe one of the most wholesome effects of emigration is this "more life and spirit" just mentioned, for here are the hopeful beginnings of a proper appreciation of the dignity and worth of a man and his work. The *contadino*'s contact with democratic, individualistic America, with its opportunities for every industrious man, no matter how lowly his birth, to become a successful, respected citizen, is creating self-respect and ambition. A spirit of hope and independence is stirring these downtrodden masses, who have been considered no better than pack-animals for centuries, and they are awakening at last to their right and the possibility of progress. That which socialism has not been able to do in any sane way, emigration is doing in a most natural manner. There are some phases of this transition which are quite amusing, and to which it is most difficult for

those who once lorded it over these poor people to accommodate themselves.

In the little town of Pulsano on the beautiful, spacious Gulf of Taranto, I roused the genial communal secretary from his midday nap. He good-naturedly showed me the registers and spoke at length of the numbers who had emigrated and of those who had returned. "Do you observe any change in the returned emigrant?" I asked. His answer was both laughable and pathetic. He nearly wept as he told me of the utter lack of respect shown by returned emigrants toward their former superiors. Said he: "I have always been good to these people and helped them, even when they were going away. Then they were very humble and always came into my office with great fear, hat in hand, hardly daring to lift their eyes from the floor. When they return, they come in here and look on me as no better than themselves. They do not even take off their hats. I can hardly endure it. Respect is due, if not to myself, at least to my official position. But in America they lose all respectfulness."

Above left: Francesco and Oliva Innocenta Contrucci in Calamecca, Tuscany, 1907/ Credit: Contrucci. Francesco Contrucci's life was typical of many other emigrants of this period. He made his first trip to the United States in 1895, finding work in the Pennsylvania coal mines. By 1902 he had become an American citizen. On his return to Italy in 1907, he married Oliva Innocenta. They came to Pennsylvania, where in 1909 she died in childbirth. Returning to Italy in 1910, he married his second wife, Francesca Benedetti. After serving in the Italian army during World War I, he again returned to the United States in 1919. In 1922 Francesca and their four children sailed from Genoa for the United States. Following this, the family remained in the United States and their first American child, a son, was born in Jeanette, Pennsylvania. In 1925 the entire family moved to Detroit, where Francesco worked as a bricklayer relining the walls of blast furnaces at the Ford Motor Company. *Above right:* Peasant women in front of the railroad station, Genoa, about 1894, photograph by Mario Nunes Vais/Credit: Gabinetto

Above left: Sidewalk vendor selling ice water and coconut slices, Naples, about 1900/Credit: Alinari. *Above right:* Piazza Campo de' Fiori, a food and vegetable market in the old section of Rome, about 1907, photograph by Mario Nunes Vais/Credit: Gabinetto. *Below right:* Selling food on the streets of Milan, about 1900/Credit: Sforzesco

Above left: Pasta drying outdoors, Naples, 1903/Credit: LC. *Above right:* Shoemaker in Milan working on the sidewalk, about 1900/Credit: Sforzesco. *Below left and right:* Selling brooms and melons from house to house in the streets of Milan, about 1900/Credit: Sforzesco

Above left: The benediction of animals, appearing in *L'Illustrazione Italiana*, 1896/Credit: Biblioteca. *Above right:* Religious procession, Ariccia (Rome), about 1895, photograph by Giuseppe Primoli/Credit: Primoli. *Below:* Playing bocce, about 1900/Credit: Fototeca 3M

Above: Street scene, Naples, about 1900/Credit: Alinari. *Below:* Peasants standing in front of a cart, near Rome, about 1900, photograph by Giuseppe Primoli/Credit: Primoli.
Opposite page: New villas in the country, appearing in *L'Illustrazione Italiana*, 1882/Credit: Biblioteca

Against the Supposed Concern of the Bourgeoisie for the Emigrants

1876. This article, which appeared in the Italian publication La Plebe *("The Crowd"), chides the bourgeoisie for its hypocritical appeals to the government to stop and prohibit the emigration of peasants because of the dangers of exploitation and suffering overseas. What really worried the landowners was the loss of cheap labor.*

The newspapers continue to print clamorous protests demanding that the government take steps to stop the flow of emigration. They vociferously condemn those monopolizers who would profit from the suffering of others, while the middle class displays signs of compassion for the unfortunate ones who are going to litter the wilderness of America with their own cadavers.

The steps that have been requested of the government—let's be logical—make no sense. Does a society perhaps have the right to impede any of its members from leaving it? Both the present laws and common sense reject such a notion. Are we to turn our society into a walled penitentiary? If it is permissible today even to commit suicide, should it not be permissible to leave? The government, by complying with these requests, can create obstacles for those who leave, but it can never prohibit emigration without violating the most fundamental principle of personal freedom.

It is appropriate to speak out against those who abuse the good faith of the emigrants in order to steal a few lire from them and later leave them in the lurch. But it is even more appropriate, recognizing the right of emigrants to emigrate, to protect them from fraud, in order to help them attain their goals freely.

And this would not prevent emigration, but rather would make it easier and safer.

Love remains the final motive of those who watch and are frightened by the dangers and death to which the emigrants expose themselves. But this gives no right to impede emigration, especially when those who cry out have not taken steps to rectify the conditions that cause emigration in the first place.

And, before believing those who bemoan the evils that await emigrants, one must demand proof that they attempted to change the circumstances that make this country a stepmother to those who abandon it. Do you think it is merely capriciousness that forces the *contadini* to abandon our land to go to America? Do you think they abandon their nest with no pangs of the heart? Do you think they seek the future and the unknown for glory, out of a desire for adventure, or for honor, like the Spanish hidalgos who sailed on the ships of Cortés, Pizarro and Ojeda? When they leave, in addition to the marks of hard work and privation, they have on their faces the signs of deep pain, poorly concealed by the mask of a smile, and it is the pain of leaving their homeland. And when they regain their cheerfulness, it is because of the hope for a better future, and of the certainty that the land that awaits them will not be as inhospitable as the one they leave behind. They become cheerful looking at their children who will grow up on a soil that will produce to compensate them for their labor, that will produce for them, not for others. They are consoled by the hope and the knowledge that here they have nothing to lose and there everything to gain. . . . And so do you really believe that they think you are warning them for their own good? One individual, in fact, told me that, while being exhorted to stay, he had decided to leave because he truly believed that both life and liberty awaited him there. Do you see?

Letter from *Contadini* in Northern Italy to the Minister of the Interior

1876. This eloquent letter from a group of farm workers appeared in La Plebe. *It enumerates their miserable economic conditions and the governmental abuses that provided them with an incentive to emigrate.*

From the *contadini* of northern Italy to the Illustrious Baron, the Honorable Minister of the Interior:

Dear Baron!

We well understand the real motive behind your circular, and you have expressed it clearly. It is *that emigration is in such alarming proportions in some provinces that it causes fear of serious damage to the economic life of the nation.*

And now, dear Baron, is precisely when we must take you aside and first of all ask you: What do you mean by "nation"?

If you mean the majority of citizens, that is, the class of oppressed, we are the nation.

Now, look at us, dear Baron! Do not our pale and yellowed faces, our sunken cheeks show with their silent eloquence our painful hard work and our utter deficiency of nutrition?

In fact, our life is so bitter that it is little better than death. Hence, for us the greatest economic damage that we can incur is to continue living under the present circumstances.

We cultivate wheat yet we don't taste white bread.

We cultivate the vine yet we don't drink its wine.

We raise livestock but never taste meat.

We wear fustian cloth, live in hovels, tormented by cold in the winter and by hunger during the long days of summer.

Our only bounty in this Italian land is a little corn, and even that is reduced by your unjust milling taxes. The inevitable consequence of all of this is pellagra in the dry regions and both pellagra and marsh fever in the wetlands.

The ultimate consequences of so much suffering are the hospital and death, without even the comfort of a last farewell from our loved ones.

With all of this do you expect that we not emigrate? . . .

If by "nation" you mean, as it seems, not the majority of the oppressed who work, but rather the minority who do nothing and grow fat from our blood and sweat, then we do agree that the exodus of *contadini* who cause *serious damage to their economic life*. . . .

But what do we care about all of them?

For almost sixteen years these people have been stuffing us with notions of country, unity, liberty and other nonsense.

In the beginning, we believed them and shed our share of blood in battles for an independent country, for which we were promised all sorts of material and moral blessings, but what have we gained? . . . Only to be swindled and exploited worse than before.

Salt, the only condiment available for our food, is raised to an impossible price.

All consumer items are enormously overpriced.

Conscription is like before, even worse.

An income tax.

A tax on grinding corn.

Family taxes and all the rest.

What has happened to all the state and ecclesiastical land which, if divided into small lots and distributed among us *contadini*, would have doubled the tax income of the state and changed radically so many families of good farmers by upraising them from misery to the state of modest landowners? . . .

But for you the misery of the poor farmers is not the principal cause of their emigrating.

For you, emigration is caused by the *manipulations of mercenary speculators.*

It is unfortunately true that there are in Italy mercenary speculators whose conscience has not prevented them from speculating even on the misery of us poor *contadini*.

However, it is not any less true that instead of punishing the delinquents, you use them as a pretext for oppressing the victims, believing that by abolishing the agencies and the agents you will suppress emigration.

But be careful—the laws of nature cannot be violated without consequence.

The Egyptians also wanted to prevent the Jews they were exploiting from leaving the land of servitude. Read the Bible.

And if Oliver Cromwell had not been prevented from emigrating, he would not have had Charles I decapitated some time later.

Emigration provides you an escape valve: we advise you for your own interests and for the lesser of evils not to close it off.

When one tries to control steam too much, the boiler blows up. We are tired of dying of exhaustion on the ground in order to maintain a hoard of lazy individuals who, decorated with stripes, stroll through our streets, as well as a flock of high- and low-level bureaucrats, three-fourths of whom are useless.

Oppressed and vexed in every way possible, we are going away in order to leave you in your comfort. What else can you want? . . .

Serious Riots in the Streets of Milan

1898. As in other parts of Europe, the urban working class mobilized to express its dissatisfaction with economic conditions such as the inflated price of bread. On May 7, there was a general strike and the streets in the city center of Milan were flooded with thousands of male and female demonstrators. This report from the Corriere della Sera *of the next day presents a completely unsympathetic view of the events.*

Yesterday morning Milan was unfortunately the site of renewed and deplorable disorder, indeed far more serious than could have been predicted.

Correctly understood, the issue of bread was secondary; indeed it was never a serious issue here. Rather, the agitators used it as a pretext to incite uninformed youths, misinformed workers, women, and children to excesses one would never have believed possible in Milan.

How much moral and material damage! How many sad, prolonged consequences from these painful events! How many ruined businesses and families in mourning!

But first, a few sincere words for our officials and soldiers.

They demonstrated truly admirable patience, endurance and discipline; thanks to them Milan escaped even more serious ills at the hands of those who resort to looting, burning, and destruction.

One newspaper reported, as a significant item, a rather strong sentence uttered by a police officer; but why did it not report the millions of insults, obscenities, and abuses hurled at the soldiers who are our brothers, our sons?

Swarms of unruly children applauded frantically as tiles

rained from roofs and stones flew through the streets; and when—after much patience, many wounds, and many bruises—the soldiers finally fired their rifles, the hysterical crowd shouted, "Scoundrels, cowards, assassins!" What degeneracy!

The women were even more out of control: they approached the troops, insulting them with every obscenity and screaming: "We work all day to pay for your leisure, you lazy brutes!"

Certain principles that have been cleverly and repeatedly preached are now beginning to bear fruit!

With a heart that aches and a hand that trembles, we write the story of these deplorable events; our account, based on notes transmitted to us by friends and reporters, is as accurate as possible. . . .

As the demonstrators moved through the suburbs, ordering and obtaining the closing of factories despite the reluctance of many workers, their numbers continued to increase until they formed a crowd of several thousand.

By 11:00 A.M., all the major industrial establishments of the city had been shut down; in addition to the Stigler, Vago, Roth, and Suffert factories, in the suburb of Porta Nova, the Miani and Silvestri, the Bocconi (Via Olona), the tobacco manufacturing company, and others were closed; according to a recent poll, these workshops account for 37,000 workers, many of them women.

As the menacing sea of protestors advanced, the doors of houses and shops were hastily locked; those who were shut out then augmented the crowds of the curious! . . .

Piazza del Duomo was occupied by the military—infantry, cavalry, and artillery.

The command of the troops was taken over by General Bava-Beccaris.

The passage that leads from the Gallery into the Piazza was blocked by *bersaglieri*; cavalry sealed off the entrance into the Corso; *alpini* and infantry closed off Via Mercanti, Via Torino, Via Carlo Alberto, and Via Rastrelli.

All of the city's gates were also under military control.

Obviously, the plan of the military authorities was to clear the center of the city, to divide the rioters while pushing them toward the gates, and to insure that reinforcements could not join them.

The preponderance of evidence indicates that although some impulsive defenders may have blindly joined the struggle, the operation was well prepared and organized; indeed many had assigned posts.

Taken by surprise by an unjustifiable revolt, the majority of citizens refrained from participating and limited themselves to the role of saddened spectators.

Above: May Day parade with the *bandiera rossa*, the red flag of the socialists, in the Piazza Santa Croce in Gerusalemme, Rome, 1891, photograph by Giuseppe Primoli/ Credit: Primoli. *Below:* Illustration of the riots in the streets of Milan on May 7, based on a photograph by Luca Comerio, appearing in *L'Illustrazione Italiana*, 1898/Credit: Biblioteca

Above: "Going to the Land of Opportunity," emigrants aboard ship on their way to America, 1909/Credit: LC. *Right:* A family of emigrants departing from the central railroad station, Milan, 1889, photograph by Giuseppe Primoli/Credit: Primoli

CHAPTER THREE

NEW LIVES
IN THE NEW WORLD
1881-1914

The Trauma of Departing from a Sicilian Village

1905. Although emigrating to America offered economic opportunities, it created crises within families, especially evident when men boarded railway trains in their native regions before embarking for America. In reporting on his tour of Italy, Italian writer Angelo Mosso described an epic departure in rural Sicily which must have been repeated thousands of times in towns and villages throughout Italy.

I heard a lot of noise in the station and was told that it was the emigrants. Looking out of the compartment window, I saw a black river of *contadini*, cloth sacks on their backs, running toward the third-class section of the train: shouting women and children followed. In the turmoil, it was impossible to understand which ones were really emigrants; many of those who entered the cars with sacks later came out crying, embracing and kissing one another, in an indescribable confusion. The railroad conductors and station-master had a hard time holding people back and making those who were not passengers leave the cars. Finally the doors closed and the departure signal sounded.

Four people passed by us carrying a woman; her lifeless head, pale as that of a cadaver, rested on her chest. Other women wept; and all those brown faces roasted by the sun, their white teeth shining in mouths rent open by screams, turned towards the other part of the train and paid no attention to us. Vigorous young men leaned out of windows to embrace the people below. Like a wave the multitude crushed against the cars, climbing up on and descending from the footboards, clutching the door-handles. . . .

The locomotive whistled fitfully with a laboring hiss, but the disorder was so great that the engineer did not dare move the train. Despite the requests and reprimands of the police, the crowd still clutched the train, embraced by the final grasps of good-bye.

The station-master told me that thirty emigrants were leaving, with seven women, for America. These

poor people had waited for two months without being able to get space on the steamer; the order finally arrived to embark from Palermo.

When the train moved, there was a heartbreaking cry like the anguished roar that bursts from a crowd at the instant of a great calamity. All the people raised their arms and waved handkerchiefs. From the windows of the cars the leaning figures of the young men and women strained; they seemed suspended in air and kissed the hands of old people as the train departed.

A woman left the crowd and ran screaming. We were already out of the station, and she was still running, saying in a loud voice: "Say hello to him, remind him that I'm waiting; make him send me the money for the trip; tell him that I'm waiting, that if I don't leave, I'll die."

Weeping and breathlessness cut off her voice; she stopped, caught hold of a telegraph pole, then suddenly bent over and fell to the ground.

On the dusty road consumed by the sun, relatives and friends from far away waited in carts to say farewell to the emigrants. Their carts were festive and characteristically Sicilian, with horses dressed up in embroidered work, red tassels and red harnesses, plumes on their heads, *siddumi* [trappings on the harness pads] on their saddles, multicolored feathers, and bells that glistened in the sun. The women heaped upon the carts pulled back their black shawls to reveal eyes made bigger and brighter by tears. And in their unbridled sorrow, all of them, men and children, wore an intense expression like a dramatic mask in order to impress a memory upon those fleeing people they saw, perhaps, for the last time.

On the embankment of the railroad tracks exotic-looking aloes formed a scrub of gigantic leaves with thorny edges culminating in black points; and from the middle of the ashen green bushes, the antennae of gigantic flowers stretched upward, like the ornaments of a fantastical decor. Then bushes of prickly pear flew past, and among the succulent leaves wild geraniums spread out cheerful festoons of purple.

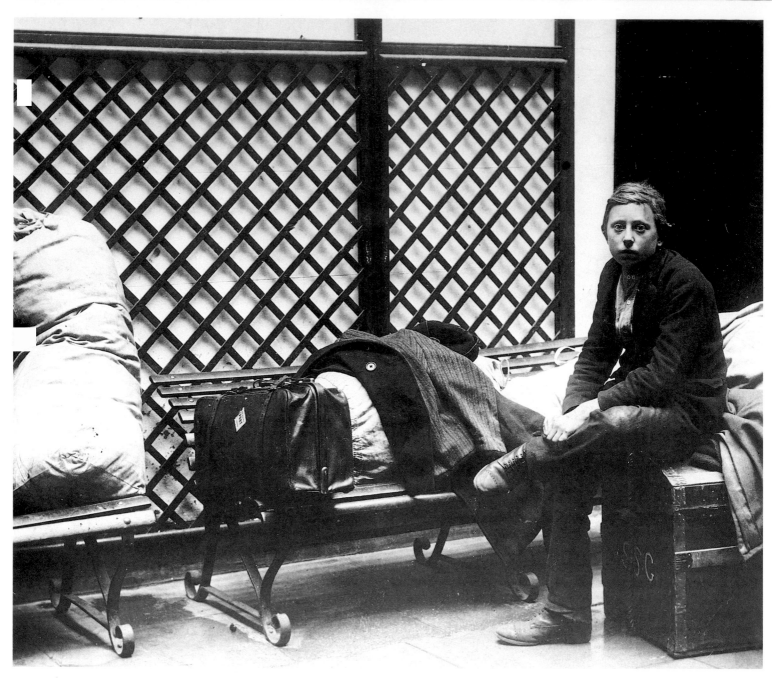

But the tears of departure and passage for the *contadini* of Castrofilippo are not yet finished. At the crossroads in the distance, next to the humble house of the signalmen, behind the gates and in the shade of melancholy eucalyptus trees, stand horses in a row, sparkling with harness-bells, embroidered martingales and collars; and the people on the carts bid farewell with cries of sadness and rejoicing.

When the train slowed down before arriving at Racalmuto, the people in front of and around the station gave a long muddled shout that grew like thunder until the engine stopped. Here six or seven emigrants reenacted the same moving scenes of good-bye. Outside the gate, in the midst of a crowd dressed in black, were other carts—arched saddles bright with little mirrors, red wheels, frames and sides painted with stories of Charlemagne and the royal family of France. It is a fantasy vision of medieval paladins and impoverished modern heroes setting off into the unknown in search of fortune. The train moved and the emigrants barely succeeded in disentangling themselves from the hands that formed a hedge around every window. The people gave a sad parting cry, and the scene grew faint in the sound of the fast-moving train and in the cloud of dust it left behind.

Far from the station of Racalmuto, where the tracks curve amidst the fields, a woman on a horse waited with a child in her arms and another behind her; a solemn cry of farewell emanated from the train. Everyone leaned out of the windows, waved caps and handkerchiefs, and shouted, "Maria." The still figure of this heartbroken mother, poised between two children who lifted their hands, moved me; I, too, extended my hand to wave, and my eyes filled with tears.

Then everything calmed down. The train raced ahead in solitude and virtual silence; a hot, dry wind moved the crops, bending the golden grain and swirling over barren furrows. Great waves like white smoke, like delicate sea-foam, rippled the surface of the fields.

Above: A young orphan going to America in search of his fortune, carrying all of his belongings with him, about 1900/Credit: TCI. *Right:* A family about to board a ship of the Red Star Line, one of the companies which specialized in transporting emigrants to the United States, Genoa, about 1894, photograph by Mario Nunes Vais/Credit: Gabinetto

The Emigrants' Lament in Song

About 1900. Folk tunes sung by departing emigrants and newly arrived immigrants expressed their hopes for a better life in the new country and their concern for the loved ones and the homeland they left behind.

I'm Leaving for America

(Brianza, Lombardy)

> *He:* I'm leaving for America,
> Leaving on the boat,
> I'm leaving and I'm happy
> Never to see you again.

> *She:* When you're gone
> You'll be sorry,
> You'll be sorry
> You let me go.

> *He:* When I'm in America
> I'll marry an American,
> And then I'll abandon
> The beautiful Italian.

> *She:* I've trampled
> The ring you gave me,
> If you don't believe me, handsome,
> I'll show it to you!

> *He:* Oh woman, you're so changeable,
> Oh woman without a heart,
> You vowed your love
> But it was a lie.

> *She:* Give me my letters,
> Give me my picture,
> Traitor, I will never
> Love you again.

> *He:* I'm leaving for America,
> I'm leaving on the boat,
> One day we will meet
> And I will love you again.

Mama, Give Me a Hundred Lire

(Northern Italy)

Mama, give me a hundred lire
Because I want to go to America.
  Mama, give me a hundred lire
  Because I want to go . . .
  Because I want to go to America.

I will give you a hundred lire
But America, no, no, no!
  I will give you a hundred lire
  But America no . . .
  But America no, again no!

Her brothers at the window:
"Mama, let her go!"
  Her brothers at the window:
  "Mama, let . . .
  Mama, let her go!"

As soon as it reached the open sea
The boat went down!
  As soon as it reached the open sea
  The boat went . . .
  The boat went down!

Mama's words
Proved true.
  Mama's words
  Proved . . .
  Proved true.

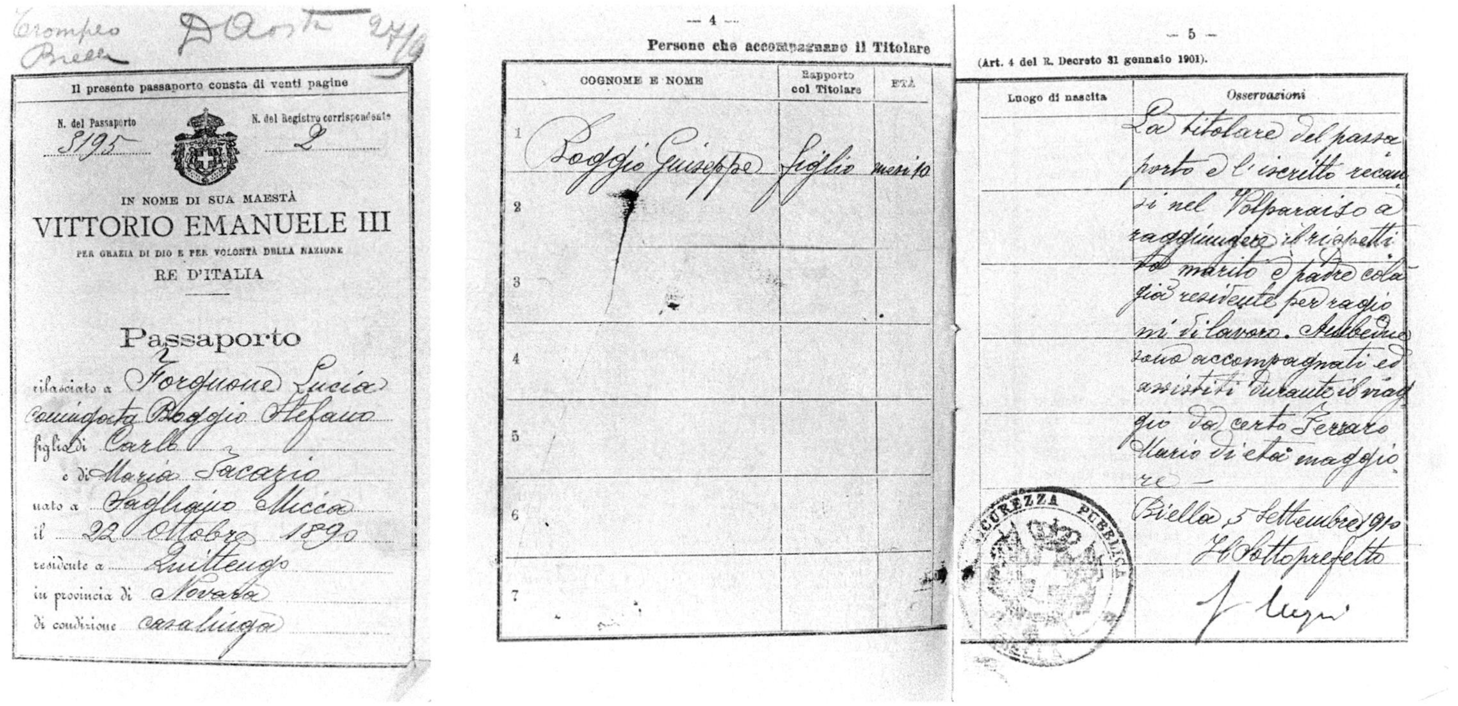

Italian Passport (top document):

Il presente passaporto consta di venti pagine

N. del Passaporto 8195   N. del Registro corrispondente 2

IN NOME DI SUA MAESTÀ

VITTORIO EMANUELE III

PER GRAZIA DI DIO E PER VOLONTÀ DELLA NAZIONE

RE D'ITALIA

Passaporto

rilasciato a Forguone Lucia
coniugata Poggio Stefano
figli di Carlo
e di Maria Sacario
nato a Tagliano Micca
il 22 Ottobre 1890
residente a Suitengo
in provincia di Novara
di condizione casalinga

— 4 —

Persone che accompagnano Il Titolare

	COGNOME E NOME	Rapporto col Titolare	ETÀ
1	Poggio Giuseppe	figlio	mesi 10
2			
3			
4			
5			
6			
7			

— 5 —

(Art. 4 del R. Decreto 31 gennaio 1901).

Luogo di nascita	Osservazioni
	La titolare del passaporto è l'iscritto recansi nel Valparaiso a raggiungere il rispettivo marito e padre colà residente per ragione di lavoro. Saranno accompagnati ed assistiti durante il viaggio da certo Ferraro Mario di età maggiore

Biella 5 Settembre 1910

Il Sottoprefetto

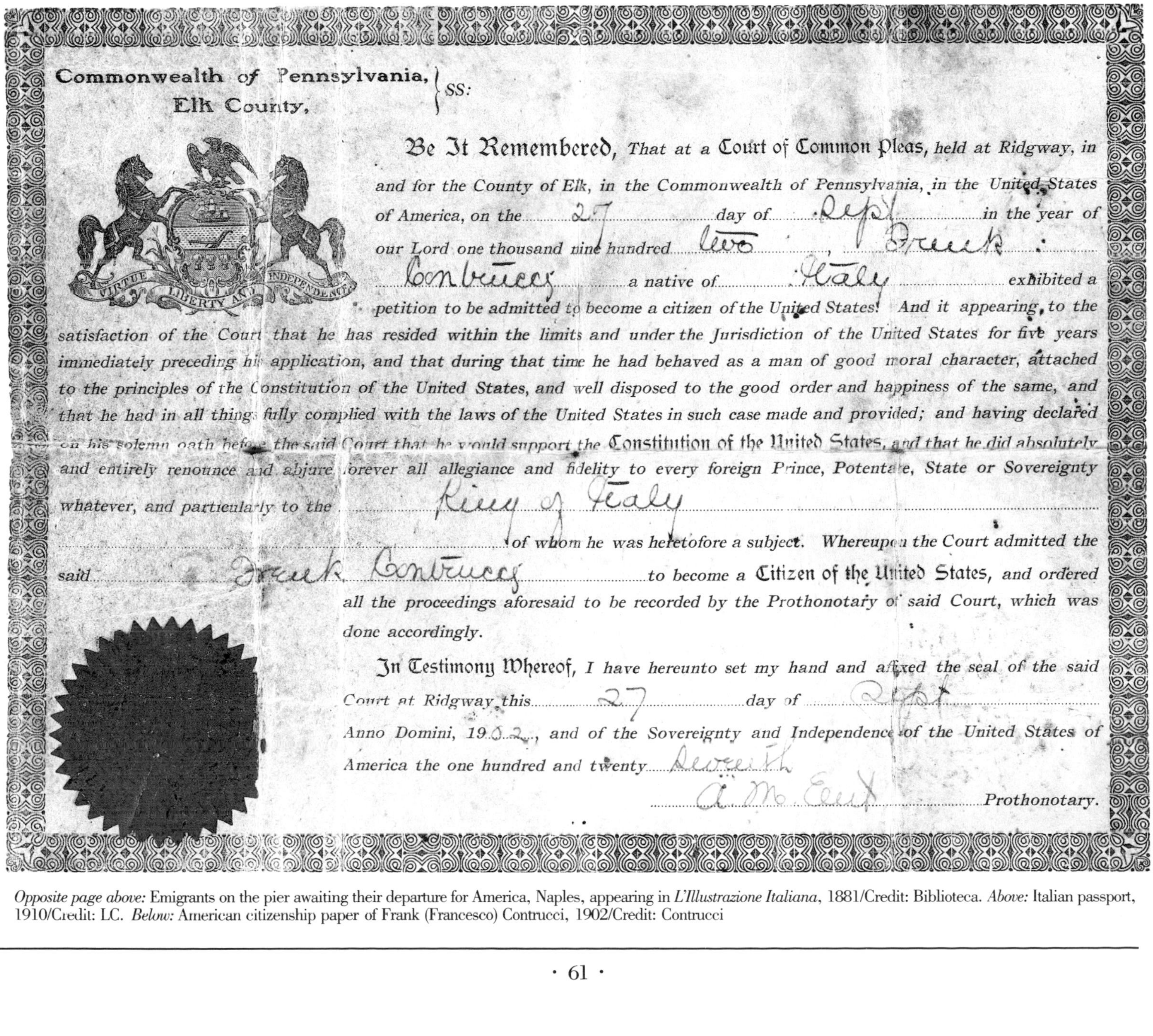

American Citizenship Paper (bottom document):

Commonwealth of Pennsylvania, } SS:

Elk County,

Be It Remembered, That at a Court of Common Pleas, held at Ridgway, in and for the County of Elk, in the Commonwealth of Pennsylvania, in the United States of America, on the 27 day of Sept in the year of our Lord one thousand nine hundred two, Frank Contrucci a native of Italy exhibited a petition to be admitted to become a citizen of the United States! And it appearing to the satisfaction of the Court that he has resided within the limits and under the Jurisdiction of the United States for five years immediately preceding his application, and that during that time he had behaved as a man of good moral character, attached to the principles of the Constitution of the United States, and well disposed to the good order and happiness of the same, and that he had in all things fully complied with the laws of the United States in such case made and provided; and having declared on his solemn oath before the said Court that he would support the Constitution of the United States, and that he did absolutely and entirely renounce and abjure forever all allegiance and fidelity to every foreign Prince, Potentate, State or Sovereignty whatever, and particularly to the King of Italy of whom he was heretofore a subject. Whereupon the Court admitted the said Frank Contrucci to become a Citizen of the United States, and ordered all the proceedings aforesaid to be recorded by the Prothonotary of said Court, which was done accordingly.

In Testimony Whereof, I have hereunto set my hand and affixed the seal of the said Court at Ridgway this 27 day of Sept Anno Domini, 1902, and of the Sovereignty and Independence of the United States of America the one hundred and twenty seventh.

A. M. Eny Prothonotary.

Opposite page above: Emigrants on the pier awaiting their departure for America, Naples, appearing in *L'Illustrazione Italiana*, 1881/Credit: Biblioteca. *Above:* Italian passport, 1910/Credit: LC. *Below:* American citizenship paper of Frank (Francesco) Contrucci, 1902/Credit: Contrucci

Conditions Endured by Emigrants Aboard Ship

1890. The noted Italian author Edmondo De Amicis decided to prepare a firsthand report of the experiences of emigrants on board a ship that traveled to America. He and the artist Arnaldo Ferraguti sailed on the Galileo, *recording in words and pictures the ordeal shared by millions of Italians.*

It was toward evening when I reached the wharf. The embarkation of the emigrants had been going on for an hour; and there lay the *Galileo* filling up with misery as there passed over her gangplank an interminable procession of people, coming in groups out of the building opposite, where the police official was examining passports. The greater part, having passed a night or two in the open air, lying about like dogs in the streets of Genoa, were tired and drowsy. Workmen, peasants, women with children at the breast, little fellows with the tin medal of the infant asylum still hanging around their necks passed on their way, and almost everyone was carrying something. They had folding chairs, they had bags and trunks of every shape in their hands or on their heads; their arms were full of mattresses and bedclothes, and their berth tickets were held fast in their mouths. Poor mothers that had a child for each hand carried their bundles with their teeth. Old peasant women in wooden shoes, holding up their skirts so as not to stumble over the cleats of the gangplank, showed bare legs that were like sticks. Many were barefoot and had their shoes hung around their necks. From time to time there passed through all this wretchedness gentlemen in natty dusters, priests, ladies in plumed hats, leading a lapdog, or carrying a satchel, or perhaps a parcel of French novels of the well-known Lévy edition. Then, suddenly, a stoppage of the procession and, amid a shower of blows and curses, a drove of cattle or a flock of sheep came

along; and when they were got on board, all frightened and straggling here and there, they mingled their bellowing and their bleating with the neighing of the horses in the forward part of the ship, with the cries of sailors and porters, and with the stunning clatter of the donkey engine that was hoisting in whole piles of packing cases. Then the train of emigrants moved on once more; faces and costumes from every part of Italy, strong, sad-eyed working men, others old, ragged, dirty; women *enceinte*, merry boys, half-tipsy youths, country fellows in their shirt-sleeves; and boys, and still more boys, who hardly had put foot on deck, amid that throng of passengers, stewards, officers, company's employees, and custom-house people, when they stood amazed or lost their way as if in a crowded square. For two hours these people had been going on board; and the great ship, moveless, like some grim sea monster that had fixed its fangs into the shore, still went on sucking Italian blood.

The emigrants, as fast as they got on board, filed in front of a table at which was seated the commissary, who told them off in messes of half a dozen persons each, writing the names upon a printed form which he handed to the eldest, that he might go at meal hours and get the ration. Families of less than six persons went in with their friends or with strangers, as the case might be. While this business was going on there was evident in everyone a lively fear of being cheated in the matter of half- and quarter-fares for children and infants; fruit of that invincible mistrust which the peasant feels for any man with a pen in his hand and a registry in front of him. Quarrels arose, there were protests and lamentations. Then the families separated; the men were passed to one side, while the women and children were shown to their cabins. And piteous it was to see these women clumsily descend the steep ladders and grope their way through the long, low between-decks among innumerable berths, arranged in tiers like the shelves in a silkworm shed. Some, all

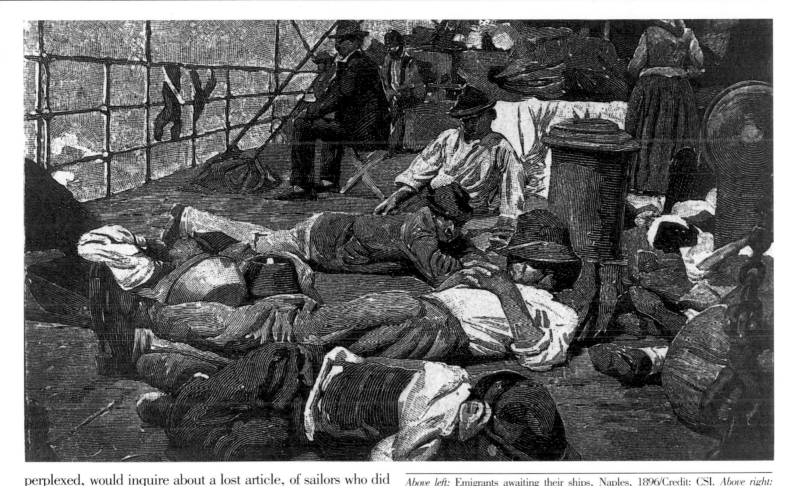

perplexed, would inquire about a lost article, of sailors who did not understand one word they said; some sat down wherever it might be, dazed and exhausted; others wandered about vaguely, looking with uneasiness at all those unknown travelling companions who were as uneasy as they; and, like them, confused and frightened in this disorderly throng. Some who had come down one ladder, and saw others leading still on, down into the dark, refused to go any farther. Through the open hatchway I marked a woman with her head in the berth and sobbing violently. I soon learned that her young child had died almost suddenly an hour or two before, and that her husband was forced to leave its little body with the police to be taken to the hospital. Most of the women remained below, while the men, having laid by their things, went on deck again and leaned against the bulwarks. It was odd enough. The huge steamer, seen by most of them for the first time, must have been like a new world, full of strangeness and of mystery; and yet not one looked about him or aloft, or paused to examine any of those many wonderful objects never seen before. Some would fix an attentive eye upon a trunk, or a neighbor's chair, or the number on a box, or whatever it might be; others munched an apple, or nibbled a crust—examining it at every bite as placidly as if they had been in front of their own stable. Some women had red eyes; some boys were giggling, but their mirth was plainly forced. The greater part showed nothing but apathy or fatigue. The sky was clouded and the night was coming on.

Suddenly furious cries were heard from the passport office, and people were seen running that way. It proved to be a peasant with a wife and four children—all found by the examining physician to have the itch. The first few questions had shown the man to be out of his mind; and, on being refused a passage, he had broken out into frenzy.

On the wharf there were perhaps a hundred persons. Very few relatives of our emigrants. The greater part loungers or relatives of our ship's company, quite used to such separations.

When all were on board there ensued a kind of quiet in the ship, and the dull rumble of the engine could be heard. Almost all were on deck, crowded together and quite silent. These last few moments of waiting seemed an eternity.

At last the sailors were heard shouting fore and aft, *"Chi non è passeggero, a terra"*—"All ashore that's going ashore."

These words sent a thrill from one end of the *Galileo* to the other. In a few moments all strangers were out of the ship, the bridge was hauled ashore, the fasts cast off, the entering port closed, a whistle sounded, and the ship began to move. Then women burst out crying, youths who had been laughing grew serious, and bearded men hitherto stolid were seen to pass a hand across their eyes. This emotion contrasted strangely with the cool salutes that passed between the ship's company and their relatives on the wharf, just as if it were a trip to La Spezia: "Don't forget me to the people at home." "You'll see about that parcel?" "Tell Gigia I'll do as she says." "Post it at Montevideo, please." "It's all understood about the wine, is it not?" "Pleasant voyage to you." "Good-bye!" A few persons who had just reached the wharf had only time to fling some bundles of cigars or some oranges on board. These were duly caught but some of the last ones fell into the water. Lights began to twinkle in the city. The ship slid softly along through the darkness of the harbor almost furtively, as it were, as if she were carrying off a cargo of kidnapped human flesh. I made my way forward through the crowd of people all turned toward the land and looking at the amphitheater of Genoa, now being rapidly illumi-

nated. A few were talking in low tones. Here and there in the dusk, women were seen with infants on their laps and their heads leaned hopelessly on their hands. From the forecastle a voice called out in sarcastic tone, *"Viva L'Italia!"* and looking up I saw a tall thin old man who was shaking his fist at his native country. As we passed out of the harbor it was night.

Saddened by this spectacle I went aft again to the first-class cabin to find my stateroom. And it must be confessed that the first descent into these submarine lodging places is deplorably like going for the first time into a prison with its cells. In those low, narrow corridors, tainted with the reek of bilge-water, the smell of oil lamps, the fragrance of sheepskins, and with wafts of perfume from the ladies, I found myself in the midst of hurrying groups who all wanted the steward, and were behaving with the low-minded selfishness which characterizes almost all travellers in the first bustle of getting settled. A half-light fell upon the confusion here and there, and I caught glimpses of a beautiful blonde lady, three or four black-bearded men, a very tall priest, and the broad, bold face of an angry stewardess. I heard Genoese, French, Italian, Spanish. At a turn of the corridor I came upon a Negress. From a stateroom came a solfeggio in a tenor voice. And opposite to that stateroom I found my own—a cage of a place, about half a dozen cubic meters in size, with a Procrustean bed on one side, a sofa on the other; on the third a barber's mirror over a fixed hand-wash stand, and beside the mirror a lamp on gimbals, swinging to and fro as if to say, "What a fool you were to set out for America." Above the sofa gleamed a round window like a huge glass eye, which seemed, as it caught mine, to wear a mocking expression. And, indeed, the idea of having to sleep for twenty-four nights in that suffocating cubiculum, and the presentiment of the deadly dullness; the heat of the torrid zone, of the bumped heads I should have in bad weather, for six thousand miles—but it was too late to repent. I looked at my baggage, which said, oh, so many things to me in that moment; I handled it as if it were a faithful dog, the last living relic of my house; I prayed God I might not repent having spurned the proposals of an insurance agent who came to tempt me the day before leaving; and then, blessing in my heart the good faithful friends that had stood by me until the last moment, I let myself be rocked to sleep upon the cradle of my country's sea.

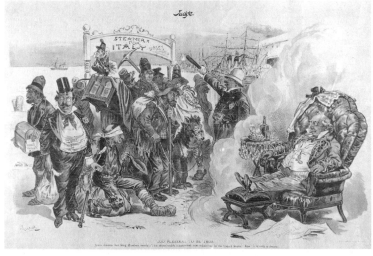

Left: Italian family on the deck of a ferry, looking at Manhattan from Ellis Island, 1905, photograph by Lewis Hine/Credit: NYPL. *Right:* Caricature depicting nativist attitude toward the influx of newly arriving Italian immigrants, appearing in *Judge*, 1888/Credit: CSI

Above: Processing immigrants in the "Great Hall" at Ellis Island, about 1910/Credit: NYPL. *Above left:* Mother and child sitting outside the detention cell at Ellis Island, 1905, photograph by Lewis Hine/Credit: NYPL. *Above right:* In the luggage storage area of Ellis Island, 1905, photograph by Lewis Hine/Credit: NYPL. The child in his mother's arms is Dominick Justave, who was raised in Scranton, Pennsylvania. *Below left:* Italian woman at Ellis Island, about 1910, photograph by Augustus Francis Sherman/Credit: NYPL. *Below right:* A newly arrived immigrant on his way to Rutland, Vermont, about 1900/Credit: Barre

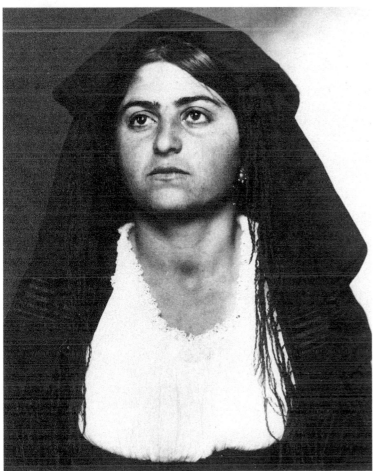

The Italians of New York

1890. Jacob Riis was born in Denmark and emigrated to the United States in 1870. Living in abject poverty for some time before becoming a reporter for The New York Daily Tribune, *he described the squalor and misery experienced by immigrants on Manhattan's Lower East Side in both his books and his photographs, which represent some of the most eloquent testimony to urban poverty ever recorded.*

Certainly a picturesque, if not very tidy, element has been added to the population in the "assisted" Italian immigrant who claims so large a share of public attention, partly because he keeps coming at such a tremendous rate, but chiefly because he elects to stay in New York, or near enough for it to serve as his base of operations, and here promptly reproduces conditions of destitution and disorder which, set in the frame-work of Mediterranean exuberance, are the delight of the artist, but in a

matter-of-fact American community become its danger and reproach. The reproduction is made easier in New York because he finds the material ready to hand in the worst of the slum tenements; but even where it is not he soon reduces what he does find to his own level, if allowed to follow his natural bent. The Italian comes in at the bottom, and in the generation that came over the sea he stays there. In the slums he is welcomed as a tenant who "makes less trouble" than the contentious Irishman or the order-loving German, that is to say: is content to live in a pig-sty and submits to robbery at the hands of the rent-collector without murmur. Yet this very tractability makes of him in good hands, when firmly and intelligently managed, a really desirable tenant. But it is not his good fortune often to fall in with other hospitality upon his

Above: Mulberry Bend in the heart of New York's Little Italy, about 1889, photograph by Jacob Riis/Credit: MCNY

coming than that which brought him here for its own profit, and has no idea of letting go its grip upon him as long as there is a cent to be made out of him.

Recent Congressional inquiries have shown the nature of the "assistance" he receives from greedy steamship agents and "bankers," who persuade him by false promises to mortgage his home, his few belongings, and his wages for months to come for a ticket to the land where plenty of work is to be had at princely wages. The *padrone*—the "banker" is nothing else—having made his ten per cent out of him en route, receives him at the landing and turns him to double account as a wage-earner and a rent-payer. In each of these roles he is made to yield a profit to his unscrupulous countryman, whom he trusts implicitly with the instinct of utter helplessness. The man is so ignorant that, as one of the sharpers who prey upon him put it once, it "would be downright sinful not to take him in." His ignorance and unconquerable suspicion of strangers dig the pit into which he falls. He not only knows no word of English, but he does not know enough to learn. Rarely only can he write his own language. Unlike the German, who begins learning English the day he lands as a matter of duty, or the Polish Jew, who takes it up as soon as he is able as an investment, the Italian learns slowly, if at all. Even his boy, born here, often speaks his native tongue indifferently. He is forced, therefore, to have constant recourse to the middle-man who makes him pay handsomely at every turn. He hires him out to the railroad contractor, receiving a commission from the employer as well as from the laborer, and repeats the performance monthly, or as often as he can have him dismissed. In the city he contracts for his lodging, subletting to him space in the vilest tenements at extortionate rents, and sets an example that does not lack imitators. The "princely wages" have vanished with his coming, and in their place hardships and a dollar a day, beheft with the *padrone*'s merciless mortgage, confront him. Bred to even worse fare, he takes both as a matter of course, and, applying the maxim that it is not what one makes but what he saves that makes him rich, manages to turn the very dirt of the streets into a hoard of gold, with which he either returns to his southern [Italian] home, or brings over his family to join in his work and in his fortunes the next season.

The discovery was made by earlier explorers that there is money in New York's ash-barrel, but it was left to the genius of the *padrone* to develop the full resources of the mine that has become the exclusive preserve of the Italian immigrant. Only a few years ago, when rag-picking was carried on in a desultory and irresponsible sort of way, the city hired gangs of men to trim the ash-scows before they were sent out to sea. The trimming consisted in leveling out the dirt as it was dumped from the carts, so that the scow might be evenly loaded. The men were paid a dollar and a half a day, kept what they found that was worth having, and allowed the swarms of Italians who hung about the dumps to do the heavy work for them, letting them have their pick of the loads for their trouble. To-day Italians contract for the work, paying large sums to be permitted to do it. The city received not less than $80,000 last year for the sale of this privilege to the contractors, who in addition have to pay gangs of their countrymen for sorting out the bones, rags, tin cans and other waste that are found in the ashes and form the staples of their trade and their sources of revenue. The effect has been vastly to increase the power of the *padrone*, or his ally, the contractor, by giving him exclusive control of the one industry in which the Italian was formerly an independent

"dealer," and reducing him literally to the plane of the dump. Whenever the back of the sanitary police is turned, he will make his home in the filthy burrows where he works by day, sleeping and eating his meals under the dump, on the edge of slimy depths and amid surroundings full of unutterable horror. The city did not bargain to house, though it is content to board, him so long as he can make the ash-barrels yield the food to keep him alive, and a vigorous campaign is carried on at intervals against these unlicensed dump settlements; but the temptation of having to pay no rent is too strong, and they are driven from one dump only to find lodgement under another a few blocks farther up or down the river. The fiercest warfare is waged over the patronage of the dumps by rival factions represented by opposing contractors, and it has happened that the defeated party has endeavored to capture by strategy what he failed to carry by assault. It augurs unsuspected adaptability in the Italian to our system of self-government that these rivalries have more than once been suspected of being behind the sharpening of city ordinances, that were apparently made in good faith to prevent meddling with the refuse in the ash-barrels or in transit.

Did the Italian always adapt himself as readily to the operation of the civil law as to the manipulation of political "pull" on occasion, he would save himself a good deal of unnecessary trouble. Ordinarily he is easily enough governed by authority—always excepting Sunday, when he settles down to a game of cards and lets loose all his bad passions. Like the Chinese, the Italian is a born gambler. His soul is in the game from the moment the cards are on the table, and very frequently his knife is in it too before the game is ended. No Sunday has passed in New York since "the Bend" became a suburb of Naples without one or more of these murderous affrays coming to the notice of the police. As a rule that happens only when the man the game went against is either dead or so badly wounded as to require instant surgical help. As to the other, unless he be caught red-handed, the chances that the police will ever get him are slim indeed. The wounded man can seldom be persuaded to betray him. He wards off all inquiries with a wicked "I fix him myself," and there the matter rests until he either dies or recovers. If the latter, the community hears after a while of another Italian affray, a man stabbed in a quarrel, dead or dying, and the police know that "he" has been fixed, and the account squared.

With all his conspicuous faults, the swarthy Italian immigrant has his redeeming traits. He is as honest as he is hotheaded. There are no Italian burglars in the Rogues' Gallery; the ex-brigand toils peacefully with pickaxe and shovel on American ground. His boy occasionally shows, as a pickpocket, the results of his training with the toughs of the Sixth Ward slums. The only criminal business to which the father occasionally lends his hand, outside of murder, is a bunco game, of which his confiding countrymen, returning with their hoard to their native land, are the victims. The women are faithful wives and devoted mothers. Their vivid and picturesque costumes lend a tinge of color to the otherwise dull monotony of the slums they inhabit. The Italian is gay, lighthearted and, if his fur is not stroked the wrong way, inoffensive as a child. His worst offence is that he keeps the stale-beer dives. Where his headquarters is, in the Mulberry Street Bend, these vile dens flourish and gather about them all the wrecks, the utterly wretched, the hopelessly lost, on the lowest slope of depraved humanity. And out of their misery he makes a profit.

Arriving in Boston

1902. Constantine Panunzio, a native of Molfetta in the province of Puglia, became a professor of sociology in this country. In his autobiography he described his first reactions, as a new arrival, to the "Little Italy" in which he found himself.

As I looked about me I said to myself: "Well, this is a real immigrant community, of which I have heard so much, in the American world!" From the moment I first set foot in it, I began to be conscious of the tremendous difficulties which on the one hand confront America in her desire and efforts to assimilate immigrant groups; and which, on the other, are in the way of the immigrants themselves in their need, and often their desire, to become an integral part of the body American.

For one thing, here was a congestion the like of which I had never seen before. Within the narrow limits of one-half square mile were crowded together thirty-five thousand people, living tier upon tier, huddled together until the very heavens seemed to be shut out. These narrow alley-like streets of Old

Boston were one mass of litter. The air was laden with soot and dirt. Ill odors arose from every direction. Here were no trees; no parks worthy of the name; no playgrounds other than the dirty streets for the children to play on; no birds to sing their songs; no flowers to waft their perfume; and only small strips of sky to be seen; while around the entire neighborhood like a mighty cordon, a thousand thousand wheels of commercial activity whirled incessantly day and night, making noises which would rack the sturdiest of nerves.

And who was responsible for this condition of things, for this crowding together? Were the immigrants alone to blame? Did they not occupy the very best tenements available, the moment they were erected and thrown open to them, even though at exorbitant rates?

Not only was all this true, but every sign of America seemed to have been systematically rooted out from this community as if with a ruthless purpose. Here still stood old Faneuil Hall, the Cradle of Liberty; here the Old North Church still lifted its steeple as if reminding one of the part it had played in the Revolutionary War; here was Copp's Hill and many other

spots of the greatest historical importance; not far away was State Street (old King Street), where the first blood of the Revolution was spilled; and here too, the spot where the Boston Tea Party, which had contributed so much to the making of America, had taken place. But while these monuments stood like sentinels reminding one of what this neighborhood had once been, now every last vestige of America was gone! All the American churches, homes, clubs and other institutions which once had graced these streets were gone forever; gone to some more favorable spot in the uptown section of the city, leaving this community to work out its own destiny as best it could. There *were* churches here, to be sure, Catholic and Protestant and Jewish, but they were representative of other than America; they were under the leadership of men who, consciously or unconsciously, stood for other than American sentiments and ideals. In the homes and on the streets no English language was spoken save by the children; on the newsstands a paper in English could scarcely be found; here were scores if not hundreds of societies, national, provincial, local and sub-local, in which English was not usually spoken and in which other than

American interests were largely represented. There were schools also in which the future citizens of America were taught in a language other than English. Here, when on a certain patriotic occasion the American flag was raised a moment sooner than another flag, the person responsible for such a "crime" was nearly rushed out of the community. Above the stores and over those infernal institutions which are permitted to bear the name of "banks," the signs were mainly in a foreign language. In a word, here was a community in America in which there was not a sign of the best of American life. Had it not been for three well-organized and splendidly equipped social service houses and for the public schools, all of which consistently upheld American traditions and standards, this might well have been taken for a community in some far-off land.

Above left: A group of children on the streets of Boston's North End, its Little Italy, about 1900/Credit: LC. *Above right:* Two unidentified Italian children in Boston's North End, about 1912/Credit: Bostonian. Although each Little Italy across the country had its own particular character, they all had something in common — street life in which children were always evident because they had no other place to play.

Above left: "Fresh air for the baby," New York, 1910, photograph by Lewis Hine/Credit: NYPL. *Below left:* "Stale bread," New York, about 1900/Credit: LC. *Above right:* Bootblacks in City Hall Park, New York, 1896, photograph by Alice Austen/Credit: NYPL. *Below right:* Organ grinder and his wife, Seventh Avenue and 48th Street, New York, 1896, photograph by Alice Austen/Credit: SIHS

A Son Writes to His Parents in Siena

1914–1918. G. Battista Turchi settled in New York City; he regularly sent postcards to his parents in Siena, reporting on his own experiences, which were often difficult and disheartening. He also discussed his opinion of conditions in Italy and the United States.

N.Y. 18.2.1914

Dear Father,

Don't worry, and be happy for me. I am in perfect health, as are my three children. I am still working in the same factory on 147th Street; the one that burned was on 63rd Street. Here there is great suffering everywhere: in the city alone there are more than 400,000 without work. I work two or three days a week since the few orders for pianos are distributed among the workers. The work crisis is frightening but they hope things will get better in April; on the basis of my experience, I am less optimistic. Three days of continuous snow; bitter cold. All the trains are blocked; and thus the Lord has provided a little bread for those who will have to remove snow from the streets for three weeks. I have sent you my picture. I had it taken on February 8; after five days of rest, I was starting to get fat. I repeat, don't think ill of me; I am fine in every way, a fact I owe to my great forbearance and my iron will put to the test from the first moment that I set foot in this land of illusions. Thank you, Papa! . . . Thank you for your thoughts. Your little angels and I pray that the Lord gives you strength, peace, and health. I embrace you and send my best wishes,

Your loving son,
G. Battista Turchi

N.Y. 1.3.1918

Dear parents,

For the moment our family is fine in every way. However, I pray that the same is true of all of you. In the piano factory where I work they will soon begin making airplanes. The government urgently needs an indefinite number to defeat our enemies as soon as possible. They have already begun to induct all those Italians who did not enlist at home. However, American conscription affects those 21 to 31 years old. Now the war has begun.

We send best wishes and kisses.

Your loving son,
G. B. Turchi

10.11.1918

Dear Father,

Thank you, dear Father, for your frequent and fond thoughts. I am altogether satisfied by what you tell me, but you must have considered my position without being able to demonstrate my legitimate reasons at the right moment. The sensational victory of the Italian forces, which destroyed one of the greatest armies in the world, made an isolated Germany put down its arms. We were delighted and joyous when we heard the news of the German surrender! Work stopped as if by magic. Banners, music, lights, parades, dances, parties, rejoicing everywhere—to the point of insanity. I will write more. Kisses and best wishes.

Your loving son,
G. B. Turchi

Above: The newly opened St. Regis Hotel, where the entire kitchen staff was Italian immigrants, is depicted in one of the postcards sent by G. Battista Turchi from New York to his parents in Siena, 1914–1918/Credit: Malandrini. *Right:* Crowded conditions on Mulberry Street in New York's Little Italy were reminiscent of busy and noisy street markets in Italy, 1906/Credit: LC

DIALOGHI (DIALOGUES).

INGLESE.	PRONUNCIA.	ITALIANO.
Madam, sir, miss, I wish you a good morning.	Mèdèm, sor, miss, ai uisc juu e good mòòning.	Signora, signore, signorina, io vi auguro il buon giorno.
I wish it to you likewise ; how is your health ?	Ai uisc et tu juu laichuais; hau es juur hèltd ?	Io ve lo auguro del pari; come sta la vostra salute ?
Quite well, I thank you. I am happy to see you enjoy such good health.	Quait uèl, ai tdènch juu. Ai èm hèppi tu sii juu engioi suec good hèltd.	Benissimo, grazie. Io son felice di vedervi in buona salute.
Thank God, I am perfectly well, and all my family is well too.	Tdènch Gòd, ai èm porfèctli uèl, ènd òl mai fèmili es uèl tuu.	Grazie a Dio, io sto perfettamente bene e tutta la mia famiglia sta anche bene.
I was just inquiring after you this morning of Mr. Brown.	Ai uès giost inquairing èfta juu tdes mòòning òv mister Braun.	Io ho chiesto di voi appunto questa mattina al signor Brown.
I thank you for your kind attention; how is your lady ?	Ai tdènch juu for juur caind ettenscion ; hau es juur ledi?	Io vi ringrazio per la vostra gentile attenzione ; come sta vostra signora ?
She has not been well for	Sci es nòt biin uèl for som deis,	Essa non è stata bene per al-

MANUALE 1093 1291
PER IMPARARE GLI ELEMENTI E LA RETTA PRONUNZIA DELLA

LINGUA INGLESE

SENZA MAESTRO.

PER USO PRINCIPALMENTE
DEGLI EMIGRANTI ITALIANI.

DEL
PROF. AUGUSTO BASSETTI.

NEW YORK:
PUBLICATO DALL' AUTORE AL
No. 20 VANDAM ST.

COPYRIGHT, 1885. BY AUGUSTO BASSETTI.

1885.

Above left: Pages from Professor Bassetti's manual prepared specifically for Italian immigrants to learn English, 1885/Credit: LC. Although its educational value is questionable, such books were available for those who had no command of the language that they found in their new homeland. *Above right:* Title page from Professor Bassetti's manual, 1885/Credit: LC. *Below right:* Advertisement for one of the many Italian-language newspapers catering to immigrants which reported on events in their distant homeland, 1890/Credit: LC. *Opposite page above and below right:* Exterior and interior of the Leonard Street Public School in New York, which catered to Italian American children. The Italian School Young Men's Association provided newspapers and useful books in a community reading room available to adults in the neighborhood, 1881/Credit: LC. *Opposite page bottom left:* Statutes and regulations of a mutual aid society which served the needs of immigrants from the province of Campobasso, about 1900/Credit: LC

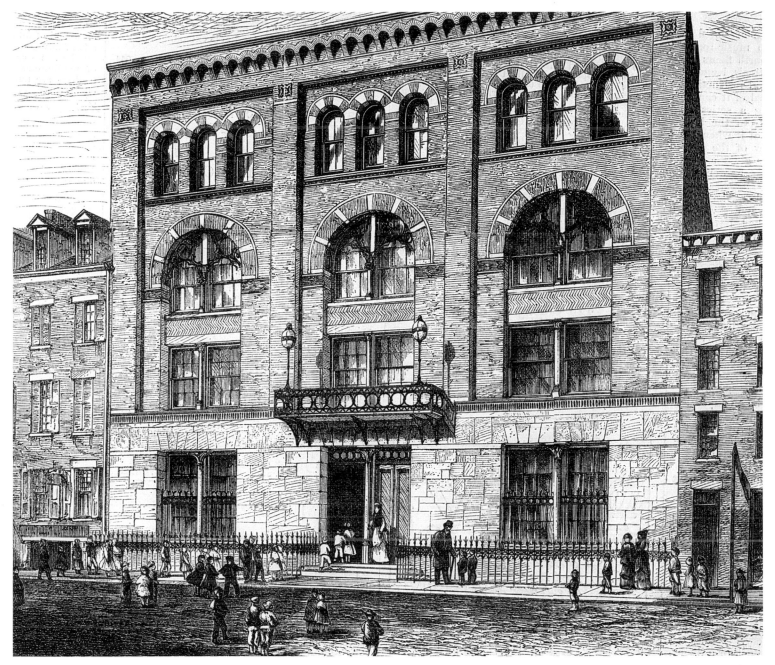

STATUTI E REGOLAMENTI

DELLA

SOCIETA' DI MUTUO SOCCORSO

PROVINCIA DI CAMPOBASSO

FONDATA IN NEW YORK
IL 14 FEBBRAIO 1895 ED
INCORPORATA IL 26 LUGLIO 1895

NAPOLI PRESS
444 E. 115th ST.
NEW YORK

Above: Class of predominantly Italian American students in a public school in New York, 1892/Credit: CSI. *Below:* Taking the Pledge of Allegiance at the Mott Street Industrial School in New York, 1892, photograph by Jacob Riis/Credit: LC

Above: "Pietro learning to write," Jersey Street, New York, about 1890, photograph by Jacob Riis/Credit: LC. *Below:* Libreria Italiana, San Francisco, about 1900, photograph by J.B. Monaco/Credit: Monaco. Italian-born Giorgio Cavalli established his Italian language bookstore in San Francisco's North Beach in 1880, where it became a cultural center for the Italian American community. One hundred years later, the store continues to operate in the same neighborhood.

Left: The Americanization class at Saints Peter and Paul Church, San Francisco, about 1910/Credit: Eureka. The instructor was Signora Adele Zabaldano. *Above:* Nina Monaco, daughter of photographer Louis Monaco, taught English to newly arrived Italian immigrants in the San Francisco region for many years, about 1900, photograph by J.B. Monaco/Credit: Monaco

Left: Lincoln's Birthday celebration at the Young Men's Lincoln Club of Little Italy, New York, 1914/Credit: Balch. Leonard Covello, a distinguished educator and later principal of Benjamin Franklin High School in East Harlem, is seated second from the right. *Above right:* Students of the Presentation Convent School performing in the convent garden, San Francisco, about 1899, photograph by Hugo Weitz/Credit: Eureka. *Below right:* The Telegraph Hill–Montgomery Street Baseball Team, San Francisco, about 1912/Credit: Eureka. The team, city champions in 1912, was organized by the Salesians of Saints Peter and Paul Church.

I CINQUE POVERI ITALIANI
⟶ Linciati a Talulah in America ⟵

E se non piangi di che pianger suoli? (DANTE).

O gioventù d'Italia
   Abbruna la bandiera!
   Chi di valor t'uguaglia,
   O gioventude fiera?
Orgoglio e speme della Nazion,
Ti prego, ascolta questa canzon!

Canto per quei linciati,
   Che laboriosi, onesti,
   Perchè Italian nomati
   Non fu pietà per questi;
In tanta strage, perfidia, orror!
Uccisi, appesi quai malfattor.

Offeso e provocato
   Un buon connazionale,
   Lo vollero salvato
   Dall'ira lor brutale.
Quella masnada, senza ragion,
Feriti a morte, li fe' prigion.

Assalta la prigione
   La folla delinquente,
   La rabbia sol è sprone
   A quella turpe gente.
La corda al collo lor fe' passar,
Condotti al campo per trucidar.

Tradotti alla foresta
   Son tutti cinque appesi,
   Di colpi una tempesta,
   Atrocità palesi.
Grida di gioia? Infamia, orror!
Aimè! che sento mancarmi il cor!

American Governo
   Perchè pietà non porti?
   Così nel canto, eterno
   V'è 'l grido di quei morti.
Delle innocenti famiglie lor,
Soccorri e vendica l'orbato onor.

O martiri sepolti
   Laggiù nella Luigiana,
   Purtroppo siete morti,
   Ma chi la piaga sana?
Erano onesti lavorator,
Eppur son morti quai malfattor!

O gioventù d'Italia,
   Abbruna la bandiera,
   E della vil ciurmaglia
   Fanne vendetta nera,
E sotto il manto del tuo valor
Soccorri e vendica il nostro onor!

CORSO ANTONIO, *Ex-sott'ufficiale di finanza.*

Torino — Tip. M. Artale, via Maria Vittoria, 17.

Left: A handbill printed and distributed in Turin, Italy, which documents and laments the lynching of five Italian Americans in Tallulah, Louisiana, 1899/Credit: CSI. Because they had allowed Blacks equal status in their shops, they were arrested. A vigilante mob dragged three Sicilian shopkeepers from their jail cells, captured two other Italian Americans, and lynched all five for this "ignominious offense." Such posters were distributed in Italy because the middle class did not want to see a complete exodus of the peasants and the working class to America, leaving Italy without manual laborers. *Above right:* A mass meeting at the Clay Statue in New Orleans, responding to advertisements in local papers to "remedy the failure of justice in the Hennessy case," from an illustration in *Harper's Weekly*, March 28, 1891/Credit: LC. What has been described as the largest lynching in American history took place on March 14, 1891, in New Orleans. Police Superintendent David Hennessy, who gained fame for his capture of a man purported to be an Italian outlaw criminal, was assassinated in 1890, a crime that remains unsolved. The city's Sicilian population was implicated in his murder. A trial was held; the jury found five men not guilty and declared a mistrial in the case of the other six. The judge ordered the eleven suspects detained in the Parish Prison. Following the mass meeting, the crowd battered down the doors of the prison and killed the eleven men, eight of whom were naturalized American citizens. *Below right:* A lynch mob battering down the doors of the Parish Prison, from an illustration in *Scribner's*, February 1896/Credit: LC

Above: Rear tenement, Roosevelt Street, New York, 1890, photograph by Jacob Riis/Credit: MCNY. *Above right:* Italian mother and child, Jersey Street, New York, 1890, photograph by Jacob Riis/Credit: MCNY. *Below right:* "Five cents a spot," New York, about 1889, photograph by Jacob Riis/Credit: MCNY

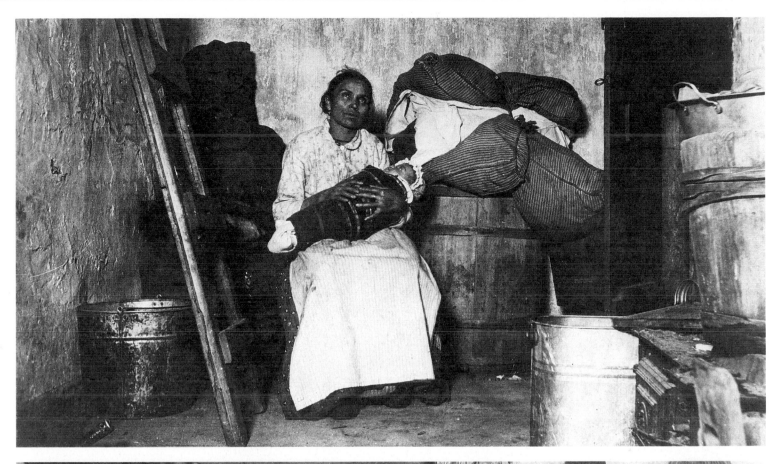

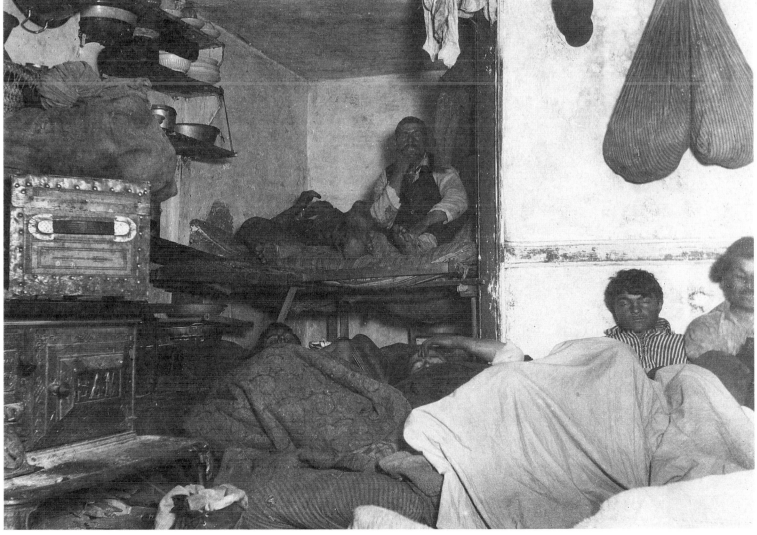

Miserable Working Conditions

1893. Although most of the Italians who emigrated to this country hoped to find better working conditions than they had left behind in Italy, many of them were bitterly disappointed to discover themselves still being exploited under different economic conditions in a foreign land.

Tradition, more than wealth, divides the Italian immigrants into laborers and contractors, and subjugates the laborers to the contractors. In the course of time some accidental changes may occur in the personnel of the two classes. The laborious and thrifty peasant of south Italy may become a shopkeeper and importer, and his son may graduate as a lawyer or a physician; the political exile from Romagna or Tuscany may become a saloon-keeper and a contractor; and teachers and members of other professions may turn street-sweepers or common laborers. Yet the initial differences in most cases become hereditary, and ultimately grow into social institutions.

The territorial divisions of Italy are reproduced by the distribution of the Italian immigrants through the States. The tailor from Naples and Palermo, the weaver from Lombardy, the hat-maker from Piedmont, all follow the tracks of those who have preceded them. When a workman earns enough to support a family and feels sure of steady employment, he generally buys a house on monthly payments and settles permanently in this country. But the common laborer—the house-painter, the stone-cutter, the job-printer—wanders from one state to another, contriving to live the whole year round on the small savings of a few working months. He has, therefore, little inducement to remain. The wages of the unskilled laborer are entirely arbitrary, the people from southern Italy receiving as a rule lower wages than their northern colleagues, even when working side by side with them.

The industry of the Italian laborer and the benefits to this country which accrue from his work cannot be disputed. He tills the soil, builds railroads, bores mountains, drains swamps, opens here and there to the industry of American workmen new fields which would not perhaps be opened but for his cheap labor. It is a mistake to believe that he causes the lowering of wages; this is due to the increase of the capitalists controlling great interests. It is equally unjust to speak of him as a pauper laborer. He becomes a pauper on landing because he receives no help, no guarantee of life and independence, and he necessarily falls a victim to the Italian contractor and the contractor's American partner or employer. There are people who would like to keep him out of this country; it would be more reasonable to keep out the contractor.

The Italian laborer does more than his share of work and receives less than his share of earnings; for as a matter of fact, the laws enacted with regard to this matter oppress the laborer

L'ITALO-AMERICANO LABOR BUREAU !

For the past ten years there has been a large influx of Italians into the State of Louisiana. In this decade there disembarked at the part of New Orleans, 4500 ITALIANS. These emmigrants are mostly STRONG, HEALTHY, ABLE BODIED INDUSTRIOUS MEN. AS LABORERS THEY HAVE NO SUPERIORS. Attracted by our temperate climate and the fertile resource of our State, they have come here in search of homes. CAPITALISTS, PLANTATION OWNERS, RAILROAD CONTRACTORS, AND, IN FACT, ALL PERSONS WHO WORK LABORERS IN GREAT NUMBERS, FIND THE ITALIAN IMMIGRANT A VALUABLE ACQUISITION, BECAUSE OF HIS WILLINGNESS AND HIS PECULIAR ADAPTABILITY TO HARD WORK. A WELL EQUIPPED AND RELIABLE LABOR BUREAU IS WANTED.

This want **L'ITALO AMERICANO** PURPOSES TO SUPPLY.

We will furnish Laborers to Proprietors, and employment to Laborers. One position is one which eminently qualifies us for the office we have elected to fill. Our circulation is not confined within narrow limits. It embraces nearly the entire United States, and our acquaintences with the Rail Road Authorities, Plantation Owners and Contractors gives us special facilities for serving satisfactorily and justly both employer and laborer.

L'ITALO AMERICANO
LABOR BUREAU

Will be in charge of a thorougly competent person, who will devote to it his constant and undivided attention. Our charges will be moderate whilst our services will be found to be of great value.

CORRESPONDENCE SOLICITED.
ADDRESS:

L'ITALO AMERICANO,
23 POYDRAS STREET,
NEW ORLEANS, LA.

and assist rather than hamper the contractor. Even supposing that the contractor does not succeed in importing contract labor, he finds in the market a large number of men entirely at his mercy, with not even the weak support of a promise to defend themselves against his greed. The few dollars which the immigrant possesses on landing are skillfully taken out of his pocket by the hotel-keeper before the hotel-keeper gives him a chance to work. When he is reduced to absolute indigence, the lowest kind of work imaginable is offered him and he has to accept it. He walks through Mulberry Street and sees a crowd around a bar in a basement. He enters the basement and finds a man employing men for a company. He adds his name to the list without knowing anything about the work he will be called upon to do, or about the place where he is to be transported, or about the terms of his engagement. Perhaps, however, he passes a banker's establishment and stops to read on a paper displayed at the window a demand for two hundred laborers, supplemented with the significant assurance that the place of work is not far distant. He enters, enlists, takes his chances, and falls in the snare set for him.

I once witnessed the departure of a party of laborers and I shall never forget the sight. In foul Mulberry Street a half-dozen carts were being loaded with bundles of the poorest clothes and rags. One man after another brought his things; women and children lounged about, and the men gathered together in small groups, chattering about the work, their hopes, and their fears. For these men *fear*. They have heard of the deceit practiced upon those who have preceded them and of their sufferings. Each man carried a tin box containing stale bread and pieces of loathsome cheese and sausage, his provision for the journey. Some had invested whatever money they had in buying more of such food, because, as they told me, everything was so much dearer at the contractor's store. The sausage, for instance, which, rotten as it was, cost them four cents a pound in New York was sold for twenty cents a pound at the place of their work. Presently our conversation was interrupted by the appearance of the contractor; the groups dissolved, the men took leave of their wives and friends, kissed once more their children, and made a rush for the carts. Then the train started for the railroad station, where the laborers were to be taken to their unknown destination. Of course, this destination and the wages and the nature of the work have been agreed upon in some informal way. But the contract is a sham. I do not believe there is a single instance in which a contract was honestly fulfilled by the contractor. When we think of law-breakers we instinctively refer to the lowest classes. But the contractors are systematic law-breakers. As a rule, the laborer is faithful to the letter of his engagement, even when he feels wronged or deceived.

The contractor is sure to depart from the terms of the contract either as to wages, or hours of labor, or the very nature of the work. Contractors have been known to promise employment, to pocket their fees, and then to lead the men to lonely places and abandon them. Some employment agencies agree with the employers that the men shall be dismissed under pretext after a fortnight or two of work, in order that the agents may receive new fees from fresh recruits. As a rule, however, the men obtain more work than they want or can stand. The contractor, who has acted thus far as an employment agent, now assumes his real functions. Him alone the employer (a railroad or some other company) recognizes, and all wages are paid to him. He curtails these for his own benefit, first by ten or twenty per cent or more, and he retains another portion to reimburse

himself for the money he has spent for railway fares and other items. Wages are generally paid at the end of the second fortnight; the first fortnight they remain unpaid till the end of the work, in guarantee of the fulfillment of the contract by the laborer. Meanwhile the men have to live, and to obtain food they increase their debt with the contractor, who keeps a "pluck-me store," where the laborers are bound to purchase all their provisions, inclusive of the straw on which they sleep. The prices charged are from twenty-five to one hundred per cent and upward above the cost of the goods to the seller, and the quality is as bad as the price is high. At sunset the work ceases and the men retire to a shanty, very much like the steerage of a third-

class emigrant ship, the men being packed together in unclean and narrow berths. The shanty is no shelter from wind or rain. Only recently the shanty where the Chicago National Gas-Pipe Company huddled its Italian workmen, near Logansport, Indiana, was blown down by a windstorm and several men were killed. Neither the number nor the names of the dead were known, as Italian laborers are designated only by figures.

The brutality of the contractors toward their subjects baffles description. The contractor is a strongly built, powerful man; he has acquired the habit of command, is well armed, protected by the authorities, supported by such of his employees as he chooses to favor, and, sad to say, by the people who are hostile to the laborers. He often keeps guards armed with Winchester rifles to prevent his men from running away. His power has the essential characteristics of a government. He fines his men and beats and punishes them for any attempted resistance to his self-constituted authority. On Sunday he may either force them to attend church service or keep them at work. I have been told of contractors who taxed their men to make birthday presents to their wives. A feudal lord would not have expected more from his vassals.

Above: Italian worker on the New York State Barge Canal, 1912, photograph by Lewis Hine. When the Erie Canal was enlarged and rebuilt as the New York State Barge Canal, Italian laborers were responsible for most of the construction work.

Left: Italian woman carrying an enormous empty dry-goods box for some distance along Bleecker Street in New York, 1912, photograph by Lewis Hine/Credit: LC. She was carrying the box to her home, where it would be used for kindling. *Above left and right:* Italian women carrying clothing to be finished by the family in tenement home-workshops, New York, 1912, photographs by Lewis Hine/Credit: LC

Group of "Breaker Boys" in the Ewen Breaker, Pennsylvania Coal Company mine, South Pittston, Pennsylvania, 1911, photograph by Lewis Hine/Credit: LC

Above left: Mrs. Palontona and her thirteen-year-old daughter, Michelina, working on "pillow lace" in the kitchen of their tenement home on the third floor of 213 East 111th Street, New York, 1911, photograph by Lewis Hine/Credit: LC. In the other photographs on this page, Lewis Hine documented the varied types of work performed by Italian American families in their homes. The young woman, *above right,* is working in a paper box factory. All photographs date from about 1910 to 1912/Credit: LC

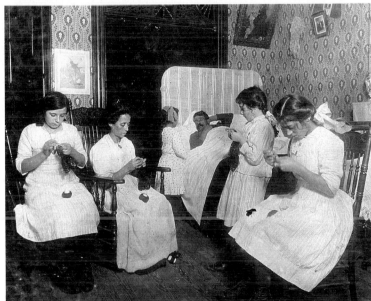

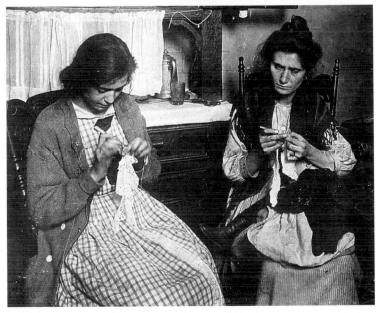

Above left: Young woman picking berries, Seaford, Delaware, 1910, photograph by Lewis Hine/Credit: LC. In addition to working tirelessly in tenement sweatshops in New York and Boston, sewing and finishing garments, as depicted in the other photographs on this page by Lewis Hine, many city children accompanied their parents as migrant laborers to pick fruit and vegetables, to clean fish and to perform other menial tasks in rural areas along the Eastern Seaboard/Credit: LC

Above: Tony Casale, called "Bologna," Hartford, 1909, photograph by Lewis Hine/Credit: LC. "Tony, eleven years old, has been selling newspapers for four years; he often works until eleven in the evening." *Below:* Finishing garments and making artificial flowers, New York, 1908–1910, photographs by Lewis Hine/Credit: LC

Above: The central figure in this photograph, Secondino Libro, "is an eleven-year-old living at 34 Walnut Street, Lawrence, Massachusetts; he works in the number four spinning room" in the textile mill, 1911, photograph by Lewis Hine/Credit: LC. *Below:* Making lace and finishing garments in New York tenements, 1910–1911, photographs by Lewis Hine/Credit: LC

Above: Carvers at the construction site of the State Historical Society Building, Madison, Wisconsin, about 1910/Credit: SHSW. *Below:* Carvers at work on sculptures for the State Capitol, Madison, Wisconsin, about 1912/Credit: SHSW

Above: Second-story stucco workshop for The Library of Congress building, 1894/Credit: LC. *Below:* Carving workshop in the northeast wing for The Library of Congress building, 1894/Credit: LC

Left: Frank Vianello of 21 Greenwich Avenue, New York, at his father's shoe-shine stand, 1910, photograph by Lewis Hine/Credit: LC. *Below left:* Shoemaker, 119 Broome Street, New York, about 1890, photograph by Jacob Riis/Credit: MCNY. *Top right:* A proclamation from the striking textile workers in Lawrence, Massachusetts, 1912/Credit: LC. One of the most bitter strikes in American labor history erupted in January 1912. Led by Joseph Ettor and Arturo Giovannitti, two experienced organizers of the IWW (International Workers of the World), thousands of unorganized men, women and children, many of whom were Italian Americans, poured out of the textile mills. The owners refused to consider the workers' grievances. The diehard attitude of the owners elicited considerable sympathy throughout the country. Strikers' children were sent to live with supporters in such dissimilar places as New York City and Barre, Vermont. Ettor and Giovannitti were put in jail on charges that they had been accessories to the murder of Anna La Pizzo, a picket shot during a clash between workers and the police. Eventually, the strikers won and much later Ettor and Giovannitti were found not guilty. *Below right:* Striking garment workers in Union Square, New York, 1913/Credit: LC. Italian Americans and Jews played a prominent role in the formation of the ILGWU (International Ladies Garment Workers Union) as both workers and organizers, as can be seen in the strikers' placards in Yiddish and Italian.

A PROCLAMATION !
IS MASSACHUSETTS IN AMERICA?

Ready to plunge the bayonets into woman's blood.

Military Law Declared in Massachusetts !

Habeas Corpus Denied in Massachusetts !

Free Speech Throttled in Massachusetts !

Free Assemblage Outlawed in Massachusetts !

Unlawful Seizure of Persons in Massachusetts !

Unwarranted Search of Homes in Massachusetts !

Right to Bear Arms Questioned in Massachusetts !

Mill Owners Resort to Dynamite Plots and Violence in Massachusetts!

Militia Hired to Break Strike in Massachusetts !
Innocent People Killed by Militia in Massachusetts !
Militia Ordered to Shoot to Kill in Mass. !

Unusual Bail and Fines Exacted in Massachusetts!
Corporations Control Administrations in Mass. !

The striking textile workers of Lawrence, Massachusetts are confronted with the above described conditions. They are making a noble fight for an increase of wages and to prevent discriminations against the members of the organization carrying on this strike. To abolish a pernicious premium system inaugurated for no other purpose than the speeding up of already overworked toilers. If you want to assist the strikers send funds to JOSEPH BEDARD, 9 Mason Street, Franco-Belgian Hall, Financial Secretary Textile Workers Industrial Union, Lawrence, Massachusetts.

Above left: Temporary office of the Bank of Italy (founded by A.P. Giannini and later renamed Bank of America) at 632 Montgomery Street, San Francisco, about 1907/Credit: BOA. *Below left and right:* Advertisements for Italian American banks in New York, 1890/Credit:LC. *Opposite page above right:* Interior of the Bank of Italy, San Francisco, 1905/Credit: BOA. *Opposite page below left and right:* Advertisements for Italian American businesses in New York and Philadelphia, 1890/Credit: LC

LXXIII

N. E. PARRAVICINO
2204 PRIMA AVENUE.
NEW YORK.
———) :o: (———

VAGLIA E TRATTE A VISTA

BANCA ITALIANA

CAMBIA VALUTE.

BIGLIETTI DI PASSAGGIO

TRADUZIONI

ASSICURAZIONE
Contro gli Incendi.

ATTI NOTARILI
In Inglese ed Italiano.

IX

BANCA ITALIANA,

CANTONI & CO.,

25 WALL STREET,   NEW YORK.

——————

COMPRA E VENDE

MONETE D'ORO E D'ARGENTO AMERICANE
ED ESTERE. FONDI PUBLICI ED A   ONI
DELLE STRADE FERRATE.

ANTICIPA

SOPRA TITOLI DI RENDITA O COUPONS,

NEGOZIA IN

LETTERE DI CAMBIO E TRATTE.

RICEVE

DEPOSITI SOGGETTI AL CHECK A VISTA

ACCORDANDO

Un interesse a seconda della loro importanza.
Si occupa infine di ogni specie d'affari Bancari.

——————

Emmette Tratte su qualunque parte d'Europa,
e sulle seguenti citta d'Italia.

Roma,	Genova,	Modena,	Biella,	Livorno,	Napoli,
Bologna,	Lucca,	Palermo,	Chiavari,	Messina,	Piacenza,
Como,	Milano,	Torino,	Firenze,	Venezia,	Brescia.

S' incarica pure delle spedizioni di denaro in carta
per qualunque Ufficio Postale d'Italia
alle condizioni piu' vantaggiose.

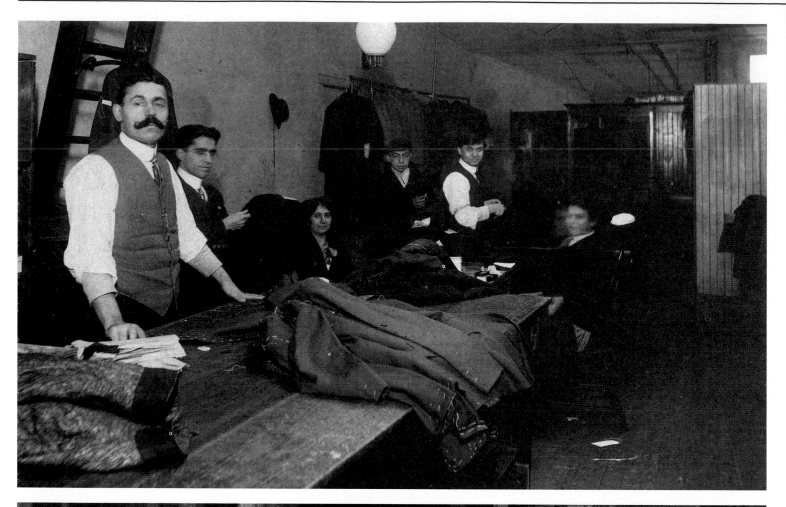

Above: Clothing factory, Philadelphia, about 1910/Credit: Balch. *Below:* M. Camica's ladies' and men's furnishings store, 1315 Grant Avenue, San Francisco, 1911/Credit: Eureka

Above: Store of V. Di Pietro, watchmaker and jeweler, Philadelphia, about 1910/Credit: Balch. *Below:* The Cataldi shoemaker and shoe store in North Beach, San Francisco, 1890/Credit: Baccari

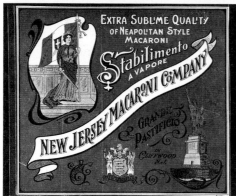

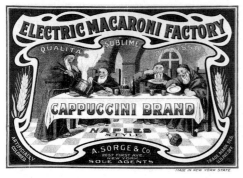

Above: Pasta labels, about 1900/Credit: Smithsonian.
Right: A thirteen-year-old Italian boy tending store, New York, 1913, photograph by Lewis Hine/Credit: NYPL.

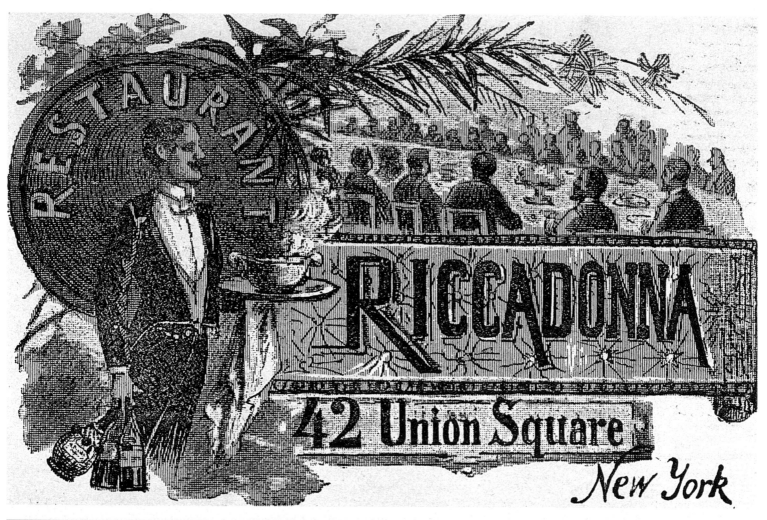

Above left: Restaurant advertisement, New York, 1890/Credit: LC. *Below left:* Fior D'Italia Restaurant, on Broadway, San Francisco, 1909/Credit: Eureka. *Above:* Interior of Solari's Restaurant, San Francisco, about 1910/Credit: Bancroft

The Italians of California

1905. Although most of the newly arrived Italian immigrants settled in the large urban centers of the East like New York, Boston, Philadelphia and Chicago, a small Italian community of considerable consequence had been established in northern California immediately following the Gold Rush in the 1850s. Marius J. Spinello, an Italian-language instructor at the University of California, described the uniqueness of this group.

California has nearly sixty thousand Italian citizens and I am in a position to assert and maintain that the economic conditions of the Italian population in this state are incomparably better than those of the Italians in the East. The greater prosperity the Italian enjoys in California is not accidental; it is the result of causes which any organization for the development of the state ought to divulge, through the Italian papers in the East, if we think that the Italians are as good citizens as any that come to our shores. Moreover, by investigating, discovering and making those reasons known, we would not only proclaim to the world in a most convincing manner the possibilities of the state, but we would also at the same time do justice to a much abused, misrepresented and undervalued portion of our population.

San Francisco has many a brilliant and highly respected professional man of Italian birth or parentage. The beautiful orchards, vineyards and gardens planted by Italians on the shifting sand dunes of San Francisco, of San Mateo, in Santa Clara Valley, around Stockton, Napa, Fresno, Tulare, Los Angeles, and on the slopes of the Sierras, tell us what the sturdy sons of the noble nation to which the world is indebted for all that makes life worth living can do wherever their lot is cast, and especially under the mild and benignant sky of California. Everywhere, we are told, the most well-kept vineyards, most luxuriant and profitable orchards belong to Italians. The Swiss-

Italian colony of Asti is another eloquent proof of what we may expect from the Italians in the land where they can have free and fair play by the side of other settlers.

The taxes collected from the Italians of California represent over $12,000,000 worth of property, real and personal. The American reference agencies have registered over eight hundred Italian business houses with a credit varying from $500 to $500,000. These facts are indisputable and show us how materially prosperous our Italian population is in California. In view of their number, the aggregate capital owned and managed by them is equally as considerable as that in the hands of the representatives of any other nationality on Californian soil. This enormous accumulation of capital is primarily due to the uncommon energy, sobriety and faithfulness which characterize the Italians, despite their decadent writers; but, when we compare their achievements here with their achievements in the East, the rapidity of their success must be recognized as due also to the youth, and to the inexhaustible wealth of this state.

The eastern Italian comes from the same country and stock from which the California Italian comes, but though very successful, he has not been able to accomplish so much in so short a time. Why? Because, in the East, he found the country thickly populated and had to begin his climbing at the lowest step of the ladder, while the people who had come before him, were well nigh the top. In California, on the other hand, he came as early as the rest of the early settlers and started alongside of them. Here, he met with no race prejudice. The virgin soil was as responsive to his toiling as it was to the labors of others. And today he finds himself on equal footing with all the other inhabitants of California. He figures as a most successful wine grower, as a prosperous farmer, as a shrewd and far-seeing business man, as a weighty capitalist, as a distinguished and well-beloved professional man and a most public-spirited citizen. He is appreciated and respected by his fellow citizens as much as any other honest, law-abiding, industrious

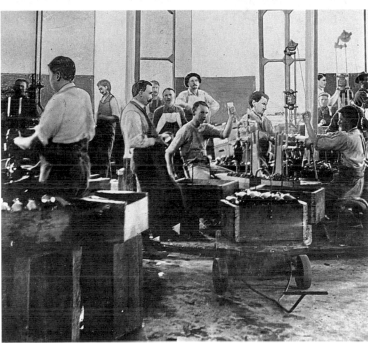

Opposite page: Dinner at the Italian Swiss Colony Vineyard, Asti, California, about 1890/Credit: CHS. *Above left and right:* Hauling grapes and separating cream of tartar from rope, Italian Swiss Colony Vineyard, about 1900/Credit: CHS. *Center left and right:* Bottling champagne at Italian Swiss Colony Vineyard, about 1910, and display truck, San Francisco, about 1920/Credit: Colony. *Below right:* Wine label, about 1910/Credit: Seagram

and intelligent Californian.

The residents of this state who have noticed, as I have, the excellent qualities of the Italian immigrants will, I am sure, welcome among us as many of them as are willing to come. Our boundless rich fields are waiting for the hands of those who, even in New England, are looked upon as the most skillful and painstaking cultivators in the country. Around New Haven, Connecticut, my former home, the Italian farms are places of great attraction. The Americans flock to see them as they would to see and admire beautiful historical monuments. Our state, with its miles and miles of unsettled territory, needs settlers to develop its unspeakable resources, to bring out its hidden treasures; and the healthy Italian race, which is three or four times as prolific as the New England Yankee, ought to be encouraged to come here.

The California Promotion Committee ought to enter upon a plan of propaganda whereby the numerous Italian colonies in the East may learn just what California has in store for all those of their members who are willing to exchange the barrenness of city life for the peace and comfort of easily acquired homes in the land of gold and sunshine. Pamphlets ought to be printed in Italian, setting forth the advantages and the rewards which California holds out to the dutiful, sober and willing immigrant. Courses of lectures should be held in the largest Italian colonies, where hundreds of hands are looking for honest employment. The diplomatic representatives of the Italian government ought to be interested in the movement, because they could, better than anyone else, direct the steps of their compatriots.

Above left: Fisherman's Wharf, San Francisco, about 1910/Credit: CHS. *Above right:* Fishermen, San Francisco, about 1891/Credit: NA. *Below left:* Fisherman's Wharf, San Francisco, about 1910, photograph by J.B. Monaco/Credit: Monaco. *Below right:* Fisherman's Wharf, San Francisco, 1902/Credit: Eureka

Above: Tending nets, Fisherman's Wharf, San Francisco, about 1905/Credit: SFPL. *Below left:* Fisherman's Wharf, San Francisco, about 1910/Credit: CHS. *Below right:* Lateen-rigged sailboat, San Francisco harbor, about 1900/Credit: Bancroft. At first the fishermen were mostly Genoese; later they were predominantly Sicilians coming from Palermo, Porticello, Sant' Elia, Isola delle Femmine and Santa Flavia.

Ten unidentified brothers from the town of Popoli (Abruzzi) who settled in Boston, 1890/Credit: Fototeca 3M. It was a common practice for the older brothers of a family to emigrate to a specific location, obtain jobs or go into business, and assist their younger siblings in coming to and establishing themselves in this country. There are a number of well-known businesses which reflect this practice. The Seven Santini Brothers moving and storage company in New York City was created by seven brothers who came from Tuscany. Pasquale emigrated in 1890 and worked for a cousin in the moving business. He sent for his brother Pietro and soon three more brothers joined them. In 1905, the five brothers decided to start their own moving business. In 1907, they sent for the remaining two brothers. From this beginning evolved one of the world's largest moving and shipping organizations.

Family outing, Barre, Vermont, about 1910/Credit: Barre

Above: Members of the "Italian Society of Victor Emanuel 3rd," Waukesha, Wisconsin, about 1919/Credit: SHSW

Above: Relaxation, Barre, Vermont, about 1910/Credit: Barre. *Below:* Lagomarsino family, north San Mateo County, California, about 1880/SMCHS

Above: Two men, San Francisco, about 1895, photograph by J.B. Monaco/Credit: Monaco. *Below:* "Prosperous Italians," identified from left to right as Martinelli, Pallavelini and Seragnoli, photograph by J.B. Monaco/Credit: Monaco

Above left: Mr. and Mrs. J.B. Monaco, San Francisco, about 1890, photograph by J.B. Monaco/Credit: Monaco. *Above right:* Mr. and Mrs. Conti, San Francisco, about 1890, photograph by J.B. Monaco/Credit: Monaco. *Below left:* Domenico Battistesa and sons, about 1890, photograph by J.B. Monaco/Credit: Monaco. *Below right:* Giovanni and Teresa Jacuzzi, San Francisco, about 1900/Credit: Jacuzzi

Above left: Mrs. Edith Fantozzi Baccari at the age of eight months, about 1905/Credit: Baccari. *Above right:* John Megna, iron worker and sweeper, sixteen years old, Fall River, Massachusetts, about 1914, photograph by Lewis Hine/Credit: LC. *Below left and right:* Children, Di Marco family, Philadelphia, about 1910/Credit: Balch

Left: Luisa D'Archia and Peter Striano, on their wedding day, Hoboken, New Jersey, 1912/Credit: Striano. *Above:* An unidentified couple of newlyweds posing after their wedding, San Francisco, about 1900/Credit: LC. *Below:* Family and friends, Bitetti's Grove, Staten Island, New York, about 1910/Credit: SIHS

Above left: Father Oreste Trinchieri, pastor of Saints Peter and Paul Church, San Francisco, about 1914, photograph by J.B. Monaco/Credit: Monaco. *Above right:* First communion for John and Charles Molinari, about 1914, photograph by J.B. Monaco/Credit: Monaco. *Below left:* Mother Frances Cabrini, the Italian immigrant who became the first American saint, founded the Congregation of the Missionary Sisters of the Sacred Heart, dedicated to the spiritual care of Italian immigrants, about 1910/Credit: NA. *Below right:* Father Raffaele Piperini, pastor at Saints Peter and Paul Church, San Francisco, about 1910, photograph by J.B. Monaco/Credit: Monaco

Above: Meeting of a women's group, Italian American parish, Boston, about 1910/Credit: CSI. *Below:* Meeting of a men's group, Sacred Heart Church, North End, Boston, about 1900/Credit: CSI

Above: Apollo Fife and Drum Corps, Chicago, 1904/ Credit: UIC. *Below:* Ettore Patrizi, publisher and editor of *L'Italia* newspaper, addressing 200,000 people who attended the Verdi Day Memorial, Golden Gate Park, San Francisco, 1914/Credit: Baccari. *Opposite page above:* Marsella Band, Philadelphia, about 1900/Credit: Balch. *Opposite page below left:* Artist Domenico Tojetti, San Francisco, about 1900, photograph by J.B. Monaco/Credit: Monaco. *Opposite page below right:* Stage actress Eleonora Duse, 1906, photograph by Mario Nunes Vais/Credit: Gabinetto. Eleonora Duse toured the United States several times. She died in Pittsburgh in 1924. A memorial service was held at the Church of Saint Vincent Ferrer in New York before her body was returned to Italy for burial at Asolo (Veneto).

METROPOLITAN OPERA HOUSE.

MR. HENRY E. ABBEY, - - - - - - - Director.
Acting Manager - - - - - MR. MAURICE GRAU.

MONDAY EVENING, OCTOBER 22, 1883,

INAUGURAL NIGHT

AND

First Night of the Subscription,

WHEN GOUNOD'S OPERA OF

"FAUST."

Will be presented with the following Cast:

FAUST, - - - - - - Sig. ITALO CAMPANINI
MEPHISTOPHELES, - - - Sig. FRANCO NOVARA
VALENTINO, - - - - Sig. GIUSEPPE DEL PUENTE
WAGNER, - - - - - - - Sig. CONTINI
SIEBEL, - - - - - - Mme. SOFIA SCALCHI
MARTA, - - - - - - Mlle. LOUISE LABLACHE
(Who has kindly consented to assume the part at short notice.)
AND
MARGHERITA, - - - - Mme. CHRISTINE NILSSON

Musical Director and Conductor, · Sig. VIANESI

WEBER PIANO USED.

Mason & Hamlin's Organ Used.

All the above Operas performed at this House can be had in every form, Vocal and Instrumental at G. SCHIRMER, No. 35 Union Square, Importer and Publisher of Music.

The Scenery by Messrs. Fox, Schaeffer, Maeder, and Thompson.
The Costumes are entirely new, and were manufactured at Venice by D. Ascoli
The Appointments by Mr. Bradwell.
Machinists, Messrs. Lundy & Gifford.

NIGHTLY PRICES OF ADMISSION:

Boxes, holding six (6) seats.................................... $50
Orchestra Stalls... 6
Balcony Stalls.. 3
Family Circle (reserved)...................................... 2
Admission to Family Circle.................................... 1

Seats and Boxes can be secured at the Box Office of the Metropolitan Opera House, which will remain open daily from 8 A. M. to 5 P. M.

Doors open at 7.15.   Performances at 8 precisely

Gunerius Gabrielson & Son, Florists to the Metropolitan Opera House.

Opera Glasses on Hire in the Lobby.

L. F. Mazette, Caterer.

Parties desiring Ices can be supplied by the Waiter, in Corridor.

Business Manager - - - - - - - - Mr. W. W. TILLOTSON.

Treasurer - - - - - - - - - Mr. CHAS. H. MATHEWS.

METROPOLITAN OPERA HOVSE

GRAND OPERA SEASON 1911~1912
GIULIO GATTI-CASAZZA, General Manager.

SATURDAY AFTERNOON, JANUARY 13TH, AT 2:15 O'CLOCK

THE GIRL OF THE GOLDEN WEST

(LA FANCIULLA DEL WEST)

(IN ITALIAN)

OPERA IN THREE ACTS——LIBRETTO BY C. ZANGARINI AND G. CIVININI

FOUNDED ON THE DRAMA WRITTEN BY DAVID BELASCO

MUSIC BY GIACOMO PUCCINI

MINNIE	EMMY DESTINN
DICK JOHNSON, (RAMERREZ THE ROAD-AGENT)	ENRICO CARUSO
JACK RANCE, GAMBLER AND SHERIFF	PASQUALE AMATO
NICK, BARTENDER AT THE "POLKA"	ALBERT REISS
ASHBY, WELLS-FARGO AGENT	ADAMO DIDUR
SONORA	DINH GILLY
TRIN	ANGELO BADA
SID	GIULIO ROSSI
BELLO	VINCENZO RESCHIGLIAN
HARRY	(MINERS)	PIETRO AUDISIO
JOE	LAMBERT MURPHY
HAPPY	ANTONIO PINI-CORSI
LARKENS	BERNARD BEGUE
BILLY, AN INDIAN	GEORGES BOURGEOIS
WOWKLE, HIS SQUAW	MARIE MATTFELD
JAKE WALLACE, A MINSTREL	ANDREA DE SEGUROLA
JOSE CASTRO, WITH RAMERREZ'S BAND	PAOLO ANANIAN
THE POST RIDER	LAMBERTO BELLERI

MEN OF THE CAMP AND BOYS OF THE RIDGE

CONDUCTOR	ARTURO TOSCANINI

STAGE MANAGER, JULES SPECK	CHORUS MASTER, GIULIO SETTI

TECHNICAL DIRECTOR, EDWARD SIEDLE

Left: Program for opening night of the Metropolitan Opera on October 22, 1883/Credit: Metropolitan Archives. *Above*: Program for Puccini's *The Girl of the Golden West* (*La fanciulla del West*), 1912/Credit: Metropolitan Archives. *Right*: Giacomo Puccini, 1914, photograph by Mario Nunes Vais/Credit: Gabinetto

Left: Giulio Gatti-Casazza, General Manager of the Metropolitan Opera, about 1912/Credit: LC. After ten years as director of La Scala in Milan, Gatti-Casazza came to the Metropolitan in 1908 and remained until 1935. His administration was notable for its artistic and financial successes. *Above:* Opera singer Luisa Tetrazzini, 1908/Credit: LC. *Following pages:* Enrico Caruso in Puccini's *The Girl of the Golden West*, 1911/Credit: Metropolitan Archives

Above: Enrico Caruso in *Pagliacci* by Ruggiero Leoncavallo, 1914/Credit: Metropolitan Archives. *Right:* Advertisement for Caruso records, 1906/Credit: Metropolitan Archives. When record players (called talking machines at that time) became generally available, there was hardly a family owning one who did not have a collection of Caruso records.

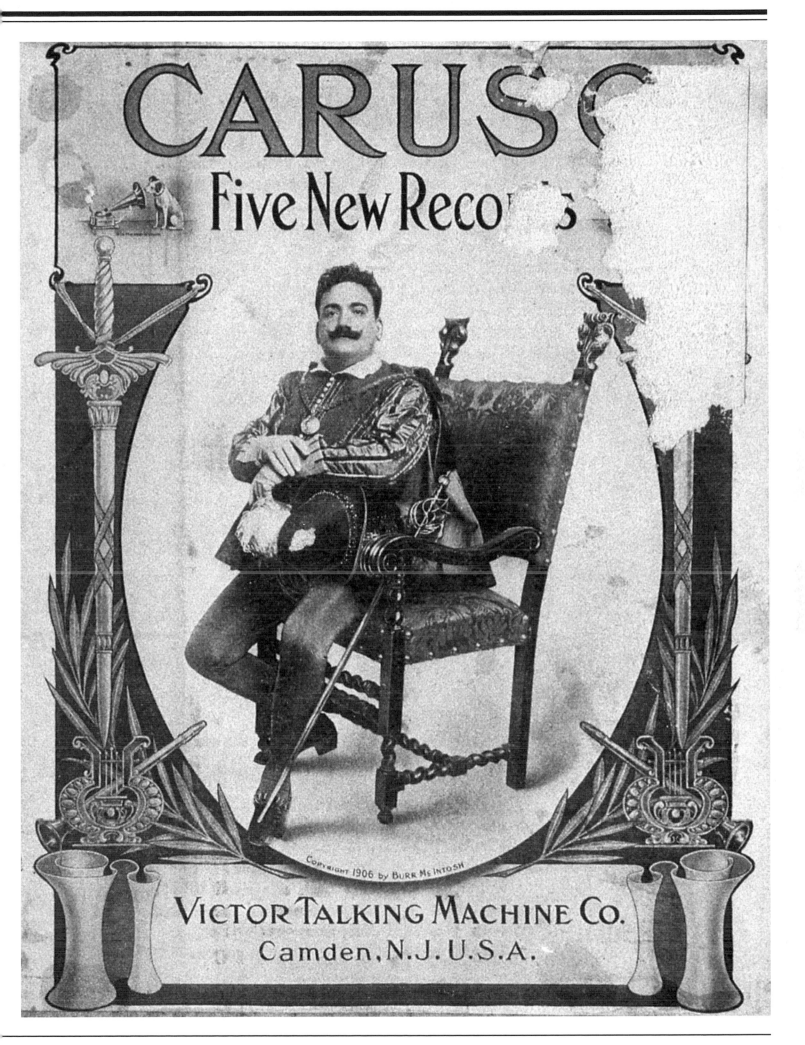

Above left: Katherine and Dante Monaco overlooking the damage caused by San Francisco's 1906 earthquake. *Below right:* Katherine Monaco, a neighbor and Dante at the family's temporary stove in front of their house on Leavenworth Street. *Below center:* Spectators on Russian Hill watching fire engulf the downtown area. Three San Francisco earthquake photographs of 1906 by J.B. Monaco/Credit: Monaco. *Opposite page top:* The town of Ottaviano (Naples), prior to 1933 called Ottaiano, ruined by the ashes of Vesuvius, 1906/Credit: LC. *Opposite page center and bottom:* Collecting money and clothing for Italian earthquake victims, Lower East Side, New York, 1909/Credit: LC

Above: Emigrants aboard the *Principessa Mafalda*, about 1920/Credit: Fototeca 3M. *Right:* "Italian child finds her first penny, Ellis Island," 1926, photograph by Lewis Hine/Credit: NYPL

SUCCESSES AND DISAPPOINTMENTS

1915-1929

Emigrating in the 1920s

1925. Luigi Barzini, an outstanding Italian writer, settled temporarily in New York with his family in the 1920s. Although he was not a typical immigrant of the period, the descriptions of his experiences, and those of his fellow countrymen, provide further insight into the acculturation of Italians moving to this country.

The inside of our new American house, in 1925, was reassuringly Italian. There were the Italian smells from the kitchen (above all the aroma of coffee, which father bought fresh-roasted at De Rosa's in Mulberry Street, near his office); there were Italian voices and occasional Victrola music; there were books, prints, our familiar paintings and old furniture. The terra incognita began beyond the front door, which, we learned, did not have to be locked and bolted as in Europe, for the same reason that there were no forbidding walls and grilled gates around the garden, our lawn merging with our neighbors' without visible markings. Apparently, there were no thieves in America, or they were too rich to bother with petty pilfering, too rich also to steal small change in the wooden cup beside the unguarded piles of morning papers on the station platform. Each customer picked up his copy, scrupulously dropped the right number of pennies (two for the *Daily News*, three for the *Times* and the *Herald*), or left a bigger coin and gave himself the correct change. We never tired of admiring the whole impossible procedure with the same amazement with which, later, I watched staunch and gallant American students fearlessly take examinations under the honor system without even considering the shabby but seductive possibility of cheating. I could not believe my eyes.

The first few weeks I spent in my room studying English or reading American books and magazines, to prepare for the imminent school term, and, feet on the window sill, raised my eyes from time to time to peer at the United States outside as an explorer prudently spies from a safe vantage point on a strange and possibly hostile territory before advancing into it. I had to admit it did not look like the efficient, inhuman, and pitiless country I had expected, where the future had

already arrived. It did not look particularly hostile either: no Indians or gangsters lurked behind tree trunks, no shooting or galloping horses could be heard in the distance. In fact, the scene was sleepy and peaceful, vaguely boring, but then it was very limited, a couple of quiet suburban blocks and five or six houses. In the tremulous speckled shadow of the immense trees I saw an occasional car or truck slowly travel the lonely road; the milkman's white wagon drawn by an old horse stop, patiently, at every door (as a devout Catholic stops at the stations of the Via Crucis); the postman in his sky-blue uniform and with his leather bag go from house to house twice a day; children in baseball uniforms going to play in some empty lot or running with their dogs; the cart of a Negro junkman on which the iron scraps bounced noisily to the rhythm of the trotting horse. In the late afternoon I could see collarless elderly men in unbuttoned waistcoats watering flowers, and old ladies with hairnets over their pale blue hair rocking themselves on their porches. My reading was desultory and intermittent; sometimes I was completely distracted by the blonde dancer in her one-piece bathing suit (a girl as unreal as the movie actresses I thought could not exist), who once in a while practiced on the lawn next door. I dreamed of her at night.

The light was definitely American, the clean transparent light of a mountain plateau in which all details were sharp and clean-cut. The fat birds and the squirrels, which would have been shot at sight and cooked succulently in the old country, were also American. The sounds were American, too: the clanking of iron garbage cans thrown around in the early morning; the elegiac lament of lawnmowers close by, distant, or very distant; the songs of the unknown appetizing birds; and the thumps of the afternoon paper pitched accurately against each front door by a boy on a bicycle. Definitely American, to be seen nowhere else, was the procession of dignified men in stiff collars and straw hats who walked to the station in the morning, swinging briefcases, and came back in the late afternoon. American, too, were the workingmen in Larry Semon overalls who were covering the road with a thick coat of new asphalt without bothering first to remove the old tram rails, further proof of American impatience

and wasteful wealth.

Very American to my eyes was the enchanting wood we discovered a few minutes' walk to the north. It looked to us exactly as the Indians, the *coureurs de bois*, and the trappers must have left it, a place for Leatherstockings. We often went there, my brother Ettore and I (we had no other place to go). We never found out how large it was. We never walked to its end. It looked immense. It was filled with tall trees, moss-covered dead trunks, unknown flowers, squirrels, and the same mouth-watering fat birds. There was a large and deep pond in the wood, a Walden Pond of our own, which froze solid the following winter. We skated on it then and made friends with young people from the neighborhood. Particularly American was, later in the fall, the tang of burning leaves, so American in fact that when I smell it anywhere in the world it always brings me back, like the taste of synthetic vanilla, to my first months in the United States. It was a strange world, as seen from my window, but it looked safe, friendly, and hospitable. . . .

Among the Italians I met who found life in America easy, profitable, and pleasurable, far easier, more profitable and pleasurable than in Italy, were the ditchdiggers, hotel and restaurant people, Sicilians, wheeler-dealers, the opera crowd, and the aristocrats.

The ditchdiggers were all called "Tony" (as Pullman porters were then called "George"). In spite of what seemed to some Americans their miserable and pitiable living conditions, they made more money, were less oppressed, and worked fewer hours than back home. They were happy and grateful. They were flattered when told they were brutally exploited. They sent money home, produced flocks of children, ate amply and succulently, made their own wine, and became very portly as soon as possible. The lucky ones were buying houses and automobiles by easy payments.

Hotel and restaurant people were in clover. They were dominating the market. New York was for them a conquered colony (Colony was, in fact, the name of one of their best restaurants). At the bottom of the ladder was the cheap one-family *trattoria*, where Mama cooked, Papa served, one always found homemade red wine served in coffee cups and homely advice on how to bear life's burden. At the top were northern Italians, mostly from Lake Maggiore, who ran and sometimes owned some of the great "French" restaurants and managed the big hotels. They had usually arrived in New York after working in Switzerland, Paris, and London, learning languages and the métier. Once a year the manager of the Biltmore, the doyen of them all, gave a stag dinner for the Italian restaurant and hotel elite. Father was one of the few nonhotel guests, probably because he was known as a good cook and an expert and insatiable gourmet. It probably was the best dinner eaten in New York in the twelve months, accompanied by the best wines, and surely the best served. The top restaurant and hotel Italians did not concern themselves with the Americans' ideals, triumphs, technical progress, and political experiments. They considered their customers strictly from the *buona cucina* angle. They saw them as primitive, naive, good-natured, and lovable barbarians, who ate anything set in front of them without complaining, people who could be awed into submission with one word or a raised eyebrow, grateful for a little attention, and wantonly generous with tips.

The Sicilian patriarchs spoke little Italian and little English. Few knew how to spell out simple headlines and street signs, or could write their own names. Like all unlettered people who make do without the prop of written words, they naturally were more sagacious, intuitive, and shrewd and had more infallible memories than the miserable people who were lost without paper and ink and printed words. The Sicilians did not need to learn anything about America, though they knew practically nothing about it. They carried on simply and imperturbably as if the street they lived on were their native village and the United States an immense Sicily. In fact, they soon discovered that the United States was a far better Sicily than Sicily itself.

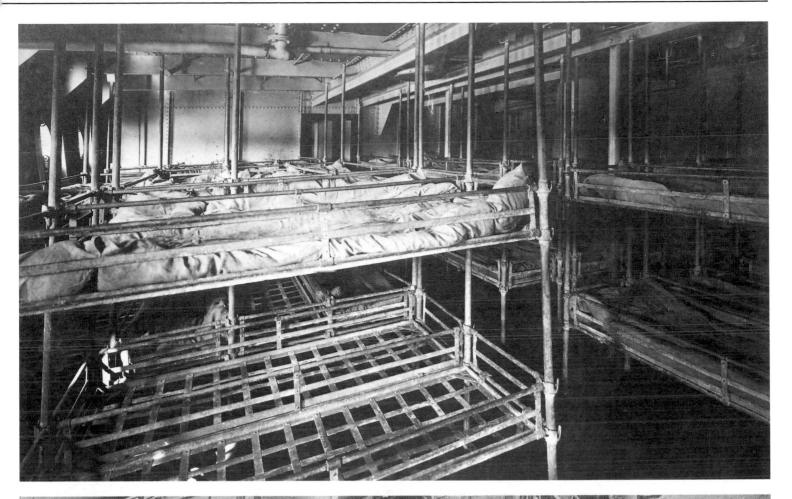

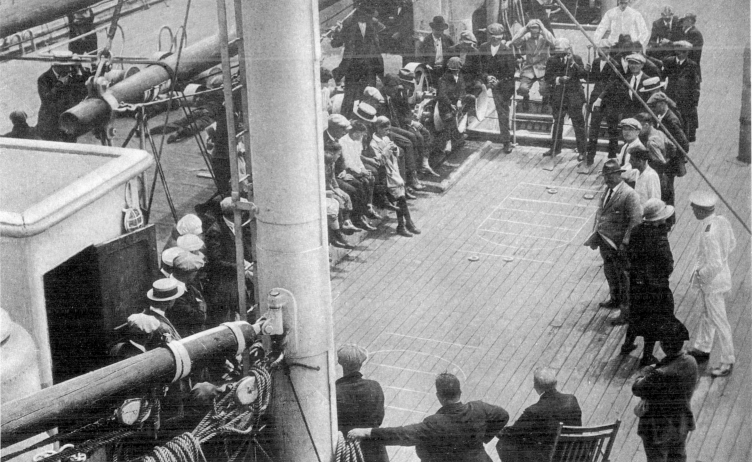

Above left: A group of emigrants on the bow of the *Conte Verde*, about 1920/Credit: TCI. *Above right:* Third-class dormitory aboard the *City of Palermo*, about 1920/Credit: TCI. *Below right:* Games on the third-class deck of the *Giulio Cesare*, about 1920/Credit: TCI

THE UNITED STATES OF AMERICA
PASSPORT

DEPARTMENT OF STATE

To all to whom these presents shall come, Greeting:

I, the undersigned, Secretary of State of the United States of America, hereby request all whom it may concern to permit *Francesca Contrucci* a citizen of the United States, safely and freely to pass, and in case of need to give *her* all lawful Aid and Protection.

This passport is valid for use only in the following countries and for objects specified, unless amended

All Countries
NAME OF COUNTRY

Temporary residence and travel enroute to the United States
OBJECT OF VISIT.

The bearer is accompanied by *her four minor children, Oscar, Gregorio, Oleda and David*

Given under my hand and the seal of the Department of State, at the City of Washington, the *28th* day of *August* in the year *22* and of the Independence of the United States the one hundred and forty- seventh

Charles E. Hughes

PERSONAL DESCRIPTION.

Age *29* years   Mouth *Medium*
Height *5 ft 5 in*   Chin *Round*
Forehead *Medium* Hair *black*
Eyes *black*   Complexion *dark*
Nose *Medium* Face *oval*
Distinguishing marks
Place of birth *Italy*
Date of birth *Feb. 20, 1893*
Occupation

X *Contrucci Frances* X
SIGNATURE OF BEARER

No *215279*

PHOTOGRAPH OF BEARER

Opposite page: Passport of Francesca Contrucci and her four children: Oscar, Gregorio, Oliva and David, 1922/Credit: Contrucci. *Above left and right:* Front and back of Francesca Contrucci's boat ticket for herself and four children from Genoa to New York on the *Conte Rosso*, 1922/Credit: Contrucci. *Below left:* The *Conte Rosso* in the harbor at Naples, about 1922/Credit: Peabody. Francesca Contucci was the second wife of Francesco Contrucci. As previously described in chapter two, he emigrated to the United States in 1895 and became an American citizen. His first wife died in childbirth in Pennsylvania. He returned to Italy in 1910 and married Francesca. After serving in the Italian army during World War I, he returned to the United States in 1919. Three years later, his wife and children joined him.

Caruso's Silver Jubilee

1919. Enrico Caruso was without question the preeminent operatic tenor of his day. His long tenure at the Metropolitan Opera was celebrated in a glowing tribute in which both his admirers and fellow musicians participated.

Enrico Caruso, at a notable performance last night at the Metropolitan Opera House, celebrated the twenty-fifth anniversary of his appearance in opera. For the occasion, which was attended by everybody in music circles who could get into the opera house, Caruso had selected to sing the third act of *L'Elisir d'Amore*, the first act of *Pagliacci* and the coronation scene from *Le Prophète*.

As the proceeds were to go to the Opera Emergency Fund, the prices were raised, but this made no difference in the number of those who wanted to cheer the great tenor.

After the operatic feature the curtain was raised and disclosed the entire Metropolitan organization, from directors down, grouped about a table loaded with gifts that were to be given to Caruso.

Otto H. Kahn, as chairman of the board of directors of the company, spoke first. He said that, in Caruso's case, "we admire not alone the voice but the art and the man." He referred to Caruso's high artistic striving, his serious artistic purpose, his generosity, his kindliness and simplicity. Mr. Kahn emphasized the tenor's loyalty to this country and this city.

"You have even managed," he said, "to find a generous thought, a pleasant gesture and a gracious word, in going through the painful process of paying an income tax running into six figures.

"As we love you and are grateful to you, and take pride in you, who are in one way or another associated with you, so does the public of New York."

James M. Beck, speaking for the people of New York, pointed out that rarely, in the history of opera, has a singer held an indisputable primacy in his art for a quarter of a century. Caruso, he said, has made an ideal of his art, and has taken his place with the great historic tenors. His art is even, Mr. Beck maintained, for it is always his best.

He said that Caruso, during his connection with the opera house, has sung at 550 performances and has appeared in thirty-six operas. In one respect, Caruso is more fortunate than his predecessors—Mario, Brignoli, Campanini and De Reszke—for where they sang to thousands, Caruso has sung to millions, by means of the phonograph. In this way, he has added to the sum of the world's happiness. Mr. Beck closed by referring to Caruso's great work during the war and extolling Italy's share in the conflict.

Caruso seldom makes an extended speech, but, with much feeling, he replied:

"My heart is beating so hard with the emotion that I feel that I am afraid I cannot even put a few words together. I am sure you will forgive me if I do not make a long speech. I can only thank you and beg you to accept my sincerest and most heartfelt gratitude for tonight and for all the very many kindnesses which you have showered upon me. I assure you that I will never forget this occasion, and ever cherish in my heart of hearts my affection for my dear American friends. Thank you! Thank you! Thank you!"

What Mr. Gatti-Casazza thinks of his leading tenor may be determined from his statement:

"Someone has said, 'Mr. Caruso no longer is what he used to be! But of course, twenty-five years have passed!'

"Nothing truer. Caruso no longer is what he used to be, for the simple reason that he has gone forward steadily and constantly, and today, on his silver jubilee, he can celebrate not only the completion of the twenty-five years of his career, but also his arrival at the zenith of his art and his physical powers.

"He is an artist who ever has in reserve for the public many varied and delightful surprises. We can await them with faith assured."

Caruso then had a chance to look over the tokens that were stacked up on the table. They comprised an illuminated parchment from the directors of the Metropolitan Opera and Real Estate Company, signed by A. D. Juilliard; an engrossed parchment, bound in blue morocco, from the Philadelphia opera directors; an illuminated scroll from the directors of the Brooklyn Academy of Music; a silver receptacle for fruits and flowers, from the Victor Talking Machine Company; a folio edition of Corrado Ricci's *Dante*, from Alfred E. Seligsberg; a gold medal, four inches in diameter, from the management of the opera house; an Italian silver vase, twenty-four inches high, from the board of directors of the opera company; a silver loving cup, eighteen inches high, from the chorus; an ornate silver floral vase from the orchestra; an illuminated parchment, with a bird's-eye view of Naples, from the administrative staff of the opera house; a gold medal and engrossed and illuminated parchment, from the chiefs of the stage departments.

From his fellow artists he received a platinum watch, set on the rim with seventy-eight diamonds and ornamented on the back with three circles of diamonds containing 140 stones, surrounding a circular monogram, with the initials "E.C." made with sixty-one square-cut sapphires. It was presented in a silver box on which are engraved the names of the donors—every member of the company.

Above left: Enrico Caruso with his family, 1920/Credit: LC. *Above right:* Mutual aid society, Scranton, Pennsylvania, 1928/Credit: Balch. *Below left:* L.M., Lloyd, Claire and Virgil Giannini, unidentified chauffeur and Reynolds Barbieri, about 1920/Credit: BOA. *Bottom right:* Street scene, Chicago, about 1925/Credit: UIC

Above left: Emilio and Grace Giaimo Panella, New York, about 1928/Credit: Sichel. *Above right:* Husband and wife, New York, about 1928/Credit: Malandrini. *Below left:* The Gustozo (Justave) family at Ellis Island, 1905, detail of photograph by Lewis Hine, Credit: NYPL. Dominick Justave is seen in the arms of his mother. *Below center:* Wedding of Dominick Justave and Rose Carlino, Scranton, Pennsylvania, 1927/Credit: Balch. *Below right:* Dominick and Rose Justave, family members and grandchildren, Scranton, Pennsylvania, 1954/Credit: Balch

Above: Saints Peter and Paul Church Altar Boys Society, San Francisco, 1924/Credit: Eureka. *Below:* Wedding photo of T.J. Lampson (Lamposona) and Mary Cangelosi, Stafford, Texas, 1927/Credit: Frank E. Tritico, Institute of Texan Cultures

Above: String quintet, Chicago, 1917/Credit: UIC. *Below:* Andrea DeLuca (third from left) and friends playing bocce, Chicago Heights, about 1920/Credit: UIC

Above: Damante Band, Chicago, about 1927/Credit: UIC. *Below:* Peter de Paolo, winner of the Baltimore-Washington 250-mile race, 1925/Credit: LC

GERHARD
SISTERS
ST. LOUIS

The Last Statement of Bartolomeo Vanzetti

1927. In what has become one of the most disputed trials in American judicial history, Nicola Sacco and Bartolomeo Vanzetti, Italian immigrant radicals, were found guilty of robbery and murder and executed, despite circumstantial evidence, after six years of protracted public protests. Vanzetti never wavered in his protestations of innocence.

What I say is that I am innocent . . . of the Braintree crime. . . . That I am not only innocent . . . but in all my life I have never stole and I have never killed and I have never spilled blood. That is what I want to say. And it is not all. Not only am I innocent . . . not only in all my life I have never stole, never killed, never spilled blood, but I have struggled all my life, since I began to reason, to eliminate crime from the earth.

Everybody that knows these two arms knows very well that I did not need to go in between the street and kill a man to take the money. I can live with my two arms and live well. But besides that, I can live even without work with my arm for other people. I have had plenty of chance to live independently and to live what the world conceives to be a higher life than not to gain

our bread with the sweat of our brow. . . .

Well, I want to reach a little point farther, and it is this— that not only have I not been . . . in Braintree to steal and kill and have never steal or kill or spilt blood in all my life, not only have I struggled hard against crimes, but I have refused myself the commodity or glory of life, the pride of life of a good position, because in my consideration it is not right to exploit man. I have refused to go in business because I understand that business is a speculation on profit upon certain people that must depend upon the businessman, and I do not consider that that is right and therefore I refuse to do that.

Now, I should say that I am not only innocent of all these things, not only have I never committed a real crime in my life —though some sins but not crimes—not only have I struggled all my life to eliminate crimes, the crimes that the official law and the official moral condemns, but also the crime that the official moral and the official law sanctions and sanctifies—the exploitation and the oppression of the man by the man, and if there is a reason why I am here as a guilty man, if there is a reason why you in a few minutes can doom me, it is this reason and none else.

I beg your pardon. [Referring to paper] There is the more good man I ever cast my eyes upon since I lived, a man that will last and will grow always more near and more dear to the people, as far as into the heart of the people, so long as admiration for goodness and for sacrifice will last. I mean Eugene Debs. I will say that even a dog that killed the chickens would not have found an American jury to convict it with the proof that the Commonwealth produced against us. That man was not with me in Plymouth or with Sacco where he was on the day of the crime. You can say of yours on the train, at the University Club of Boston, on the Golf Club of Worcester, Massachusetts. I am sure that if the people who know all what you say against us would have the civil courage to take the stand, maybe, Your Honor—I am sorry to say this because you are an old man, and I have an old father—but maybe you would be beside us in good justice at this time.

When you sentenced me at the Plymouth trial you say, to the best of my memory, of my good faith, that crimes were in accordance with my principle—something of that sort—and you take off one charge if I remember it exactly, from the jury. The jury was so violent against me that they found me guilty of both charges, because there were only two. But they would have found me guilty of a dozen of charges against Your Honor's instructions. Of course I remember that you told them that there was no reason to believe that if I were the bandit I have intention to kill somebody, so that they will take off the indict- ment of attempt to murder. Well, they found me guilty of what? And if I am right, you take out that and sentence me only for attempt to rob with arms—something like that. But, Judge Thayer, you give more to me for that attempt of robbery than all the 448 men that were in Charlestown, all of those that attempt- ed to rob, all those that have robbed, that have not such a sentence as you gave me for an attempt at robbery. . . .

We were tried during a time that has now passed into history. I mean by that, a time when there was a hysteria of resentment and hate against the people of our principles, against the foreigner, against slackers, and it seems to me— rather, I am positive of it, that both you and Mr. Katzman has done all what it were in your power in order to work out, in order to agitate still more the passion of the juror, the prejudice of the juror, against us. . . .

But her children were not unmindful of her long yearning, and when . . . family prosperity seemed sufficiently founded to permit a luxury for our mother's sake, we ourselves pleaded with her to take a summer off for a visit to Italy with her aged parents and her sister. She allowed herself at length to be persuaded.

Thus Mother went to Italy. And for two months we received breathless letters from an Alice writing home from her Wonderland. Now for the first time she visited Rome, and the Romans became for her a people among the ruins of Pompeii. But Florence, Venice, Milan, Assisi, Perugia, these were not on her itinerary, and she would hardly have known what to do with a Raphael or a Michelangelo. No, my mother's itinerary was restricted to the region about Gaeta: a few trips in the environs, a few visits to marvelous places of pilgrimage, and she was content. Culture, tradition, and poetry were for her exhausted in a native village by the sea in the company of her aged mother and father, a sister, and a sister-in-law. For the first time in her life she was treated with open deference as a person of consequence, and her letters were delightful in innocent avowal of the satisfactions of being a personage. Meanwhile she collected hangings and tapestries for her home, gifts and souvenirs for her children, and, in gratitude, an effigy of the Virgin in gesso and had them all packed in her trunk two weeks before the day of her departure.

And then it happened—and the pathos of it shook the little village so that people spoke of it to me three years afterward in accents beyond politeness and facile resignation. She suddenly felt a pain in the region of her stomach and her right side and she treated it herself as a digestive disturbance or as an untimely recurrence of her old trouble. For three days she suffered as an Italian peasant knows how to suffer. She applied hot olive oil on the exterior of the ache, she was devotedly nursed by her people with the household remedies their ancestors might have used. But to no avail. And then, by the time they were able to transfer her to the poor local hospital and call the specialist from Naples, the ache had swollen and burst and it was too late. They say that toward the end she opened her eyes and cried: "I shall never see my children again, I know it now." But whether there was resignation in her voice or a final peace in her eyes we cannot tell. We were not there to see.

Three years later I opened the niche in the mortuary chapel where her bones lie in a white sheet beside those of her aged father, stricken immediately in sympathy with his oldest daughter's death. They were bones, physically and logically related to her whom I had loved alive. But her death I remember in another fashion. I saw it in her eyes as her ship drew away from the Boston docks. Then she seemed to clasp the rail half-faint and draw back terrified. On her face was the expression of one who has spoken a word impossible to gainsay. Was it natural fear of departure or especial premonition? This last image of my mother has haunted me since. Like her life, it portrayed courageous acceptance of tragedy humanized by the simplicity of instinct, while the flesh shrank unashamed from the pain it would ultimately master thanks to some unobtrusive grace of its own nature.

The De Nora family, Colchester, Connecticut, 1940, photograph by Jack Delano/ Credit: LC

"Breaking Away"

1942. In this excerpt from his autobiographical novel, Mount Allegro, *Jerre Mangione raises the sensitive issue of how the immigrant Italian American family deals with the dichotomy of the desire to be separated from "Little Italy" while fearing what lies ahead in the unfamiliar territory of the broader American community.*

A few of my relatives began breaking away from Mount Allegro to live on the outskirts of town where they could enjoy the luxury of a vegetable garden. At first they seemed lost in their new American surroundings, where there were no guitar sessions and no storytellers like Uncle Nino. Every few evenings they would come bounding back to the neighborhood with tall stories about the joys of suburban life and bring generous gifts of fruits and vegetables.

But as they became acquainted with their new American neighbors—most of them families of German and Irish origin—their visits to Mount Allegro became less frequent. Some of them grew quite aloof and did their best to forget they had ever lived in a poorer environment. Others, like *compare* Calogero and Rosario Alfano, couldn't bear to be away from their Sicilian neighbors and moved back into Mount Allegro.

Those who left it for good developed strange habits and tastes. They took to drinking fruit juices at breakfast and tea with supper. They wore pajamas to bed, drank whiskey with soda, and learned to play poker.

My relatives pretended to be scandalized by the foreign customs of these renegades, but at heart they were envious and gradually they too adopted some of them. The most popular of all was poker. The Unholy Three began to play less *briscola* and more *pochero*, as they pronounced it, and my Uncle Luigi shone as a *pochero* expert because he had often watched the game played at his union's headquarters and naturally knew more of the rules than anyone else. He knew what it took to make a *fulla-hausa*, a *straighto*, and a *flosho* long before the others did. For a while he won the most money.

If the children had had their own way, my parents would have dropped all their Sicilian ideas and customs and behaved more like other Americans. That was our childhood dream. Yet, as much as we wanted them to be Americans and as much as we wanted to live an American life, we did not have the vaguest notion as to how to go about it. I used to wonder how it would be if our family moved out of Mount Allegro, as some of the other relatives had done, but the idea of leaving playmates behind was too painful. Besides, it was clear to me that those who had moved into American neighborhoods didn't seem any more American than they ever had, in spite of their tea and pajamas.

Gathering on Fisherman's Wharf, San Francisco, 1941, photograph by John Collier/Credit: LC

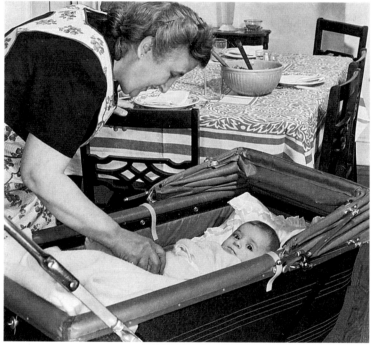

Although no one seemed to approach them in real life, the movie stars came closest to our idea of what Americans were like. I tried to imitate some of my favorite stars, but in the face of having to speak Sicilian and eat Sicilian food it seemed futile. In my imitations, no one pointed to me and said: "Look, that boy must be American. He has dark eyes and an olive skin, yes, but probably some of his Mayflower ancestors intermarried with the Indians.". . .

Our general attitude toward all Americans was bound to be distorted, for, not knowing any of them well, we could not make independent judgments and were influenced by the confused opinions our elders had of them. On one hand, my relatives were cynical about *Americani:* they had no manners; they licked their fingers after a meal and they chewed gum and then played with it as though it were a rubber band. Also, *Americani* were *superbi* (snobs) and looked down on people who didn't speak their language fluently. On the other hand, they feared and respected *Americani* and there were times when they emulated them.

If a Sicilian began to behave like an *Americano*, they said he was putting on airs but, actually, they had great admiration for anyone who achieved any degree of Americanization. After all, to be an *Americano* was a sign that you were getting on in the world. The bosses were Americans. The police were Americans. In fact, nearly anyone who had plenty of money or a good steady job was either an American or was living like one.

You had only to look at the example set by the sons of poor Italians who became doctors or lawyers in the community. As soon as they had established themselves, they married blonde American girls and moved as far as possible from their former neighborhoods. Some of them dropped the vowels from the end of their names, so that people would think they had always been American. They stopped associating with their relatives. Their wives got their pictures in society pages and, instead of having a raft of children, they bought wire-haired terriers and walked them around the block, like many other prosperous Americans. The only times they liked dealing with Italians was when it meant money in their pockets.

Opposite page above left: Anthony Parisi, a fisherman's son, Gloucester, Massachusetts, 1943, photograph by Gordon Parks/Credit: LC. *Opposite page above right:* Mr. Caputo reading the comics to his daughter, Brooklyn, 1942, photograph by Arthur Rothstein/Credit: LC. *Opposite page below left:* Mrs. Rose Carrendeno playing with her grandchild, New York, 1943, photograph by Gordon Parks/Credit: LC. *Opposite page below right:* Mrs. Marinana Costanzo in her living room, New York, photograph by Marjorie Collins/Credit: LC. *Above left:* Cowpuncher Frank Latta, Bozeman, Montana, 1939, photograph by Arthur Rothstein/Credit: LC. *Above right:* Nick Grillo, developer of the "Thornless Rose," Southington, Connecticut, 1942, photograph by Fenno Jacobs/Credit: LC. *Below:* Bratta family picnic, Chicago, about 1939/Credit: UIC

Emigrating in 1939

1939. The restrictive immigration laws of the 1920s were aimed at putting a complete end to the massive wave of southern, central, and eastern European immigration to the United States. Riccardo Massoni, who later became a surgeon, was one of the relatively few Italians able to enter this country at this time.

When he knew the war was going to break out, my father took the whole family to Paris. I was walking on the Champs Elysées the day war was declared. That's when the idea crystallized in my father: that the two young male members of our family—I was nineteen and my cousin was seventeen—would come to the United States. We were both medical students, and we would continue medical school. We were of age to serve in the army and we would have been put in the Italian army. And Dad said, "No, if you have to fight, you might as well fight where you believe in and go on the winning side and fight for the side that you want to fight for. And if you can continue your studies, fine. And if you can't, then you can serve wherever you are expected to." So we came.

You know, those were tragic times. It was very difficult to get passage. Poland had already been taken, and the Germans were pretty close to Holland. They were expected momentarily to move into Holland. There were an awful lot of Germans in Rotterdam, where we went to get the boat. German Jews particularly. Passages on the boat were very difficult to obtain. We had two tickets, and we were with two other young men who also had tickets, and at the last minute, as we were ready to board, there was a family who really—if they had been caught

by the Germans, they would have been exterminated. They were German Jews. So we gave them our tickets because we were young men. We felt, "Well, we can always make a go of it." But here was a father, a mother, a daughter, another kid. We gave them our tickets. The boat pulled out and hit a mine in the harbor and sank while we were watching. We could see it. You never know how things will come out. They had thanked us and we had felt generous. . . .

We took the next boat and it turned out to be the last boat to leave Rotterdam. That boat was like a Grand Hotel. There were refugees from all over Europe: American citizens getting home, Cubans going back to Cuba, Jewish refugees from Germany, and political refugees, young and old, all mixed together. There was the Russian Ballet of Monte Carlo who performed at the Met many times and a band from Cuba that was leaving Europe. Everybody else was older, so they sort of adopted us, and we used to eat with the Cuban band and had it nice. We had good times on that boat. And when we got into New York City everyone was going. Everyone had a place to go. Everybody knew where to go except us. The Cuban boys were getting their instruments, and the Russian Ballet was getting ready to perform at the Metropolitan, and all of a sudden I realized that that was *it*. My last contact with Europe was over. I felt afraid.

We had a little cash and some things we planned to sell— gold cigarette lighters, a fine leather briefcase, that sort of thing. I remember going into a telephone booth and trying to figure out how to dial a hotel and find out if they had a vacancy, in broken English. I said to myself, "This is really going to be rough." We took a cab, and immediately you change your way of thinking. What in Paris cost a few francs, here it looked very little, but

MADE JULY 8-1935 BY G. SIMONE

then you translate it into francs and Italian lire and you say, "You mean to tell me I've already spent this much just to take a cab? I'm not going to last a week."

The hotel was on Eighty-eighth Street, right off Broadway. It was a real rathole. We unpacked enough to change, and I said, "Okay, let's go take a look now. Get the first glimpse of New York." We went down to the street and we looked up and saw the sign BROADWAY. I said, "Don't tell me this is Broadway, what we have heard so much in songs." Remember we were at Eighty-eighth Street. It wasn't uptown. We were flabbergasted by the poor taste of the shops. We were fresh from Paris, from the Rue de la Paix. I remember there was a window and a shop full of junk. Dust and dirt all over. It was unbelievable, you know, and I said, "My God! Where on earth did we come?" If we had been off Park Avenue or Fifth Avenue or Madison Avenue, the impression would have been different, but that first taste was absolutely terrible. That first impression. And I said, "Oh, if I was only walking down the Champs Elysées instead of this place. Or the Via Veneto in Rome. What are we doing here?"

We had to get used to eating very little. The food was so different and, of course, we didn't have much money. You'd go into a cafeteria for instance and you'd ask for a sandwich and they'd say, "Rye or white?" and you don't know what they're talking about. What is that? A sandwich is a sandwich. There is no such thing in Italy as rye bread or white bread or whole-wheat bread; it's bread. Bread is bread. Now what is he asking me about the bread? And they say it so fast. I couldn't under-stand a word. I would just mumble anything. Imitate the first word that he said and if he didn't come back at me with another

thing, otherwise I would say anything, you know? Because I just didn't know. And, of course, things that I knew, like spaghetti or macaroni, they were so terrible. But then little by little I learned.

We moved out to Brooklyn, and I remember the delight I used to have in going to delicatessens somewhere there and really loving those hot pastrami sandwiches as if there was no tomorrow. In those days that particular part of Brooklyn was nice. It was cheaper and we liked it. I remember there were small little homes, one after another, and clean streets. Very orderly. The people that rented us a room in their house, they were nice people of Russian origin. Very cordial, really nice. It was like a little bit of the country. And then little by little we began to realize that all the world is alike, you know. We saw some nice people, we saw people that we didn't like as much, but by and large they were friendly.

We found out that people here were terribly ignorant of what was going on in Europe. And so were the newspapers. They seemed to have no idea what Nazis were, or Mussolini. The only one that was making any sense was FDR; the others just had no idea. They didn't know what was going on in Europe. People thought it was a war that didn't concern them.

Opposite page: Class in citzenship and English, New York, 1943, photograph by Marjorie Collins/Credit: LC. *Above:* An embroidery by Gaetano Simone, Westville, Connecticut, 1940, photograph by Jack Delano/Credit: LC

Above left: Carving a statue of Ethan Allen for the Vermont state capitol building in Montpelier at the Vermont Marble Company works, Rutland, about 1940/Credit: LC. *Above right:* Cabinet maker, New York, photograph by Lewis Hine, 1943/Credit: LC. *Below left:* Luigi Antonini, vice-president of International Ladies Garment Workers Union, on the picket line, about 1935/Credit: ILGWU. *Below right:* Poster for ILGWU Italian Local No. 89 "Bread and Roses" festival, 1937/Credit: ILGWU

Above: Day laborers at Seabrook Farms, Bridgeton, New Jersey, 1941, photograph by Marjorie Post Wolcott/Credit: LC. Some are brought by truck from nearby towns and others come in their own cars from Philadelphia. *Below*: House on a small farm owned by Italian Americans, Santa Clara County, California, photograph by Dorothea Lange/Credit: LC

Above left: Angelo Cribari being photographed in his vineyard after Sunday church service, 1942/Credit: Cribari. *Above right:* Pruning grapes in the vineyard, Sonoma County, California, 1942, photograph by Russell Lee/Credit: LC. *Below left:* Young day laborer carrying a basket of beans to be weighed, Seabrook Farms, Bridgeton, New Jersey, 1941, photograph by Marjorie Post Wolcott/Credit: LC. *Below right:* Young man picking cranberries, Burlington County, New Jersey, photograph by Arthur Rothstein/Credit: LC

Above: Vineyards, Sonoma County, California, 1942, photograph by Russell Lee/Credit: LC. *Below:* Young Michael Mondavi accompanies the planter at the Krug Winery, California, about 1949/Credit: NA

Opposite page above left: Italian cheese store, Bleecker Street, New York, 1937, photograph by Berenice Abbott/Credit: MCNY. *Opposite page above right:* De Martino's fish market, New York, 1943, photograph by Gordon Parks/Credit: LC. *Opposite page below left:* Bakery on First Avenue, New York, 1943, photograph by Marjorie Collins/Credit: LC. *Opposite page below right:* Hanging out pasta to dry at the Atlantic Macaroni Company, Long Island City, New York, 1943, photograph by Marjorie Collins/Credit: LC. *Above:* Street procession of the Blessed Mother Incoronata with Knights of Columbus, Chicago, 1945/Credit: UIC. Joseph Vernerri, on the left, is the only person permitted to take the statue down from the altar. *Below right:* Street procession of the Blessed Mother Incoronata in the town of Ricigliamo (Salerno), 1925/Credit: UIC. The Chicago statue is patterned after this one. *Below left:* Feast, Melrose Park, Illinois, 1944/Credit: UIC

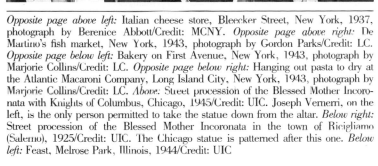

Arturo Toscanini, New York, photograph by Horst, 1940/Credit: NYPL Music. The legendary Toscanini is often considered to be the greatest symphony conductor of modern times. Born in Parma in 1867, he died in New York a few weeks before his ninetieth birthday. When Gatti-Casazza became General Manager of the Metropolitan Opera in 1908, he invited Toscanini to be principal conductor. After the combination of the New York Philharmonic with the New York Symphony in 1928, Toscanini became permanent conductor. In 1937 he became music director of the NBC Symphony Orchestra, a radio orchestra that had been organized especially for him. "The Maestro," as he was affectionately called, demanded absolute perfection; he would erupt into violence when he could not get what he wanted from an orchestra. No one, even the most celebrated opera stars or instrumental soloists, ever dared to question his authority.

Above: Conducting the NBC Symphony Orchestra, New York, about 1940, photograph by Joe Lawrie, Jr./Credit: NYPL Music. *Below:* With his granddaughter, New York, about 1950, photograph by Herbert Geher/Credit: NYPL Music

Italian Americans, Fascism and the War

1942. Constantine Panunzio, who arrived in Boston as an immigrant in 1902, later became a preacher, a teacher and eventually a professor of sociology at the University of California. He surveyed the complexities of Italian American attitudes toward both fascism and World War II.

The response which the Italian Americans have given to fascism, or are giving to it in the present crisis, has passed through three well-marked phases: early indifference, passing interest, and mild antagonism; partial acceptance and participation; and withdrawal and repudiation. During the years in which fascism was in its formative stages, by far the great majority of Italian Americans regarded the movement with indifference, or passing interest, or mild antagonism. Although on this issue no Gallup poll was ever taken, all the available evidence of their literary and social expression points to such a conclusion. At least four factors helped to produce it. First, the Italians who came to the United States before 1920 were almost wholly late-nineteenth century liberals. In their home land they had been influenced by the American and French Revolutions, had participated in the agrarian, proletarian, and cooperative movements, and had in other ways inclined toward democracy. Italy had adopted a constitutional monarchy in 1861–1870, but considerable segments of the Italian working and middle classes, to which the immigrants belonged, had continued to hope for some form of democratic government. Garibaldi and Mazzini were their political heroes: Garibaldi, who in Italy and elsewhere had fought valiantly in behalf of democracy, and Mazzini, who had devoted his entire life to working for the establishment of a republic in Italy and a federation of free nations in Europe. There were some among the Italian immigrants who came to the United States before 1920 who leaned toward socialism, or syndicalism and the economic revolution,

or philosophical or active anarchism; but democracy as such stood above all their other political interests. Concrete evidence of this is found in their publications, in the names which they gave to their numerous mutual-aid, political, and social organizations, and in the democratic manner in which they conducted them. When fascism arose, these early Italian Americans almost to a man reacted negatively to the movement. . . .

About 1926 the picture started to change. More Italian Americans began to lean toward fascism. In this shift also several factors were at work.

First among these was the psychological effect of the immigration restriction movement. The restriction movement, it will be recalled, though primarily economic in its purpose, was largely colored by the inferiority-superiority doctrines of Gobineau and company, which labeled the Italians, along with several other peoples, as inferior. Italian Americans did not oppose restriction per se, since they themselves, being largely of the laboring classes, were interested in preventing additional workers from entering the country. But they were humiliated by the underlying discrimination, especially when that discrimination was given national expression and confirmation in the Immigration Acts of 1921 and 1924.

The fascist doctrine, on the other hand, gave them strength, endowed them with a sense of ethnic dignity and pride, by proclaiming the greatness of the Italian people and of the contribution they had made to culture. It encouraged Italians the world over to return to their native land and not subject themselves to indignity abroad; it promised them an empire of their own, a new Roman empire, in which they could toil in their own right and reap the fruit of their labor for themselves and the motherland. As knowledge of these fascist doctrines and promises permeated the thought of the Italians in this country—and the fascists saw to it that it did—many Italian Americans, being human and needing a prop to sustain them in a world where many people with whom they had to deal

regarded them as inferior, looked on fascism as their savior. They turned to it simply as a means of recovering their sense of human importance. If the facts were known, it would probably be found that there were many who, like Domenico Trombetta, editor of the New York weekly *Grido della Stirpe* ("Cry of the Race"), became fire-eating fascists and agitators against democracy as a result of this process. . . .

This activity continued to gain momentum until about 1935. In 1931 Foreign Minister Grandi came to the United States, ostensibly to discuss peace with President Hoover. Grandi was accompanied by his wife—an unheard-of arrangement for an Italian on a diplomatic mission—to assist in social propaganda. Then in 1933 the fascists sent Italo Balbo flying over the Atlantic to the United States and the Chicago Fair. This glorified propaganda stunt made some converts. Finally, in January 1934 the fascists confidently sent over Piero Parini, Director General of Italian Fasci Abroad, to consolidate the fascist forces in the United States. There were in this country at that time 125 principal fascist centers, having headquarters, regularly elected officers, and a membership of about 500,000.

The Parini visit, however, marked the turning point in this movement. Instead of consolidating fascism among Italian Americans, it actually sounded the first peal of the death knell of the movement. The antifascists, who had been looking for just such an opportunity, warned of the danger. The House Committee investigating un-American activities looked into the matter. Parini was scarcely out of the country when fascist propagandists started to run for cover. Italian Americans all over the land, beginning to realize the full significance of fascism, commenced to withdraw from fascist groups. American reaction to the Ethiopian war accelerated that movement. Many Italians took out their naturalization papers and brought over their families. They knew where they stood. . . .

In 1938 an increasing number of Italian Americans perceived the real meaning of fascism, for Italy as well as for the rest of the world. First came the Austrian *Anschluss* and the occupation of the Brenner Pass by the Nazis in March, with the fascists' tacit acceptance of that fact, and then Hitler's descent into Italy, in May, at the invitation of the fascists. These events made it clear that fascism, wittingly or unwittingly, was betraying Italy. At first, Italian American newspapers and radio programs were on the defensive; later they became half apologetic; and as time passed they gave fainter and fainter praise to fascism. Prominent Italian Americans changed overnight from fascists to ardent advocates of democracy.

Meantime the Italian antifascists, who for nearly two decades had been looked down upon and who had waged a losing fight as individuals, now became articulate. They initiated a broad movement to counteract the fascist propaganda. Outstanding in this connection is the Mazzini Society organized in 1939 by such men as Salvemini, Sforza, Venturi, and others, most of whom are American citizens of Italian extraction. The Mazzini Society now has about fifty centers and over 3,000 members or associate members. It devotes itself to educating Italian Americans in the fundamentals of American democracy. It conducts meetings, publishes literature, assists Italians needing services once performed by the consulates; and in other ways, it aids Italian Americans in the name of democracy.

It is safe to assert that at present the Italian American community as a whole is almost to a man disillusioned as to fascism. There are those who are watching the way the wind blows and who still hope for an Axis victory. But they are few and very far between. The vast majority of Italians in this country today are unequivocally for democracy.

Opposite page above left: Italian fascist dictator Benito Mussolini, 1936/Credit: LC. *Opposite page above right:* Al Capone, the notorious Chicago criminal gang leader, after his arrest, 1930/Credit: NA. *Above:* A group of men listening to a radio speech by Mussolini, San Francisco, about 1935/Credit: SFPL

Above: A shoemaker serving as an air-raid warden during World War II, New York, 1942, photograph by Marjorie Collins/Credit: LC. *Below:* An Italian butcher shop on First Avenue, near Tenth Street, New York, 1943, photograph by Marjorie Collins/Credit: LC

Above: Helen Guermotti and Mary Migogna were employed as car repairmen's helpers at the steel car shop of the Pennsylvania Railroad yard, replacing men who had gone into the armed forces during World War II, Pitcairn, Pennsylvania, 1943, photograph by Marjorie Collins/Credit: LC. *Below:* Leni Autorino polishing a searchlight at the General Electric plant, Verona, New Jersey, about 1942/Credit: Autorino

Above left: Platoon Sergeant John Basilone, who was awarded the Congressional Medal of Honor "for extraordinary heroism and conspicuous gallantry in action against the enemy" at Guadalcanal in 1942, later died in the battle for Iwo Jima/Credit: NA. *Below and above right:* Corporal Salvatore DiMarco, a member of the American armed forces who liberated Italy, pointing to the sign of his hometown, Mezzojuso (Palermo), and later as he was greeted by his parents and sister at the door of their home in Mezzojuso, 1943/Credit: NA

Above: Private Frank Provenzano of Brooklyn sings an Italian folksong with a local accordion accompanist in Pozzilli (Isernia), 1944/Credit: NA. *Below:* Felix Giannetto, formerly of Jackson Heights, Queens, New York, and his daughter, Adeline, showing Pfc. John Peacock a welcome sign which was on his door as the first American troops entered Messina, 1943/Credit: NA

ITALIAN-AMERICANS
Coming Into Their Own

Above: Cover of *The New York Times Magazine*, May 15, 1983/Credit: Daniel Maffia and The New York Times. *Appearing on the cover from left to right and from top to bottom:* "Martin Scorsese, Film director, Governor Mario Cuomo, Democrat of New York, Salvador E. Luria, Nobel Prize winner for medicine, Eleanor Curti Smeal, Former President of NOW, Lee A. Iacocca, Chairman of Chrysler, Joseph V. Vittoria, President of Avis, Representative Geraldine A. Ferraro, Democrat of New York, Robert Venturi, Architect, Joseph Cardinal Bernardin, Archbishop of Chicago, A. Bartlett Giamatti, President of Yale, Senator Pete V. Domenici, Republican of New Mexico, Senator Alfonse M. D'Amato, Republican of New York." *Right:* Choir boys, Little Italy, New York, about 1955, photograph by Leonard Freed/Credit: Magnum

CHAPTER SIX

FROM LITTLE ITALY TO FRONT PAGE

Since 1946

Second-Generation Teenagers

1961. In Italy at the turn of the century, the Italian peasant family had been a patriarchal, well-integrated economic and social unit. When these families emigrated to the United States, they settled in cities where the family-centered life they had led in Italy was no longer possible. Dr. Francis A. J. Ianni provided a sociological interpretation of adolescence as experienced by the children of these families.

With the emergence of the second-generation Italo-American teenager, whose parents were American-born children of Italian-born parentage, the family had moved even further from the traditional Italian pattern. This movement was physical as well as cultural, for, by the 1930s, Italo-Americans had begun to move in increasing numbers out of the colonies. The degree of this movement can be appreciated if we consider one example covering the period 1900 to 1950. A study conducted by the writer in Norristown, Pennsylvania, indicated that in 1900 all 87 Italo-American residential units in this city-sized borough were within the confines of the Italian colony. By 1930 only 12.5 percent of the 1,247 family units had moved out of the colony, but by 1950 nearly 42 percent of the 2,161 Italo-American families lived outside the colony. Recent visits to Norristown reveal that, today, fewer than 50 percent of the Italo-American families in Norristown remain in the colony.

This residential mobility was accompanied by occupational and social mobility as well. The Italian immigrants who came to America's cities worked in ethnically homogeneous labor crews. In 1910, for example, 77 percent of the 592 Italo-American males in the labor force in Norristown worked as laborers. By 1930 this proportion had fallen to 55.5 percent of the 1,680 Italo-American males in the labor force as the results of the entrance of the second-generation children of the immigrants into the labor market became apparent. By 1950, when the Italo-Americans in the labor market were almost all at least second-

generation, the proportion had dropped to 38.9 percent of 3,840 Italo-American males in the labor force.

The forces which molded the second-generation teenager were as much, if not more, lower-class urban American as traditional Italian. In his childhood, he attended an American public school or a parochial school where the nun teachers and usually the pastor were Irish-American rather than immigrant Italian or even Italo-American. The few Italian priests and nuns who had come to the United States were dying off, and they were not being replaced by Italo-Americans in anywhere near sufficient numbers to staff the churches in the colonies. In these churches, he was encouraged to join a host of new church-centered social, religious, and recreational groups, such as the Catholic Youth Organization. Such groups, along with youth centers, school-centered social groups, and the other civic activities designed to keep him off the streets, brought him into increased and intensified contact with parent substitutes who conveyed the values of urban American rather than Italo-American culture. For those who had moved out of the colonies, the acculturative contact was even greater. Their peer group associations were with non-Italo-American youngsters. The old immigrant provincial mutual-benefit societies and the *bocce* clubs, organized to keep nostalgic contact with the old-country values, were as alien to the second-generation teenager as to the American young people.

In some cases, the adjustment of the second generation to this conflict was extreme—the name was changed, all association with the colony was cut off, and the individual rushed to become an American. In some cases, the reaction was extreme in the other direction—the second-generation families reembraced the Italo-American cultural pattern, preferred to remain in the colony close to the parental home, and insulated themselves against further pressures toward acculturation. The most common reaction, however, was to attempt some compromise adjustment, earnestly to seek integration into the American culture while still retaining intimate contact with the immigrant family and way of life.

These second-generation teenagers, many of whom married outside their ethnic group and many of whom served in armed services in World War II, are the parents of today's third-generation Italo-American teenagers. The adjustment which they made to the conflict between the small-village peasant Italian culture of their parents and the predominantly lower-class urban American culture in which they were reared represents the cultural baseline for the third-generation teenager.

Today's Italo-American teenager is, then, the third-generation product of this heritage of peasant-village Italian culture exposed to forty-odd years of acculturation in the United States. A third set of forces, the general social change which has taken place in the teenage culture of the United States over the last half-century, combines with the forces previously discussed to shape his cultural milieu. How individual Italo-American teenagers respond to these forces is, of course, dependent in large part upon the type of adjustment made to them by their second-generation parents.

For those teenage members of second-generation families who sought complete integration into the American culture, residual Italian cultural characteristics are minimal or nonexistent. Living outside the ethnic colony, often with new or anglicized names, their only association with the Italo-American culture is the infrequent contact they have with their immigrant grandparents. On these occasions, the grandparents are often proud of the advances made by their "American" descendants but still retain some degree of resentment over the abandonment of the "old family" and its traditions. During a recent visit to a large Italian colony in Pennsylvania, the writer was introduced to the immigrant grandfather of a popular Italo-American rock-and-roll singer. The old man gave a lengthy description of the beautiful and costly home bought by the young star for his parents. His obvious pride in the accomplishment of his grandson was somewhat conditioned, however, by ill-hidden disappointment, for he added, "Of course, in that beautiful house with all those paintings and pictures he didn't put up one saint or even a crucifix."

For those Capobiancos who became "Whiteheads" and the Campanas who became "Bells," the transition is almost complete. This total rejection of Italo-American ethnicity has been relatively rare, but where it does exist, it necessarily becomes even more complete in the third-generation teenager. His parents have rejected Italo-American culture, and he has been reared as an American. If his parents were accepted as Americans, then he has no ties with the immigrant culture. These teenagers are Italo-American only in ancestry and are virtually indistinguishable from their non-Italo-American peers.

In those few families which sought to maintain and, indeed, to reembrace the Italian cultural pattern by a closer orientation with the Italian neighborhood, the course of social change and the compelling forces of acculturation have worked against any further re-Italianization. As movement out of the colonies continues, along with increasing dilution of the cultural baseline of their ethnicity, they are now forty years removed from the traditional environment. Warm, family-centered life remains, but the importance of interfamilial community relationships has all but disappeared. The traditional religious *feste* where *paisani* from the same province celebrated the feast of the patron saint, the provincial mutual-benefit societies, and the interlocking system of godparenthood are becoming rarities. And even where they do exist, the bonds they once signified are alien and meaningless to today's teenager. Even the neighborhoods are beginning to disappear as Italo-Americans move up the ladder of social acceptance and are replaced in the slum areas by recent Spanish-speaking immigrants and Negroes. As the immigrant grandparents die off in increasing numbers, there is no place to turn but to greater integration into the American culture. These teenagers may well become the new Italo-American generation in conflict, for the decision of their parents to resist acculturation has merely postponed its inevitable occurrence.

The vast majority of today's teenage Italo-Americans, how-

ever, come from neither of these two types of second-generation families but, rather, from the marginal families which, both in and outside the colonies, sought Americanization while still retaining a bond with the old family and culture. The teenagers of this group are best described as typically American while still retaining certain elements of ethnic identification.

Since these Italo-American families fall predominantly in the lower socioeconomic classes, their teenage children have greater representation in the earlier phases of teenage culture. By late adolescence, they have usually entered the labor market, and those who do go on to college have no distinctive ethnic patterns to follow. Italo-Americans are still underrepresented in the higher socioeconomic classes, and, so, Italo-American teenagers are not a significant group in the middle- and upper-class-oriented later-teen culture.

The role of the younger Italo-American teenager in the family is much the same as in other lower-class families. There is, perhaps, greater warmth and a stronger affectional bond, but only the affectional function remains of the once strong family. The family is slightly more patriarchal than other lower-class families but still strives toward the "democratic family" ideal.

Today's Italo-American teenager is also much more Irish-American in religious orientation than either his father or grandfather. The effect of religious and often academic education by the predominantly Irish Catholic Church in the United States has been to give this generation of Italo-American teenagers a much stronger religious orientation to life than previous generations. It is this orientation, more than any other, which will shape their attitudes toward family life and the rearing of the coming fourth generation.

Another factor which affects Italo-American participation in teenage culture is their high degree of urbanization. Most Italo-American families continue to live in large and medium-sized cities, so that third-generation teenagers are under-represented in the suburban and rural patterns of teenage culture. . . .

The final factor which preserves some element of ethnicity in the Italo-American teenager is the fact that he is still identified as being an Italian American by his peers and their parents. Attitudes toward Italo-Americans have changed over the last forty years, and social acceptance is much greater today than in the past. Certainly, active discrimination against the group is no greater than that for similar groups such as the Poles, Ukrainians, and Greeks. But while there is not the same hostility and social distance that existed for the second-generation teenager, Italo-Americans are still considered to be "different." Most Italo-American teenagers accept this differentiation as a relatively minor part of American life. Being considered as different, however, cannot help but influence the teenager's self-concept, and so he does not participate as an equal in teenage culture.

Most of these changes have been the result of the acculturative experience of the Italian family in the United States. Equally important, however, has been the role of the general social change which has taken place during this half-century. Recent visits to Italy by the writer have indicated that many of the changes described above are also taking place among teenagers in the Italian cities. In fact, the orientation of Italian urban teenagers is almost as much to American teenage culture as it is to Italian culture.

Over the last forty-odd years, then, Italo-American teenage culture has changed to the point where the third-generation teenager is quite similar to other lower-class teenagers. Those characteristics which do not set him apart are the result of the general position of the group in the American social structure. As the process of assimilation continues, even these differences will disappear, and he will soon be indistinguishable from other teenagers.

Above left and above right: Nuns and groups of men and women on Mulberry Street, Little Italy, New York, 1955, photographs by Leonard Freed/Credit: Magnum

Opposite page: Actress Anne Bancroft visiting her family, New York, 1960, photograph by Dennis Stock/Credit: Magnum. *Above:* Jacuzzi family reunion, Oakland, California, 1958/Credit: Jacuzzi. *Below:* Leone family, Philadelphia, about 1950/Credit: Balch

Opposite page above left: Jockey Eddie Arcaro after winning the Diamond Jubilee Preakness at Pimlico, 1951/Credit: Bettmann. *Opposite page above right:* Yankee catcher Yogi Berra attempts to catch a foul ball hit by Ted Williams, 1951/Credit: Bettmann. *Opposite page below:* Heavyweight champion Rocky Marciano defending his title against Ezzard Charles, New York, 1954/Credit: NA. *Above:* Joe DiMaggio connects to hit a home run against the Philadelphia Athletics in Shibe Park, 1950/Credit: Bettmann

Above left: Opera singer Lucia Albanese in *Traviata*, about 1950/Credit: Metropolitan Archives. *Above right:* Ezio Pinza in *Boris Godunov*, about 1948/Credit: Metropolitan Archives. *Below left:* Thirteen-year-old coloratura soprano Anna Maria Alberghetti looking at poster announcing her Carnegie Hall debut, 1950/Credit: Bettmann. *Below right:* Flamenco dancer Jose Greco, about 1950/Credit: NYPL Dance. *Opposite page above left:* Mario Puzo proudly holds his Oscar, won for the script of *The Godfather, Part II*, 1975/Credit: Bettmann

"I Am Another Italian Success Story"

1970. Mario Puzo, a native of New York City, reflected on the struggle to realize his talents and on his relationship with his family as he rose from the tenements of Hell's Kitchen to the top of the best-seller lists.

As a child and in my adolescence, living in the heart of New York's Neapolitan ghetto, I never heard an Italian singing. None of the grown-ups I knew were charming or loving or understanding. Rather they seemed coarse, vulgar, and insulting. And so later in my life when I was exposed to all the clichés of lovable Italians, singing Italians, happy-go-lucky Italians, I wondered where the hell the moviemakers and storywriters got all their ideas from.

At a very early age I decided to escape these uncongenial folk by becoming an artist, a writer. It seemed then an impossible dream. My father and mother were illiterate, as were their parents before them. But practicing my art I tried to view the adults with a more charitable eye and so came to the conclusion that their only fault lay in their being foreigners; I was an American. This didn't really help because I was only half right. I was the foreigner. They were already more "American" than I could ever become.

But it did seem then that the Italian immigrants, all the fathers and mothers that I knew, were a grim lot; always shouting, always angry, quicker to quarrel than embrace. I did not understand that their lives were a long labor to earn their daily bread and that physical fatigue does not sweeten human natures.

And so even as a very small child I dreaded growing up to be like the adults around me. I heard them saying too many cruel things about their dearest friends, saw too many of their false embraces with those they had just maligned, observed with horror their paranoiac anger at some small slight or a fancied injury to their pride. They were, always, too unforgiving. In short, they did not have the careless magnanimity of children.

In my youth I was contemptuous of my elders, including a few under thirty. I thought my contempt special to their circumstances. Later when I wrote about these illiterate men and women, when I thought I understood them, I felt a condescending pity. After all, they had suffered, they had labored all the days of their lives. They had never tasted luxury, knew little more economic security than those ancient Roman slaves who might have been their ancestors. And alas, I thought, with newfound artistic insight, they were cut off from their children because of the strange American tongue, alien to them, native to their sons and daughters.

Already an artist but not yet a husband or a father, I pondered omnisciently on their tragedy, again thinking it special circumstance rather than a constant in the human condition. I did not yet understand why these men and women were willing to settle for less than they deserved in life and think that "less" quite a bargain. I did not understand that they simply could not afford to dream. I myself had a hundred dreams from which to choose. For I was already sure that I would make my escape, that I was one of the chosen. I would be rich, famous, happy. I would master my destiny.

And so it was perhaps natural that as a child, with my father gone, my mother the family chief, I, like all the children in all the ghettos of America, became locked in a bitter struggle with the adults responsible for me. It was inevitable that my mother and I became enemies.

As a child I had the usual dreams. I wanted to be handsome, specifically as cowboy stars in movies were handsome. I wanted to be a killer hero in a worldwide war. Or if no wars came along (our teachers told us another was impossible), I wanted at the very least to be a footloose adventurer. Then I branched out and thought of being a great artist, and then, getting ever more sophisticated, a great criminal.

My mother, however, wanted me to be a railroad clerk. And that was her *highest* ambition; she would have settled for less. At the age of sixteen when I let everybody know that I was going to be a great writer, my friends and family took the news quite calmly, my mother included. She did not become angry. She quite simply assumed that I had gone off my nut. She was illiterate and her peasant life in Italy made her believe that only a son of the nobility could possibly become a writer. Artistic beauty after all could spring only from the seedbed of fine clothes, fine food, luxurious living. So then how was it possible for a son of hers to be an artist? She was not too convinced she was wrong even after my first two books were published many years later. It was only after the commercial success of my third novel that she gave me the title of poet.

My family and I grew up together on Tenth Avenue, between Thirtieth and Thirty-first Streets, part of the area called Hell's Kitchen. This particular neighborhood could have been a movie set for one of the Dead End Kids flicks or for the social drama of the East Side in which John Garfield played the hero. Our tenements were the western wall of the city. Beneath our windows were the vast black iron gardens of the New York Central Railroad, absolutely blooming with stinking boxcars freshly unloaded of cattle and pigs for the city slaughterhouse. Steers sometimes escaped and loped through the heart of the neighborhood, followed by astonished young boys who had

never seen a live cow.

The railroad yards stretched down to the Hudson River, beyond whose garbagey waters rose the rocky Palisades of New Jersey. There were railroad tracks running downtown on Tenth Avenue itself to another freight station called St. John's Park. Because of this, because these trains cut off one side of the street from the other, there was a wooden bridge over Tenth Avenue, a romantic-looking bridge despite the fact that no sparkling water, no silver flying fish darted beneath it; only heavy dray carts drawn by tired horses, some flat-boarded trucks, tin-lizzie automobiles, and, of course, long strings of freight cars drawn by black, ugly engines.

What was really great, truly magical, was sitting on the bridge, feet dangling down, and letting the engine under you blow up clouds of steam that made you disappear, then reappear all damp and smelling of fresh ironing. When I was seven years old I fell in love for the first time with the tough little girl who held my hand and disappeared with me in that magical cloud of steam. This experience was probably more traumatic and damaging to my later relationships with women than one of those ugly childhood adventures Freudian novelists use to explain why their hero has gone bad.

My father supported his wife and seven children by working as a trackman laborer for the New York Central Railroad. My oldest brother worked for the railroad as a brakeman, another brother was a railroad shipping clerk in the freight office. Eventually I spent some of the worst months of my life as the railroad's worst messenger boy.

My oldest sister was just as unhappy as a dressmaker in the garment industry. She wanted to be a schoolteacher. At one time or another my other two brothers also worked for the railroad—it got all six males in the family. The two girls and my mother escaped, though my mother felt it her duty to send all our bosses a gallon of homemade wine on Christmas. But everybody hated their jobs except my oldest brother who had a

night shift and spent most of his working hours sleeping in freight cars. My father finally got fired because the foreman told him to get a bucket of water for the crew and not take all day. My father took the bucket and disappeared forever.

Nearly all the Italian men living on Tenth Avenue supported their large families by working on the railroad. Their children also earned pocket money by stealing ice from the refrigerator cars in summer and coal from the open stoking cars in the winter. Sometimes an older lad would break the seal of a freight car and take a look inside. But this usually brought down the "Bulls," the special railroad police. And usually the freight was "heavy" stuff, too much work to cart away and sell, something like fresh produce or boxes of cheap candy that nobody would buy.

The older boys, the ones just approaching voting age, made their easy money by hijacking silk trucks that loaded up at the garment factory on Thirty-first Street. They would then sell the expensive dresses door to door at bargain prices no discount house could match. From this some graduated into organized crime, whose talent scouts alertly tapped young boys versed in strongarm. Yet despite all this, most of the kids grew up honest, content with fifty bucks a week as truck drivers, deliverymen, and white-collar clerks in the civil service.

I had every desire to go wrong but I never had a chance. The Italian family structure was too formidable.

I never came home to an empty house; there was always the smell of supper cooking. My mother was always there to greet me, sometimes with a policeman's club in her hand (nobody ever knew how she acquired it). But she was always there, or her authorized deputy, my older sister, who preferred throwing empty milk bottles at the heads of her little brothers when they got bad marks on their report cards. During the Great Depression of the 1930s, though we were the poorest of the poor, I never remember not dining well. Many years later as a guest of a millionaire's club, I realized that our poor family

on home relief ate better than some of the richest people in America.

My mother would never dream of using anything but the finest imported olive oil, the best Italian cheeses. My father had access to the fruits coming off ships, the produce from railroad cars, all before it went through the stale process of middlemen; and my mother, like most Italian women, was a fine cook in the peasant style. . . .

Forty years ago, in 1930, when I was ten, I remember gaslight, spooky, making the tenement halls and rooms alive with ghosts.

We had the best apartment on Tenth Avenue, a whole top floor of six rooms, with the hall as our storage cellar and the roof as our patio. Two views, one of the railroad yards backed by the Jersey shore, the other of a backyard teeming with tomcats everybody shot at with BB guns. In between these two rooms with a view were three bedrooms without windows—the classic railroad flat pattern. The kitchen had a fire escape that I used to sneak out at night. I liked that apartment though it had no central heating, only a coal stove at one end and an oil stove at the other. I remember it as comfortable, slum or not.

My older brothers listened to a crystal radio on homemade headsets. I hitched a ride on the backs of horses and wagons, my elders daringly rode the trolley cars. Only forty years ago in calendar time, it is really a thousand years in terms of change in our physical world. There are the jets, TV, penicillin for syphilis, cobalt for cancer, equal sex for single girls; yet still always the contempt of the young for their elders.

But maybe the young are on the right track this time. Maybe they know that the dreams of our fathers were malignant. Perhaps it is true that the only real escape is in the blood magic of drugs. All the Italians I knew and grew up with have escaped, have made their success. We are all Americans now, we are all successes now. And yet the most successful Italian man I know admits that though the one human act he could

never understand was suicide, he understood it when he became a success. Not that he ever would do such a thing; no man with Italian blood ever commits suicide or becomes a homosexual in his belief. But suicide has crossed his mind. And so to what avail the finding of the dream? He went back to Italy and tried to live like a peasant again. But he can never again be unaware of more subtle traps than poverty and hunger.

There is a difference between having a good time in life and being happy. My mother's life was a terrible struggle and yet I think it was a happy life. One tentative proof is that at the age of eighty-two she is positively indignant at the thought that death dares approach her. But it's not for everybody, that kind of life.

Thinking back, I wonder why I became a writer. Was it the poverty or the books I read? Who traumatized me, my mother or the Brothers Karamazov? Being Italian? Or the girl sitting with me on the bridge as the engine steam deliciously made us vanish? Did it make any difference that I grew up Italian rather than Irish or black?

No matter. The good times are beginning. I am another Italian success story. Not as great as DiMaggio or Sinatra but quite enough. It will serve.

Yet I can escape again. I have my retrospective falsification (how I love that phrase). I can dream now about how happy I was in my childhood, in my tenement, playing in those dirty but magical streets—living in the poverty that made my mother weep. True, I was a deposed dictator at fifteen but they never hanged me. And now I remember, all those impossible dreams strung out before me, waiting for me to choose, not knowing that the life I was living then, as a child, would become my final dream.

Above: Producer-director Francis Ford Coppola in his office at Zoetrope Studios, Los Angeles, 1982, photograph by Raymond Depardon/Credit: Magnum. *Below:* Actor Robert De Niro and director Michael Cimino during filming of *The Deer Hunter*, 1980, photograph by Philip Jones Griffith/Credit: Magnum

Above: Film director Martin Scorsese in his editing room, about 1980, photograph by Sylvia Plachy/Credit: Archive. *Below:* Actors Sylvester Stallone and John Travolta at the premiere of *Staying Alive*, New York, 1983/Credit: Bettmann

Above: Opera singer Luciano Pavarotti, about 1980/Credit: FD. *Below:* Conductor Riccardo Muti of La Scala and the Philadelphia Orchestra, 1985/Credit: Philadelphia

Above left: Painter and sculptor Corrado Marca-Relli, about 1950. *Above right:* Painter Frank Stella, 1982. *Below left:* Sculptor Mark Di Suvero, 1983. *Below right:* Painter and sculptor Robert De Niro, 1980. Photographs on this page are by Hans Namuth.

A Recent Immigrant

1972. Mario Lucci, a suburban Boston high school student, recounted the story of his family's move to this country and his experiences as a new arrival.

My mother's father lived in Boston. He lived there for many years. I think it was in 1967—I was either five or six years old—my mother got a telegram saying that her father died. It was at night. I remember that scene. It was about ten at night, and the church bells ring. You know, when the bells ring everybody wants to go up and see what happened. So my mother went up there, and I went up with her. One lady had a telephone, and this lady told my mother that something drastic happened. She didn't want to tell us, but she wanted us to go to the church. The priest told us that my grandfather died. My mother was pretty upset, and she lit some candles.

Then one of the aunts—she lives in the United States—wrote and told my mother that she's got the citizenship from my grandfather. So my father got the wild idea, "Why don't we go check it out?" He decided to come here to the United States and see what it's like, because everybody said that the highways are paved with gold—that old story. Yeah, it's still going around.

My father says he'll move here first, then later he'll send us the papers and we'll come, too. That's how come me and my mother came after. First my father. Then my brothers Gino and Sal. Then, a couple years later, me and my mother and my grandmother.

We came by plane—Alitalia. I got on the plane, and then, when we were about two hours away from Rome, the engineer tells us there's something wrong with the plane. I got scared. We started going toward Rome again. As soon as we got down, I see my brother. He's still there. I guess he was just kind of sad to see us leave. When I saw him, I said, "Mom, let's go back home. I don't want to go to the United States." But we got on a different plane and we took off again.

We came in about two in the morning, and we went through—you know, when they open the baggage. I think we brought some oregano and some laurel leaves. They took those. You couldn't bring those in. Then we saw my brother and got the baggage and went to his car. It was the biggest car I ever seen in my life—a Pontiac Catalina. I heard they had big cars in America, and I said, "Wow!" I was interested to see all the people. In the early 1970s, you know, girls were still walking around in miniskirts. My mother was looking at them, and she put her hand over her eyes and said, "I don't want to see this." I saw people staying up in the street till three, four in the morning, just talking to each other and eating watermelons. I said, "That's weird." It was much different than the town I came from.

I came February 22, and March 1 started school. The shock! Well, in Italy people are really quiet in school, and they dress nice. But here—I think I was one of the politest kids in school! Everybody I saw I used to salute them, even though I didn't know them, because that's the way we were taught. The teacher's name was Miss Kiefer. It sounded like *schifo*. In Italian that means something of no value, bad. And in Italy the students are taught to say just *Signorina*—that means teacher. You can't call a teacher by their name, because to her it's like—I don't know how to say it here—like it's not nice. Every time she talked to me, I go, "Yes, teacher," because I don't want to get spanked. I finally straightened that out.

In Italy, if you start acting bad they smack you. I used to be one of those. I didn't take work serious. But when I did, I would really get down to it, and I wrote some nice poems. Well, in school they teach you to write little poems that rhyme, something sweet. I used to write it, and the teacher used to say I used to do pretty good work in poetry. Then, every time I went to school I used to go by a field, and I picked three or four flowers and take it to the teacher. They would like to have new flowers on the desk every day. It gave you the feeling of spring. Once I did it here. I was walking by this yard and I saw some nice flowers—tulips, I think it was. I went over there and I ripped them out. The teacher said, "Where'd you get these?" I didn't really understand what was wrong. Then Sal, my brother, told me. First he started laughing. I said, "What's the matter?" He goes, "You don't bring flowers in the United States." I said, "Why not?" He goes, "They're going to think you're a sissy." . . . One of the boys on my street used to ask me to play baseball, and I used to make up excuses, because I didn't know how to play and I was scared to play with them. Plus, I couldn't speak, so I felt bad. I would stay inside. I was ten years old, and I used to play with this kid that was three years old. He was Italian, so I used to play with him. I didn't want to play with anybody else. He used to come over my house in the morning around seven—this was in the summertime—and we used to eat breakfast over my house. Then we used to watch TV from seven till five, and that's how I would spend my summer.

After a year, I started going to a special class, with Miss Gorelli. She used to teach me English. Then this other girl from Italy came. She was crying and I was trying to teach her, because I knew the way she felt. But *I* wasn't crying, because, you know, what are you going to cry for? You got to learn. You got to get accustomed to everything.

I really tried hard in school, and I tried to be good. I've been a good English student. The third year, I got a B-minus, and then I improved to an A. Yeah, I feel good in English. I can still read and write and speak Italian, but it's kind of blurry.

I was making friends and I started playing baseball, but I never learned how to play real good baseball, like hard hitting, fast pitching, and everything. After I found out that soccer was kind of dead in the United States, I started playing basketball, and after a couple of years I became a good basketball player.

When I went to junior high I used to go by bus. I stayed after one day, and when I walked out to get the bus, I still had some time, so I walked around the school. I wanted to see what it was like. I saw a bunch of guys kicking balls around. I said, "Are they playing soccer, or are they playing soccer?" So I got out there, and for the first time in the United States, I picked up a soccer ball. I still had a magic touch—after three years almost, yeah. That same season I played right wing. That was the best thing that could happen to me in the world, almost. I was happy.

My coach asked me if I wanted to teach some little kids. So after soccer practice I used to take these little guys—I actually teach them, from about six till seven—till it got dark.

By eighth grade, when the soccer season came, everybody came to watch me play, because—no bragging or nothing—I used to take the ball from everybody. I used to write the plays for my coach, and he used to send orders to the other guys to put in this kind of play. I was pretty good with that. Everybody knew me. I started feeling more—I was really Americanized almost. I figured those were my best years in the United States —in my life, really, so far.

Above: "The Little Carabiniere," Little Italy, New York, 1983. *Below:* Friends, Brooklyn, 1983. Photographs on this page are by Ernesto Bazan/Credit: Archive

Above: Grandmother and child, East 187th Street, The Bronx, 1986, photograph by Ethel Wolvovitz. *Below:* Grandmother and granddaughters, Brooklyn, 1983, photograph by Ernesto Bazan/Credit: Archive

Above: Friends, Michael Farella on left and John Polzella on right (unidentified man in center), Arthur Avenue, The Bronx, 1986, photograph by Ethel Wolvovitz. *Below:* Two men, Brooklyn, 1983, photograph by Ernesto Bazan/Credit: Archive

Neighbors, Marion Vaudo on left and Lucille Pulgniano Handlowitz on right, Bensonhurst, Brooklyn, 1986, photograph by Ethel Wolvovitz

Above: Interior, Queens, 1983, photograph by Ernesto Bazan/Credit: Archive. *Below:* Interior, Brooklyn, 1983, photograph by Ernesto Bazan/Credit: Archive

Above: Sylvia, Newburgh, New York, 1977, photograph by Susan Sichel. *Below:* Bridesmaids, from left to right: Lari Solamon, Doreen Faul and Sandy Buono, Dyker Heights, Brooklyn, 1986, photograph by Ethel Wolvovitz

Mafia Myths and Mafia Facts

1980. The Mafia does exist; however, there are serious questions to be raised by the exaggerated, often officially endorsed view that one ethnic group, the Italian Americans, is fully responsible for every event associated with organized crime in the United States. Attenzione, *a leading Italian American magazine, organized a symposium in which these issues were explored in depth.*

Taking part in the *Attenzione* symposium were

FRED FERRETTI—reporter at *The New York Times* for almost ten years and a frequent analyst of media coverage of organized crime.

RICHARD GAMBINO—professor of Italian American studies at Queens College, author of *Blood of My Blood* and *Vendetta*, and moderator of this symposium.

VICTOR NAVASKY—editor in chief of *The Nation* and author of *Kennedy Justice*, an analysis of Robert Kennedy's performance as United States attorney general.

THOMAS PUCCIO—United States attorney in charged of the Organized Crime Strike Force of the Eastern District.

RALPH SALERNO—a member of the New York City Police Department's organized crime unit for twenty years, until his retirement in 1967 at the rank of supervisor of detectives. Coauthor of the book *Crime Confederation*.

DWIGHT SMITH—associate professor of criminal justice at Rutgers University and author of (among numerous publications) *The Mafia Mystique*.

GAMBINO: In American history, we have had all kinds of organized crime. We have that of the large trusts, the railroads and others in the nineteenth century. We had organized crime in the form of outlaw banditry in the West and Midwest in the nineteenth and twentieth centuries. We have had organized crime in the White House with Richard Nixon and his campaign committee. Why then does the FBI, when it gives testimony on organized crime, make it synonymous with Italian ethnic organizations?

SALERNO: That's a statement I have never heard made.

GAMBINO: If I were holding a committee hearing and I asked the FBI to come and testify on organized crime, do you think they'd bring me testimony about the oil companies? Or do you think they'd come in with Italian names and charts?

PUCCIO: I don't think anyone in the Justice Department with half a brain believes that organized crime is exclusively Italian. But I'll admit I was sort of shocked to read such an assertion in the 1967 report of the President's Commission on Law Enforcement and Administration of Justice. This report, to my mind, clearly says that organized crime is exclusively

Italian, which all available evidence indicates was as preposterous back in 1967 as it's preposterous today. Certainly I've never encountered anyone with any authority or with any intelligence in the Justice Department who thinks that that's so.

GAMBINO: Have you found anybody *without* intelligence in the Justice Department who thinks that's so?

PUCCIO: I think there was a tendency as a result of the Joe Valachi revelations and other very media-charged events to point to the Mafia as organized crime. [In 1963, federal prison inmate Joseph Valachi testified at the McClellan Senate Subcommittee hearings on organized crime, naming hundreds of individuals who, he claimed, were part of an extensive organized crime network.] It makes very good copy. And there's no question in my mind that there *is* a Mafia and that there are Mafia families. I think there is indisputable evidence on that. But not for one moment do I accept the fact that they are the real force anymore in organized crime in the country. Even in 1967 I think the importance of these people was greatly overestimated.

GAMBINO: That may very well be, but it was only a couple of months ago that Jonathan Kwitny, in his book *Vicious Circles*, could declare, and I quote, "Italian Americans haven't produced the most crooks, or necessarily even the best—just the most powerful." Now this comes from a highly respected journalist working for *The Wall Street Journal*.

PUCCIO: If I were looking to analyze organized crime in the country today, I would probably look closer at the Fortune 500 than at the Five Families. I think that economic control is organized crime at this point. Groups of people of all ethnic persuasions. More than likely, depending on the region of the country, you're going to find Mafia people involved, but they by no means control it. People of various ethnic groups that have assembled to accomplish certain ongoing criminal purposes are organized crime in the country, and it has to do with politics, it has to do with labor unions, and it has to do with corporations. But I don't think that, at this time, there is any dominant group of people who sit around coffee houses Mafia-style in New York or San Francisco and plot the big economic crimes in this country.

GAMBINO: But there is that national perception, isn't there?

PUCCIO: I think there is a national perception. I think it's going to change, though. Ten years ago, the priorities of the organized-crime strike forces throughout the country were loan-sharking, gambling, extortion cases. Every strike-force chief was given a list of the people that Valachi had named as being members of organized crime. And what a strike force would do, they'd go out and the attorneys would get together and see how many people on the list they could convict. These were so-called "made" members of organized crime, exclusively Mafia family. And I think that experience has conclusively shown that this was nonsense, that many of the people who were on this list hadn't made a nickel of illegal income in ten or fifteen years. There were certain names on that list practically on welfare.

SMITH: The interesting thing about the use of the term "Mafia" in public discourse is that it has usually had very little to do with crime control. In 1890, when the term was first used in this country in connection with the murder of [New Orleans Police Chief David C.] Hennessy, the purpose of the word for

Above: U.S. Attorney Rudolph Giuliani, left, and FBI Director William Webster, right, examining a chart describing the purported organization of the Mafia crime families, New York, 1985/Credit: Bettmann. Speaking at Rutgers University on March 3, 1987, Rudolph Giuliani said: "My father was the first one to tell me the Mafia existed and that I should not be ashamed of it. It is a very small percentage of the Italian Americans, less than one percent of one percent."

focusing public opinion was not to improve law enforcement in New Orleans, but to restrict immigration. In the 1930s, on the other hand, you had Italian gangsters running around all over the place, very visibly so, but there was no use of the word "Mafia" in connection with them. Why do you not find the word in one case, when you do find it in another? Two reasons. One is that between those two times immigration laws had been tightened up, so that the conflicts between "native" Americans and newly arrived immigrants were abating. The other was that in the 1930s, instead of being the personification of evil, the gangster was the servant, in the sense that Walter Lippmann referred to him. You can't use such a pejorative label for someone whom you appreciate, who supplies you with what you want. And so he was called a rumrunner, gangster, whatever.

It wasn't until 1945 that the word "Mafia" came back into the language again. And why did it come back then? Because the Federal Bureau of Narcotics insisted on using it. And until 1963, the Federal Bureau of Narcotics was the only agency in the government using the word. It wasn't until Joe Valachi came along that control of the concept passed out of Narcotics Bureau hands and into the larger hands of law enforcement, which is how it existed until 1967, the year of the presidential report.

SALERNO: Let me tell you something about that report. I worked on the thing. When the president's crime commission report was formulated, there was no intent, there was no desire, on the part of the president who formulated it or the leadership of his Department of Justice, to include any components of organized crime. And so when the money was allocated and the staff was divided into task forces, there was no task force on organized crime. That was added months later, when more than half of the study-period time had elapsed. The total amount of resources allocated was $30,000, which at the time was the salary of two patrolmen in the New York City Police Department and less money than one heroin addict has to steal to support his habit. Those were the priorities that were finally given to organized crime. You know that this was hurried work. It was a rush job.

SMITH: What does it say about the product?

SALERNO: The product is limited, and that's why you say there's a concentration here on the Italians. True, true, true. Because there wasn't time, there weren't resources, and there certainly was no intent to *do anything* on organized crime, let alone something comprehensive. And I say that by way of explanation, not apology.

PUCCIO: If you work on Italian criminals you're going to find out about Italian crime. You look at Polish criminals, you're going to find out about Polish crime.

NAVASKY: One of the interesting little things that happened during the Robert Kennedy years at the Justice Department—and he was the first one who decided to make a national crusade of it—was that in 1962 when J. Edgar Hoover was going to publish an article in *Reader's Digest* for the first time using the words "La Cosa Nostra," he was told by Kennedy's press secretary to take out the words "Cosa Nostra" because the attorney general wanted to be the first one to reveal this national conspiracy and to put out the Valachi story. And they subsequently gave [journalist] Peter Maas that exclusive. In effect, the United States government gave Maas the right to the story in order to dramatize what it considered to be and believed to be the criminal conspiracy of the so-called Cosa Nostra.

GAMBINO: When did Valachi first use the term "Cosa Nostra"?

SALERNO: He first used it when he was being interrogated by FBI agent James Flynn. Valachi was beating about the bush, and Flynn says to him, "You mean La Cosa Nostra?" And Valachi's response is, "Oh, shit, you know about that?"

GAMBINO: He did not use it until he heard it from an FBI official?

SALERNO: That's right. In that context.

SMITH: Where did Flynn get it?

SALERNO: Off the wires.

SMITH: Which one?

SALERNO: All of them. James Flynn's job in the New York office was to prepare a composite report every six months for file 9064, the Cosa Nostra file. And he would have made available to him the summaries of all the electronic surveillances, all the key numbers. Everything from all the offices was sent, strangely enough, not to Washington, D.C., to be assembled, but to the New York office of the FBI. And Flynn prepared a report semiannually.

NAVASKY: That's not my understanding of how it happened. But even if it happened that way, it doesn't contradict the basic flow of events, which was that the FBI never mentioned those words until the Justice Department was ready to launch its campaign on the Valachi case and wanted to get out there first with those three little words.

SALERNO: The FBI was averse to the public even hearing it in 1963. They were against Joe Valachi testifying publicly.

NAVASKY: That's the next point. The government tried to manage that story down to its last detail, including picking the writer who would tell the story. So they picked Peter Maas, who is, you know, a solid character and who had his own career as an investigative journalist prior to that time. And they gave Maas access to Valachi while Valachi was in prison, which is a violation of federal prison policy. No one else was able to do that for many years before or after.

When Maas finally finished his book [*The Valachi Papers*] and was ready to publish it, the government didn't want him to. They maintained that they didn't want him to publish because they thought he was going to go out and do independent research work. In fact, all he did was he let Valachi tell his story. The result of it was that what we got was this unidimensional story. It may or may not be true, but it was never checked out at the time.

PUCCIO: I think that there is no question that the Mafia or Cosa Nostra was, and is, a potent force. But I also think that if you can identify the solution to a problem by saying, "All right, this is the group, they're the ones who are doing it, let's investigate them," it's convenient. You solve the problem. It's much more difficult to sit down and really figure out what are the economic forces that make up the problem. Valachi made it very easy. "These are all the people. You got a list. You have names. Go out and get them."

SMITH: The Italians are an easy target of opportunity.

PUCCIO: I think that the Mafia, being what it was and what it is, was a target of opportunity in a sense. I think that's a fair statement. I don't mean to imply that the Mafia is some benevolent organization, okay, but I think that it was very convenient to identify them as the culprits. . . .

FERRETTI: A year ago, CBS News here in New York, Channel 2, did a story about the beginning of casino gambling in Atlantic City. It was done by a correspondent who shall be nameless for the purpose of this discussion, because I don't want to embarrass him.

He stood up on the boardwalk and talked about how Atlantic City was being divided up, and how so and so came down from Philadelphia and was going to get from Eighteenth Street down to the pier, et cetera et cetera. Halfway through, they switched to a piece of film. To illustrate a news story about Atlantic City, they used film clips from *Godfather II*, of Al Pacino sitting there saying, "we're going to divide this up"! And this was done two or three times in the course of a stand-up report on news. What happened with that report? It was given an Emmy as a piece of news!

So when I talk about basic perceptions, I don't care, Tom, that people in government now, the Justice Department, really don't believe it. *Everybody else does.*

And one step further. If you say that the Justice Department does not believe it, and regards it as a specious saying, why is it so passive? If they think it's nonsense and foolishness, say it.

PUCCIO: I don't quarrel with you for a moment that the perception, even among people in law enforcement, is that the Mafia is the most important criminal force in the country. I don't quarrel with you. And I think what I believe to be the correct point of view is something that's received less attention. But it's going to receive more and more attention.

I think the number of people that became interested in the assassination of Carmine Galante [thought by some to be a second-in-command in the so-called Bonanno family] was ridiculous. I agree with [*Village Voice* writer] Jack Newfield, that Galante was one of the most overrated people in the United States. His influence, as far as I was concerned, was nonexistent.

NAVASKY: But, aside from government decisions to promote anti–organized crime campaigns in terms of the dominant image, why is it that people are focusing on the Italian community? One reason may be that the Mafia or La Cosa Nostra, or the family system, or whatever you want to call it, is organized as a secret organization. And when you deal with secret organizations, just as when the government dealt with the Communist party in the forties and fifties, a whole set of myths grows up. In the same way that a number of people have suggested that the Mafia is a convenient excuse for a whole set of ills that it has nothing to do with, the Communist party was used as a convenient excuse. And you never could get a straight answer because they weren't allowed to talk about what they were doing and you had to rely only on defectors or informers who were notoriously unreliable, or electronic surveillance which was, until last year, illegal in most of its uses.

PUCCIO: Can I respond to that? I think that informers and surveillance can be very reliable. If I burglarize an apartment, it might violate your civil rights, but certainly the items that I find there are going to be reliable. If it's your diary, let's say, then it's pretty reliable evidence of what you've been doing.

NAVASKY: I don't find that to be true.

PUCCIO: Well, it depends on who they're talking to, I suppose, but the picture you're getting of the Mafia, I think, is a reliable picture. Now maybe not everybody agrees with who occupies what position, but these people, these Mafia informers, to them that's their only world and they truly believe the Mafia controls the United States. What it actually controls is their little world.

SMITH: There are a lot of opportunities for people to speak knowledgeably and authoritatively about criminal conspiracies, and the tendency in this country has been to accept what they say without ever asking them, "What makes you think that?" There had been a two-year study program behind that 1967 presidential report, and the big question that had come up was, how do we educate the public? Well, the way you educate the public is to turn out something that a government commission is able to endorse.

Now they did not mean educate. They meant indoctrinate. This is a common problem of the law-enforcement community that mixes the two terms. But they were presenting a point of view. They weren't saying let's examine the evidence in an objective way. They were saying we have concluded and we are now going to tell people what we have concluded. Their conclusions were based on the assumption that the most important thing about organized crime was that it was an alien conspiracy. That it's something out there which is foreign to our own economy, to our own culture, which has come in and done this thing to us.

The influence, if you carry it out to its ultimate conclusion—which the commission was smart enough not to do—is to say that, if we can ever destroy this group, then we won't have organized crime anymore. The commission didn't say that.

GAMBINO: All right, but what is the dynamic behind the ethnic factor? Some scholars, for instance, have leaned heavily on the theory of ethnic succession—that those on the bottom, those who were ghettoized, those persecuted, turned to organized crime in different periods of the histories of ethnic groups. As the usual story goes, it was the Irish and the Jews at one time, then the Italians took over, and now it's the blacks and Hispanics. . . .

SALERNO: Well, if you want to get into the ethnic succession thing, I'd have to say that the Italians have been important, and for a longer time than their predecessor groups, long after their immigrant experience. I think a contributing factor to that is the membership organisation they have which tends to make it dynastic. . . .

GAMBINO: Well, I'm very suspicious of the whole notion of ethnic succession. To me it smacks of the typical American game of picking on the most vulnerable group. We'll take the onus off the Italian Americans now, because we have the West Indians or the Colombians to point to as the evil corrupters of American society. I think it's absolute nonsense. Not the least convenient aspect to this notion is that organized crime is always the guys at the bottom. It is never, for instance, the great railroad tycoons, the oil companies, et cetera. It is immigrants who are introducing such evil practices into our country.

SMITH: Well, as somebody said to me recently, the largest area of criminal recidivism in this country are the oil industry, the automobile industry, and the drug industry. Now there are undoubtedly factors of ethnicity and conspiracy—in the sense that we usually attribute them to organized crime—in each of these areas which we could focus in on as the major characteristics which set them apart, but we don't, because they're white-collar crimes.

FERRETTI: I want to cite another example of what you are talking about. It's a piece I did for the *Columbia Journalism Review* after the shooting of Galante, who was such a powerful criminal that he spent perhaps a third of his life in jail. What I did was talk to the reporters—from newspapers, radio and television—and ask them why they thought he had been shot. And don't forget that we're talking here about *The New York Times*, the *Daily News*, the *New York Post*, CBS, NBC, and all those people.

Anyway, some of them told me that he was killed by executioners on behalf of a national commission of organized crime. Or leaders who deemed him a high-handed gangster who was inching into territory belonging to other gangsters. No, said somebody else: he was assassinated on orders from his own crime family because he had ignored a decree that he step down as boss. No, said somebody else: everything had happened because, though he was boss of his own family, he wanted to be boss of all bosses. No, it was because he was a boss of all bosses and he wasn't filling the job as well as Vito Genovese had done it. No, because he refused to get out of the illegal drug traffic when they told him. No, for any combination of the above. That's pure nonsense.

SALERNO: I agree.

FERRETTI: Let me just go a little further. The *Times* and the *News* had family trees drawn. According to one paper, the Gambino family boss was Agnello Della Croce and his underboss Paul Castellano. The other said the Gambino family boss was Paul Castellano and his underboss Agnello Della Croce. Everybody told me they knew. But as for the people who read it, well, if I'm a *News* reader, I know now why he died. If I'm a *Times* reader, I also know, but I don't know the same thing the *News* reader knows.

GAMBINO: Several questions emerge out of this which I want to get into. First, how does the press deal with news on organized crime? And, connected to that, what is the relationship between the press and the law enforcement agencies on how they deal with organized crime?

FERRETTI: I think the media deal with it with great insensitivity. In the first place, there is no investigation, no adhering to the general rules that any reporter should follow in any other case. In other words, if I report on a politician who is doing something at City Hall, I talk to that politician. I don't make any assumption, because I cannot make any assumptions in a news story. And I just put down all I have. If I'm writing about someone who is in "organized crime," I can do anything I want. I can say anything. I can quote unnamed sources. I can libel him. And this is done.

GAMBINO: Let me pose a question. Galante is murdered and the *Times* sends out a reporter. What does he do?

FERRETTI: Well, you have to ask that reporter. All I can do is judge by his product. And I think his product is not what he would produce if he were sent out to cover an automobile accident.

NAVASKY: The tradition is that people who are so-called investigative journalists of organized crime really have sources within the law enforcement community. They don't have sources within organized crime. They get their information third-hand.

PUCCIO: I could declare myself an organized-crime reporter tomorrow and just get everybody's books and write stories. Nobody's going to sue me. It's not like something you might say about the governor or about the head of US Steel, where you're going to get sued. You can go on and on; it's not even new stuff. What you're reading today, you read ten years ago. Same names. Whether it's true or not true, it's there. And the outrageous fact is that newspapers don't care about intelligent articles. They just print it and reprint it.

FERRETTI: In the course of a news article, a person will be identified. Let's say, John Fortunato. The article will say John Fortunato of so-and-so, Red Hook or Williamsburg, comma, who law enforcement authorities say is something or other in the so-and-so family. You can do it at will when you're reporting this kind of thing. And let's not just talk about the reporter; there is also the editor. On a normal news story, you write that a guy is a child molester and the editor will nail you. Who said so? How do you know that? Who's charging him? Did you get his side of the story? All of those questions which are basic to my business are not asked when a John Fortunato is involved.

GAMBINO: But what in fact are the procedures they use to go out and investigate . . . ?

FERRETTI: You're asking the wrong question. The point I'm making is that there should be no different procedures in reporting on that kind of a story [from those in reporting] on a two-car accident on the West Side Highway.

SALERNO: You'll find the same kind of thing in popular history as you will in the daily papers. Former Attorney General Ramsey Clark wrote a book on crime, and it had a chapter where he insisted upon repeating something that has been repeated dozens of times in literature: the American version of the so-called "Sicilian Vespers." That's where it's alleged that, in a forty-eight-hour period in September 1931, forty to sixty people were wiped out in a power struggle in twenty-four different cities. But flying only by the seat of my pants, I came up with six bodies. Five in the New York–New Jersey area, and the other a man en route to Denver, Colorado.

PUCCIO: During what time period was that?

SALERNO: September 10 to 11. About a forty-eight-hour period. Umberto Nelli, who is a historian, University of Kentucky, did a much more academic, clinical study. He went and read the newspaper files in all the morgues of the newspapers in the twenty-four cities usually cited. He spoke to policemen, he checked the homicide files, and he came up with the same six. What I'm suggesting to you today is that there are books not yet written which will talk about forty or sixty people wiped out simultaneously all over the United States in that forty-eight-hour period.

SMITH: Let's say something more about this, because other people did the same thing independently and came to the same conclusion. Which is that the Sicilian Vespers, or the "Night of the Long Knives," as it is sometimes referred to, simply did not exist.

PUCCIO: It didn't exist at all?

SMITH: Oh, there was a conflict between the Maranzano and Masseria forces, and there were some people killed in the course of it. But the popularly accepted version simply didn't happen. That story first appeared in Turkis and Feder's book *Murder Inc.* [Manor Books, 1951], and they got it from Dixie Davis, who was Dutch Schultz's lawyer. But you find that Joe Valachi repeats it in 1963 before the McClellan Committee. Don Cressey repeats it again in *Theft of a Nation* [Harper & Row, 1969], and it became for Don, as it has for so many other writers, the event that distinguishes and illustrates that the Sicilian Mafia became Americanized. Once you've accepted that much, it also becomes a significant piece in explaining the development of organized crime.

SALERNO: The only dispute I have is that forty to sixty people were killed in a forty-eight-hour period. I *do* believe that a transition took place in that era.

GAMBINO: Yes, but a transition involving whom? Is there a national syndicate, organization, association, whatever name you want to give it, that does control serious crime?

PUCCIO: No, I don't believe that. No, there is no national conspiracy.

Coming Into Their Own

1983. Stephen S. Hall, the grandson of Italian immigrants, surveyed the recent achievements of Italian Americans who have moved to the forefront in politics, business, the arts, sports and education.

There are a number of ways to assess the quiet yet spectacular rise of Italian Americans in the United States today, but one of the best perspectives is from the fifty-seventh-floor windows of the governor's New York City office in the World Trade Center. The view takes in Ellis Island, twin symbol of opportunity and pain to countless immigrants, and, beyond, the flat and colorless industrial precincts of Jersey City.

It was there that young Andrea Cuomo, a recent arrival in 1926 from the south of Italy, toiled as the classic pick-and-shovel immigrant. He dug ditches and cleaned sewers and became, in the words of social historians who came later, part of the human "dung" that fertilized America's industrial growth.

Andrea Cuomo's son—whose birth was attended by midwives, who spoke only Italian until the age of eight, who was counseled by "well-intentioned" law school officials to change his vowel-laden last name if he wanted to get ahead in life—now occupies the governor's chair. From this eyrie of power, with its clear vista upon emblems of his personal past, it is tempting to suggest that Mario M. Cuomo has traveled a great distance in one generation.

"Very little distance," he says, quietly disagreeing. "Very little distance. If my father had had my education, it would have been *no* distance. In terms of economic condition, we've improved. But as a family, as individuals, as people of merit and excellence, I don't think I've yet improved on my father."

Italian Americans have sometimes been regarded as being slow to assimilate and climb America's social and economic ladders, even by their own historians, but now—as they swell the ranks of the middle class, amass power and wealth, and help set the decade's social and political agendas as never before—it may be that they have simply measured success, as Mario Cuomo has done, by a different yardstick, and made their way to the mainstream by a slightly different route.

Barely a century ago, in 1880, the number of Italians in the United States totaled a mere 44,000. Now, Americans of Italian descent represent an estimated 7 percent of the population, and in recent years they have attained a kind of critical mass in terms of affluence, education, aspiration and self-acceptance—so much so that the political analyst Theodore H. White, in his 1982 book *America in Search of Itself*, identifies Italian Americans as "the most important among the rising ethnic groups."

To be sure, the Italian American community has never been slack in the production of distinguished individuals, but those of earlier generations flourished—like the Italians themselves—in highly circumscribed worlds. In stadiums, it was Joe DiMaggio; under the spotlights, it was Frank Sinatra; and in city government, it was Fiorello H. La Guardia, the consummate local politician of his era. But today's Italian Americans have stepped out, as it were; and become prominent players with national impact as well as a national following, taking the initiative in crucial political and social issues.

Lido (Lee) A. Iacocca, chairman of the Chrysler Corporation, has come to represent a no-nonsense integrity and can-do dash in the executive suite. Joseph Cardinal Bernardin, Archbishop of Chicago, has brought humanism and militance together in the movement of Roman Catholic bishops opposed to nuclear arms. Eleanor Curti Smeal, who recently concluded five years as president of the National Organization for Women, is credited with giving feminism a grass-roots appeal attractive to middle-class housewives. Perhaps more important, they represent merely the brightest lights in a general fluorescence of Italians in American life, a fluorescence confirmed almost on a daily basis.

If it isn't Jim Valvano coaching North Carolina State to the college basketball championship, for example, it is Joe Paterno coaching Penn State to a national title in college football, or Tommy LaSorda and Billy Martin managing world series teams. If it isn't a new movie by Francis Ford Coppola or Martin Scorsese, it is a new interpretation of architecture by the architect Robert Venturi, the "father of postmodernism." If it isn't a new Broadway musical by Michael Bennett (*Dreamgirls*), it is a new shopping mall built by Edward J. DeBartolo, Sr., the Youngstown, Ohio, businessman and sports magnate who is probably the wealthiest Italian American in the country—reportedly worth more than $500 million. And in the world of higher education, there are now such names as A. Bartlett Giamatti of Yale and John Lo Schiavo of the University of San Francisco.

Is there a single thread that runs through these people? If anything, it is the unusual propensity to merge, rather than separate, the professional and the personal. Borrowing from a culture in which the extended family can easily include thirty to forty "close" relatives, Italians thrive on community. They are accustomed to large numbers of people, and they seem to have developed an emotional facility in dealing with them. Even in large companies, they have a knack for keeping things on a human scale. "The professional community," explains one Italian American psychotherapist, "becomes the next family."

Probably the most significant symbol of the Italian American emergence is Governor Cuomo, who has practically made a political doctrine out of the concept of family. "With us, it's going from small family to big family, the state of New York. Everything I do revolves around the notion of sharing benefits and burdens in the community. And that's family."

He remains comfortably aware of his ethnic background and easily interprets the historical moment through a familial lens. "Most of the Italians who came through Ellis Island were like my mother and father," says the fifty-year-old governor, whose parents abandoned two mountain villages in the Campania region south of Naples. "No education. No skills. They called them *cafoni* [rubes]. They were the lowest strata, economically and socially.

"We are their sons and daughters, educated for the first time," he continues. "What's happening now is that the generation of turn-of-the-century Mediterranean immigrants is just now gathering to itself the kind of strength, affluence and comfort that allows it to reach out for power."

That process, in fact, has been perceptible for more than a decade. Italian Americans no longer resemble the stereotypical image of opera-loving blue-collar ethnics airing laundry, and

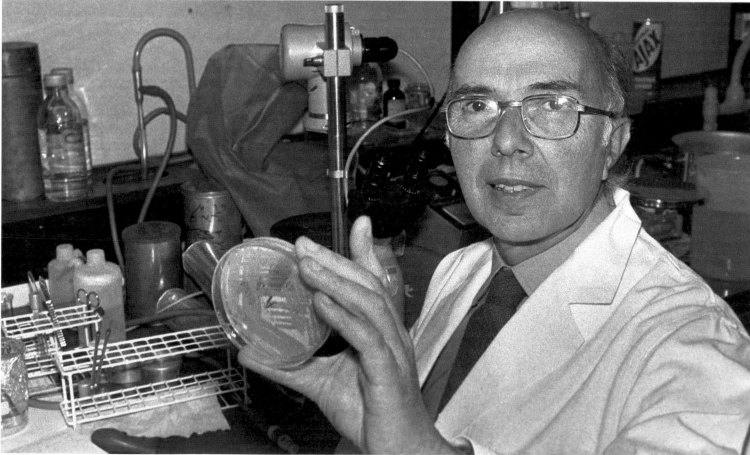

Above: President Jimmy Carter congratulates Joseph Califano and his wife after Califano was sworn in as Secretary of Health, Education and Welfare, Washington, 1977/ Credit: Bettmann. *Below:* Renato Dulbecco. Nobel Prize winner in Medicine, 1975/Credit: Bettmann

Above: Governor of New York Mario Cuomo and his family in the Executive Mansion, Albany, 1982, photograph by Joe Traver/Credit: Gamma-Liaison. *Below:* Antonin Scalia being sworn in as associate justice of the United States Supreme Court, Washington, 1986/Credit: Bettmann

personal grievances, from the windows of Italian ghettos. Instead, they are upwardly mobile—doggedly so. According to Alfred J. Tella, special adviser to the director of the Census Bureau, their presence in white-collar positions now appears to mirror national averages, they have moved to the suburbs, and they have no more children than the average American family. As breadwinners, they have made steady but striking progress: in 1979, Americans of purely Italian ancestry had a median family income of $16,993, outearning all other ethnic groups except the Scots and Germans (both of whom arrived well ahead of the Italians).

"It's the story of a three-generation success," says Mr. Tella, who estimates the number of Italian Americans at approximately 15 million. "Around the turn of the century, menial labor was synonymous with Italians. But they sacrificed a lot to get an education for their children; and they all wanted to own their own houses. Those were the twin drives. Now Italians have fully caught up with non-Italians in the upper echelons of professional and managerial occupations."

Among white ethnic groups, there is probably no other culture that has so conscientiously and successfully husbanded its traditional values—from the close-knit family structure to the exuberant celebration of feasts—into the present moment. To be sure, some traditions, such as the use of the Italian language, have eroded, prompting some observers to regard ethnic identity in the later generations as mainly cosmetic. But surveys over the last two decades by the National Opinion Research Center in Chicago, for example, consistently show that Italian Americans retain closer family ties than virtually every other ethnic or religious group. It has been a happy accident, in fact, that the Italians, by stubbornly refusing to abandon their old customs, have hung on long enough to see those values take on enhanced value as they move more boldly into the mainstream. "A sense of respect and loyalty, a respect for family members, the cohesiveness of the family—I think of these values as fundamental to our interactions with other people," says Aileen Riotto Sirey, a psychotherapist and president of the National Organization of Italian-American Women.

Those attitudes reflect a particularly Italian way of looking at things. "Italian Americans are not generally rigid in terms of their professions being all-consuming—you'll seldom find a single-faceted Italian American who devotes twenty hours a day to one narrow activity," notes former United States Attorney General Benjamin R. Civiletti, forty-seven, whose ancestors came from Palermo and Genoa. "That gives them not only a diversity of views, and a healthiness of mental outlook, but also the ability to endure problems and cope."

And cope they did, during a long and painful journey to social acceptance in this country. Given the cachet that all things Italians enjoy today—from food to fashion to a certain vivaciousness of life-style—it is difficult to conceive of just how great a liability it once was to be Italian in this country. . . .

If you had been out of the country for the last two decades, like Joseph V. Vittoria, the progress of Italian Americans would hardly seem *pian piano*. "When I came back from Europe," says Mr. Vittoria, president of Avis and former president of Hertz, "I was almost overwhelmed by the growth of Italian influence. There was a tremendous increase in the Italian presence here."

Perhaps the single most important change in Italian Americans over that period is the way they perceive themselves. Self-esteem, once weighted down by ethnicity, now fairly soars in an atmosphere where cultural pluralism has supplanted the melting-pot ideal. A recent survey of 213 third-generation Italian Americans in their early thirties, all of whom had grown up in the heavily Italian Bensonhurst neighborhood of Brooklyn, revealed overwhelmingly positive feelings about their Italian roots. To the question "Would you change your ethnic identity?" not a single person in the sample said yes—a possibility almost inconceivable a generation ago. "This is a group," says Carmela Sansone-Pacelli, who conducted the survey, "that has come a *long* way."

And that is what William D'Antonio learned, in a more personally profound way, last fall. Mr. D'Antonio, executive officer of the American Sociological Association, visited his two college-age daughters on successive weekends. At the University of Vermont, his daughter Raissa told about a psychology paper she had written on the theme "Five Things I Like About Myself"; one of those things was that she liked being Italian. Mr. D'Antonio reacted with surprise: "You said *that*?"

The following weekend, he visited his daughter Laura at Yale. "I'm the only one hundred–percent Italian in my dorm," she announced at one point, "but I know at least a dozen people who *wish* they were Italian." This final observation had double significance for Mr. D'Antonio. Forty years ago, he was a struggling, self-conscious scholarship freshman at Yale himself, steeped in ambivalence about his ethnic background. To put it simply, he was ashamed to be Italian.

"In 1943, I would not have been able to admit that *I* was Italian, much less imagine any dozen people who *wished* they were Italian," he muses now, still shaking his head at the novelty of the thought. "It really does signify a change in how we think about ourselves."

Right: Head of a Manteo marionette, 1984, photograph by Martha Cooper/Credit: City Lore. Mike "Papa" Manteo, his family and assistants continue a Sicilian marionette theater tradition, of which he is the fifth-generation practitioner, in their Gravesend, Brooklyn, workshop. The medieval world of chivalry and romance, with its knights and ladies, kings and giants, dragons and battles, is recreated with some two hundred life-size marionettes patterned after the main characters in a centuries-old folk theater tradition.

Above left: Yard shrine, Brooklyn, 1985, photograph by Martha Cooper/Credit: City Lore. In 1984, Salvatore Borgia, a furniture finisher living in Carroll Gardens, carved this wooden shrine. *Above right:* Yard shrine depicting St. Paulinus of Nola, Williamsburg, Brooklyn, 1981, photograph by Martha Cooper/Credit: City Lore. Each year on the feast day, Molly Nanna places this statue, a family heirloom, on an outdoor altar. *Below left:* Yard shrine, Brooklyn, 1985, photograph by Martha Cooper/Credit: City Lore. This wrought-iron shrine to St. Lucy, a fourth-century Sicilian martyr, was built at the corner of Court Street and Third Place in Carroll Gardens by Salvatore Balsamo and his friends. *Below right:* Detail of shrine to St. Cono, Brooklyn, 1985, photograph by Martha Cooper/Credit: City Lore. Cherubs overlook contributions for blessed bread made by neighbors at this home shrine.

Above: Interior shrine, Brooklyn, 1985, photograph by Martha Cooper/Credit: City Lore. In September, Agnes Vassella's Willià̀msburg, Brooklyn, home is transformed into a public shrine for relatives and neighbors. Family and friends gather here for prayer, food and company. *Below:* Shrine to Our Lady of Mt. Carmel, Rosebank, Staten Island, 1985, photograph by Lillian Caruana. This monumental structure, some twenty feet high, was begun in the early 1930s by Sicilian immigrant Vito Russo. A local religious society maintains the shrine and sells candles to pilgrims who return annually on July 16.

Above: Friends, Brooklyn, 1985 from left to right, Sam Cangiano, Salvatore "Sarge" Mirando and Jimmy Smith, photograph by Martha Cooper/Credit: City Lore. *Below:* Playing bocce, Brooklyn, 1982, photograph by Martha Cooper/Credit: City Lore. Italian immigrants transformed abandoned railroad tracks into a bocce court.

Above: Children are an important part of Italian religious festivals and are often outfitted in costumes, Brooklyn, 1981, photograph by Martha Cooper/Credit: City Lore.
Below: Woman looking out of window, Brooklyn, 1981, photograph by Martha Cooper/Credit: City Lore. House fronts are decorated for *feste* in Italian neighborhoods.

Mark Parente, Fulton Fish Market, New York, 1986, photograph by Bruce Davidson/Credit: Magnum. Mark Parente represents the third generation of his family at the Fulton Fish Market.

The Sciorra family at the dining room table, Brooklyn, 1981, photograph by Martha Cooper/Credit: City Lore. All of the baked goods were prepared as holiday gifts by Mrs. Sciorra.

Above: Stuffed bell peppers, and *below:* Striped bass *alla Marechiaro*, 1983, photographs by Mark Ferri. Both dishes were prepared by Dominick Ianniello of Teresa and Mimmo's at 181 Grand Street in Little Italy, New York.

Both pages: The *giglio* festival, Williamsburg, Brooklyn, 1981, photographs by Martha Cooper/Credit: City Lore. At some time after the death of St. Paulinus, bishop of Nola (Naples) from 409 to 431, the festival of the *giglio* was established. Since that time descendants of immigrants from Nola have reenacted this event on a massive scale, carry-

ing two monumental structures, a boat and the *giglio* tower, through their communities. Street bands ride on the structures, providing musical accompaniment. Each July, as part of this feast, a huge tower surmounted with the saint's statue is carried through the streets of Williamsburg.

Fireworks celebrating the Centennial of the Statue of Liberty, July 4, 1986, photograph by Neil Leifer/Credit: Time. Among those involved in planning this event were Lee Iacocca, Chairman and Chief Executive Officer of The Statue of Liberty–Ellis Island Foundation, and Stephen Briganti, Executive Vice-President of the Foundation. The International Fireworks spectacular was produced and directed by Tommy Walker and Omar Lerman; it was sponsored by Abraham & Straus and Bloomingdale's, Francesco Cantarella, Senior Vice-President for Regional Government Relations. The fireworks were presented by a triumvirate of leading American fireworks companies: Fireworks by Grucci, Zembelli International and Pyrospectaculars.

EPILOGUE
by Lee Iacocca

This is a book about Italians who became Americans, people like my parents who were equally proud of the old culture they brought with them and the new one they helped to create in this country. I don't know when they stopped being Italians and started being Americans. Maybe it was the minute they set foot on Ellis Island. Or maybe they never did. Maybe the miracle of America is that they didn't have to stop being one to become the other.

Whatever bridge it was they crossed, it was too important to be reduced to a simple hyphen. I don't know any Italian-Americans. I've never met one in my life. I wouldn't know how to describe one.

That's why the story of the Italians who came to America needs all the words and pictures in this book, and more. It's not one story, but millions of them. They defy generalization and stereotypes. They range from squalor to splendor without skipping a step. Some of the characters are saints and some of them are scoundrels.

Every ethnic group that came to this country has its own unique story, and yet most aren't really unique at all because although they may start differently, they all end the same. And so does this one about people who were Italians and became Americans.

BIBLIOGRAPHY

1 GENERAL WORKS

(a) Histories dealing with Italian Americans in the United States

Amfitheatrof, Erik. *The Children of Columbus: An Informal History of the Italians in the New World*. Boston: Little, Brown, 1973. 371 pp. A well-written and well-documented popular history of the Italians in America from its discovery to the 1970s.

Bosi, Alfredo. *Cinquanta anni di vita italiana in America*. New York: Bagnasco Press, 1921. xix, 530 pp. Italian life in America from 1870 to 1920, with a historical chapter on Italian political exiles from 1830 to the U.S. Civil War.

Caporale, Rocco, ed. *The Italian Americans Through the Generations*. New York: American Italian Historical Association, 1986. 236 pp. Proceedings of the Fifteenth National Conference.

Caroli, Betty Boyd, Robert F. Harney & Lydio F. Tomasi, eds. *The Italian Immigrant Woman in North America*. New York: American Italian Historical Association, 1978. 386 pp. Proceedings of the Tenth Annual Conference.

De Conde, Alexander. *Half-Bitter, Half-Sweet: An Excursion into Italian American History*. New York: Scribner's, 1971. vii, 466 pp. Comprehensive, scholarly examination of the Italian immigrants' economic, political, social and cultural contribution and the relations between Italy and the United States from the beginning to the 1960s.

DeMichele, Michael D. *The Italian Experience in America: A Pictorial History*. Scranton, PA: Ethnic Studies Program/University of Scranton, 1982. 144 pp. Popular history from Columbus to the present, based on secondary sources and complemented by 232 illustrations and photographs.

Gallo, Patrick, ed. *The Urban Experience of Italian Americans*. New York: American Italian Historical Association, 1977. 177 pp. Proceedings of the Eighth Annual Conference.

Gambino, Richard. *Blood of My Blood: The Dilemma of the Italian Americans*. Garden City, NY: Doubleday, 1974. viii, 350 pp. Sociological-psychological examination of Italian Americans from their Sicilian roots to their lives in American cities and suburbs, enriched by the author's personal experience in the Red Hook section of Brooklyn.

Giordano, Joseph, ed. *The Italian American Catalog*. Garden City, NY: Doubleday, 1986. ix, 246 pp. "A celebration of Italian American lifestyles and culture," its six parts deal with Family, Neighborhood, Food & Drink, Culture, History, Italian Heritage. Illustrated with many photographs.

Giovannetti, Alberto. *L'America degli Italiani*. Modena: Edizioni Paoline, 1975. 339 pp. Available also in an English translation by the author. *The Italians of America*. New York: Manor Books, 1980. 318 pp. A clear, intelligent discussion of the hardships and satisfactions of immigrants from their arrival, through rejection, assimilation and eventual success.

IMAGES: A Pictorial History of Italian Americans. New and rev. ed. New York: Center for Migration Studies/Rome: *Italy, Italy* magazine, 1986. 255 pp. The 344 photographs, 62 in color, with the brief introductions to the twelve chapters, represent the passage of four generations of Italians in America.

Iorrizzo, Luciano, & Salvatore Mondello. *The Italian Americans*. Rev. ed. Boston: Twayne, 1980. 348 pp. Comprehensive survey, based on original research integrating the story of the Italian Americans with American history.

Remigio U. Pane, Professor of Italian Emeritus, Rutgers University, in his study, Highland Park, New Jersey, 1984, photograph by Frank Wojchiechowski/Credit: News Tribune.

Gli Italiani negli Stati Uniti. Florence: Istituto di Studi Americani/Università di Firenze, 1972. 585 pp. Repr. New York: Arno Press, 1975. Proceedings of the Third Symposium of American Studies, with papers presented by American and Italian specialists.

Gli Italiani negli Stati Uniti d'America. New York: Italian American Dictionary Co., 1906. 473 pp. A survey of Italian life in America at the turn of the century, with many photos of people mentioned.

Juliani, Richard N., ed. *The Family and Community Life of Italian Americans*. New York: American Italian Historical Association, 1983, xii, 191 pp. Proceedings of the Thirteenth Annual Conference.

La Sorte, Michael. *La Merica: Images of Italian Greenhorn Experience*. Philadelphia: Temple University Press, 1985. xiv, 234 pp. The story of the privations in Italy, the struggle to survive and sometimes to succeed in America, told by the protagonists themselves, make this history an intimate and authentic documentary record of the period up to the First World War.

Lopreato, Joseph. *Italian Americans*. New York: Random House, 1970. xiv, 204 pp. Excellent up-to-date sociological study which summarizes previous studies and evaluates them.

Mondello, Salvatore A. *The Italian Immigrant in Urban America, 1880-1920, As Reported in the Contemporary Periodical Press*. New York: Arno Press, 1980. 264 pp.

Moquin, Wayne, ed., with Charles Van Doren. *A Documentary History of the Italian Americans*. New York: Praeger, 1974. 448 pp. The diversity of Italian American life is presented through selected readings from institutional records, private letters, magazine and newspaper articles and other sources.

Nelli, Humbert S. *From Immigrants to Ethnics: The Italian Americans*. New York: Oxford University Press, 1983. viii, 225 pp.

Prezzolini, Giuseppe. *I trapiantati*. Milan: Longanesi, 1963. 476 pp. An illustrated, detailed study of the Italian American lifestyle in the fifties, by a keen observer and scholar who directed the Casa Italiana of Columbia University in the thirties.

Rolle, Andrew F. *The American Italians: Their History and Culture*. Belmont, CA: Wadsworth, 1972. ix, 130 pp. The best text on the subject, based on Rolle's research and the latest finds of other scholars in the field.

Scarpaci, Vincenza. *A Portrait of the Italian Americans*. New York: Scribner's, 1983. xxxiii, 240 pp. The clear and informed text and the 293 photographs and their captions document vividly all phases of Italian American life from the 1870s to the 1980s.

Schiavo, Giovanni E. *Four Centuries of Italian American History*. 5th ed. New York: Vigo Press, 1958. 468 pp. The most useful, informative and important sourcebook on Italians in America, with many reproductions of documents, illustrations and photographs.

—————. *Italians in America Before the Civil War*. New York, Vigo Press, 1934. 399 pp. Repr. New York: Arno Press, 1975. A pioneer work documenting the Italian contribution to America through its discovery, exploration and development up to the Civil War.

Tomasi, Lydio F., ed. *Italian Americans: New Perspectives in Italian Immigration and Ethnicity*. New York: Center for Migration Studies, 1985. x, 486 pp. Proceedings of the International Conference on the Italian Experience in the United States, held at Columbia University, October 13-14, 1983. Thirty papers included.

—————, ed. *The Italians in America: The Progressive View, 1891-1914*. New York: Center for Migration Studies, 1978. 309 pp. Articles selected from the Progressives' journal *Charities*, dealing with the Italian immigrants.

Tomasi, Silvano, ed. *Perspectives in Italian Immigration and Ethnicity*. New York: Center for Migration Studies, 1977. viii, 216 pp. Proceedings of the Symposium held at Casa Italiana, Columbia University, May 21-23, 1976. Sixteen papers included.

Tropea, Joseph, et al., eds. *Support and Struggle: Italians and Italian Americans in a Comparative Perspective*. New York: American Italian Historical Association, 1986. 312 pp. Proceedings of the Seventeenth National Conference.

(b) Surveys of Italian Social History as Relevant to American History

Banfield, Edward C. *The Moral Basis of a Backward Society*. New York: The Free Press, 1958. 188 pp. Sociological study of a single village in southern Italy in 1944-1945, which concludes that family loyalty prevents villagers from acting together for the common good.

Barzini, Luigi. *The Italians*. New York. Atheneum, 1961. 352 pp. Does not concern Italian Americans directly, but is most helpful in understanding the Italian character.

Ciuffoletti, Zeffiro, & Maurizio degl'Innocenti, eds. *L'emigrazione nella storia d'Italia, 1868-1975*. Florence: Vallecchi, 1978. 2 vols. Excellent documentary history of Italian emigration and the reasons and conditions leading to it.

Cresci, Paolo, & Luciano Guidobaldi. *Partono i bastimenti*. Milan: Mondadori, 1980. 230 pp. Picture history of emigration, featuring especially scenes at the Italian ports of embarkation as the ships sail.

Douglass, William S. *Emigration in a South Italian Town. An Anthropological History*. New Brunswick, NJ: Rutgers University Press, 1984. xvi, 283 pp.

Foerster, Robert F. *The Italian Emigration of Our Times*. Cambridge, MA: Harvard University Press, 1919. 556 pp. Repr. 1924; also New York: Russell & Russell 1969; New York; Arno Press, 1975. Comprehensive scholarly study of causes of Italian emigration and the status of the emigrants in the various countries abroad.

Kertzer, David I. *Family Life in Central Italy, 1880-1910*. New Brunswick, NJ: Rutgers University Press, 1984. xvii, 250 pp. Background information on Italian Americans of the mass immigration period.

Lopreato, Joseph. *Peasants No More: Social Class and Social Change in an Underdeveloped Society*. San Francisco: Chandler, 1967. Changes caused by emigration in southern Italy.

Nichols, Peter. *Italia, Italia: Modern Italy and the Contemporary Italians*. Boston: Little, Brown, 1973. 346 pp. One of the best and most readable books to understand today's Italians.

1946-1986: Quarant'anni di repubblica, l'Italia è cresciuta. Rome: *Vita Italiana*, Supplement No. 3/1986. 196 pp. A concise and well-illustrated summary of events in Italy during its first forty years as a republic.

Villari, Luigi. *Italian Life in Town and Country*. New York: G. P. Putnam's Sons, 1902. Important for background information of the conditions in the hometowns of the immigrants of the time.

2 REGIONAL STUDIES

Barberio, G. Chiodi. *Il progresso degli Italiani nel Connecticut*. New Haven, CT: Maturo's Printing & Publishing Co., 1933. 802 pp. History of Italians in Connecticut, which includes biographical information of many leading citizens.

Belfiglio, Valentine. *The Italian Experience in Texas*. Austin, TX: Eakin Press, 1983. viii, 229 pp. Illustrated with many photographs.

Biagi, Ernest L. *The Italians of Philadelphia*. New York: Carleton Press, 1967. 289 pp.

_____. *The Italians of Philadelphia and the Delaware Valley, Vol. II*. Philadelphia: The Author, 1973. xxiv, 426 pp.

Bianco, Carla. *The Two Rosetos*. Bloomington, IN: Indiana University Press, 1974. xv, 234 pp. Comparison of the people of Roseto Valfortore, Foggia, Italy, and the people of Roseto, Pennsylvania, a town founded in 1882 by immigrants from the Italian town.

Bohme, Frederick G. *A History of the Italians in New Mexico*. New York: Arno Press, 1975. Emphasizes the "bridge" provided by Italian churchmen and settlers between Anglo-Saxon and Hispanic cultures.

Briggs, John W. *Immigrants to Three American Cities, 1890-1930*. New Haven, CT: Yale University Press, 1978. xxii, 348 pp. Illus. Based on archival materials, shows that immigrants in Rochester, Utica and Kansas City were capable of initiative and accommodation and had a viable culture that gave a sense of continuity between their old and new milieu.

Brown, Kenny L. *The Italians in Oklahoma*. Norman, OK: University of Oklahoma Press, 1980. vi, 79 pp.

Burattini, Roberto. *Italians and Italo Americans in Vermont*. Barre, VT, 1931.

Churchill, Charles W. *The Italians of Newark: A Community Study*. New York: New York University Press, 1942. Repr. New York: Arno Press, 1975. 220 pp. Illus.

Ciccolella, Erasmo S. *Vibrant Life: 1886-1942. Trenton's Italian Americans*. New York: Center for Migration Studies, 1986. 165 pp.

Cinel, Dino. *From Italy to San Francisco: The Italian Immigration Experience*. Stanford, CA: Stanford University Press, 1982. xviii, 328 pp.

Cordasco, Francesco, ed. *Italians in the City: Health and Related Social Needs*. New York: Arno Press, 1975. An anthology reprinting four contemporary texts dealing with health and social problems faced by Italians in New York City and originally published between 1903 and 1934.

Crispino, James A. *The Assimilation of Ethnic Groups: The Italian Case*. New York: Center for Migration Studies, 1980. xxiii, 205 pp. Study of the Italian Americans in Bridgeport, Connecticut.

De Marco, William M. *Ethnic and Enclaves: Boston's Italian North End*. Ann Arbor, MI: University of Michigan Press, 1982. 176 pp. with 58 illustrations.

Di Leonardo, Micaela. *The Varieties of Ethnic Experience: Kinship, Class & Gender Among California Italian Americans*. Ithaca, NY: Cornell University Press, 1984. 272 pp.

Ferroni, Charles D. *The Italians in Cleveland: A Study in Assimilation*. New York: Arno Press, 1980. 288 pp.

Fiore, Alphonse T. *History of Italian Immigrants in Nebraska*. Lincoln, NB: University of Nebraska Press, 1942.

Gambino, Richard. *Vendetta: A True Story of the Worst Lynching in America. The Mass Murder of [11] Italian Americans in New Orleans in 1891, the Vicious Motivations Behind It and the Tragic Repercussions That Linger to This Day*. New York: Doubleday, 1977. xi, 198 pp.

Gumina, Deanna Paoli. *The Italians in San Francisco, 1850-1930/Gli Italiani di San Francisco, 1850-1930*. New York: Center for Migration Studies, 1978. xiii, 230 pp. Bilingual edition.

Handlin, Oscar. *Boston's Immigrants, 1790-1880: A Study in Acculturation*. Cambridge, MA: Belknap Press, 1959. 382 pp. Repr. Cambridge, MA: Harvard University Press, 1964. First historical case study of the impact of immigrants upon a society and of the adjustment of the immigrants to the society.

Juliani, Richard N. *The Social Organization of Immigrants: The Italians in Philadelphia*. New York: Arno Press, 1981. xxxi, 229 pp.

La Piana, George. *The Italians in Milwaukee, Wisconsin*. Milwaukee, WI: Asso. Charities, 1915. 85 pp. Repr. San Francisco: R & E Research Associates, 1970.

Martellone, Anna Maria. *Una Little Italy nell'Atene d'America. La comunità italiana di Boston dal 1880 al 1920*. Naples: Guida Editori, 1973. 608 pp. A scholarly study in Italian of Boston's Italian community from 1880 to 1920.

Marzulli, Orindo. *Gl'Italiani di Essex. Note storiche e biografiche con l'aggiunta di un business directory. Riccamente illustrata*. Newark, NJ: P. Matullo, [1911]. 117 pp. An excellent history of the Italian Americans in Essex County, New Jersey, up to 1910.

Mormino, Gary Ross. *Immigrants on the Hill: Italian Americans in St. Louis, 1882-1982*. Champaign, IL: University of Illinois Press, 1986. 289 pp. Illus.

Mormino, Gary Ross, & George Pozzetta. *The Immigrant World of Ybor City: Italians and Their Latin Neighbors in Tampa, 1885-1985*. Champaign, IL: University of Illinois Press, 1986. 430 pp. Illus.

Nelli, Humbert S. *The Italians of Chicago, 1880-1930: A Study in Ethnic Mobility*. New York: Oxford University Press, 1970. xx, 300 pp. How the urban surroundings affected the assimilation of the rural newcomers. Excellent documentation and bibliographies.

Nicandri, David. *The Italians of Washington State: Emigration 1853-1924*. Washington State American Revolution Bicentennial Committee, 1977. 96 pp. Illus.

Perilli, Giovanni. *Colorado and the Italians in Colorado. Il Colorado e gl'Italiani nel Colorado*. Denver: Smith Brooks Publishing Co., 1922.

Pesaturo, Ubaldo. *The Italo-Americans in Rhode Island: Their Contribution and Achievements*.

Providence, RI: Tip. Pesaturo, 1937. 172 pp. 2nd ed. Providence: Vivitor Printing Co., 1940. 193 pp.

Re, Vittorio. *Michigan's Italian Community: A Historical Perspective*. Detroit, MI: Wayne State University Press, 1981.

Riis, Jacob A. *How the Other Half Lives: Studies Among the Tenements of New York*. New York: Scribner's, 1890. Repr., with 100 photographs from the Jacob Riis Collection, the Museum of the City of New York. New York: Dover, 1971. viii, 223 pp. The most comprehensive and objective report on how the southern Italians lived when they reached the United States.

Rolle, Andrew. *The Immigrant Upraised: Italian Adventurers and Colonists in an Expanding America*. Norman, OK: University of Oklahoma Press, 1968. xvi, 391 pp. Repr. 1970. An enlightened and scholarly account of the Italian contribution in the country's westward expansion. Deals with the twenty-two states west of the Mississippi. Translated into Italian as *Gli emigranti vittoriosi*. Milan: Mondadori, 1972. 415 pp.

Sandler, Gilbert. *The Neighborhood: The Story of Baltimore's Little Italy*. Baltimore, MD: Bodine, 1974.

Scarpaci, Jean A. *Italian Immigration in Louisiana's Sugar Parishes: Recruitment, Labor Conditions, and Community Relations, 1880-1910*. New York: Arno Press, 1980. vii, 333 pp. 1972 Rutgers University dissertation.

Scherini, Rose D. *The Italian Community of San Francisco: A Descriptive Study*. New York: Arno Press, 1980. vi, 246 pp. 1976 Berkeley dissertation.

Schiavo, Giovanni E. *The Italians in Chicago: A Study in Americanization*. With a preface by Jane Addams. Chicago: Italian American Publishing Co., 1928. 207 pp. Illus. Repr. New York: Arno Press, 1975.

_____. *The Italians in Missouri*. Chicago: Italian American Publishing Co., 1929. 216 pp. Illus. Repr. New York: Arno Press, 1975.

Schiro, George, *Americans by Choice: History of the Italians in Utica*. Utica, NY: T. J. Griffiths, 1940. 183 pp. Repr. New York: Arno Press, 1975.

Sickels, Alice L. "The Upper Levee Neighborhood: A Study of an Isolated Neighborhood of about One Hundred Italian Families in Saint Paul, Minnesota, Known as 'The Upper Levee.' " Master's thesis, University of Minnesota, 1938.

Starr, Dennis J. *The Italians of New Jersey: A Historical Introduction and Bibliography*. Newark, NJ: New Jersey Historical Society, 1985. 130 pp. Illus.

Tricarico, Donald. *The Italians of Greenwich Village: The Social Structure and Transformation of an Ethnic Community*. New York: Center for Migration Studies, 1984. 184 pp.

Valletta, Clement L. *A Study of Americanization in Carneta: Italian American Identity Through Three Generations*. New York: Arno Press, 1975. Family life from 1860 to 1965, unified through immigration. Carneta is the pseudonym of a town in eastern Pennsylvania.

Vecoli, Rudolph. *The People of New Jersey*. Princeton, NJ: Van Nostrand, 1965. 299 pp. An excellent scholarly history of the many ethnic groups making up the New Jersey population, with a very good chapter on the Italians.

Veronesi, Gene P. *Italian Americans and Their Communities of Cleveland*. Cleveland, OH: Ethnic Heritage Studies Center, Cleveland State University, 1977. 358 pp.

WPA Federal Writers Project. *Copper Camp Stories of the World's Greatest Mining Town, Butte, Montana*, New York: 1943.

_____.*The Italian Theater in San Francisco*. San Francisco, 1939.

_____. *The Italians of New York: A Survey*. New York: Random House, 1938. 241 pp. Repr. New York: Arno Press, 1969. Published also in Italian as *Gli Italiani di New York*. New York: Labor Press, 1939.

_____. *The Italians of Omaha*. Omaha, NB: Independent Printing Co., 1941. Repr. New York: Arno Press, 1975. 111 pp.

_____. *New Jersey: A Guide to Its Present and Past*. New York: Viking Press, 1939, 735 pp. Rev. ed. New York: Hastings House, 1959. Repr. of 1939 edition, New Brunswick, NJ: Rutgers University Press, 1986.

Yans-McLaughlin, Virginia. *Family and Community: Italian Immigrants in Buffalo, 1880-1930*. Ithaca, NY: Cornell University Press, 1977. 286 pp. Paperback ed. Champaign, IL: University of Illinois Press, 1981.

3 SOCIOLOGICAL STUDIES

Albini, Joseph L. *The American Mafia: Genesis of a Legend*. New York: Appleton-Century-Crofts, 1971. xi, 345 pp. Repr. paperback ed. New York: Irvington, 1979. Scholarly examination of the subject; points out that many beliefs about the Mafia are based on hearsay, and tries to separate the myths from the facts.

Alissi, Albert S. *Boys in Little Italy: A Comparison of Their Individual Value Orientations, Family Patterns, and Peer Group Associations*. San Francisco: R & E Research Associates, 1978. ix, 119 pp.

Antonini, Luigi. *Dynamic Democracy*. New York: Eloquent Press, 1944. Deals with the growth and dynamism of the Italian American labor movement.

Caroli, Betty Boyd. *Italian Repatriation from the United States, 1900-1914*. New York: Center for Migration Studies, 1973. viii, 110 pp.

Cerase, Francesco. *L'emigrazione di ritorno. Innovazione o reazione? L'esperienza dell'emigrazione di ritorno dagli Stati Uniti d'America*. Rome, 1971. 302 pp. A sociological study of immigration and the effects of immigrants returning to their hometowns.

Child, Irving Long. *Italian or American? The Second Generation in Conflict*. New Haven, CT: Yale University Press, 1943. 206 pp. Repr. New York: Russell & Russell, 1970. Examines the psychological reaction to acculturation of a group of second-generation male Italians in New Haven.

Clark, Francis E. *Our Italian Fellow Citizens in Their Old Homes and Their New*. Boston: Small, Maynard & Co., 1919. ix, 217 pp. Repr. New York: Arno Press, 1975. An early sympathetic treatment of Italian immigrants, commenting on their continuing contributions.

Coleman, Terry. *Going to America*. New York: Pantheon Books, 1972. 317 pp. Describes travel conditions for immigrants, including Italians, at the turn of the century.

Concistré, Marie J. *Adult Education in a Local Area: A Study of a Decade in the Life and Education of the Adult Immigrant in East Harlem, New York City.* Unpublished doctoral dissertation, New York University, 1944. 531 pp.

Cordasco, Francesco, & Eugene Bucchioni. *The Italians: Social Backgrounds of an American Group.* Clifton, NJ: A. M. Kelley, 1974. xx, 598 pp. A diverse collection of documents which recreates the period of immigration and describes the new community of settlers.

_____. *Protestant Evangelism Among Italians in America.* New York: Arno Press, 1975. Reprints Protestant literature dealing with the Italian immigration published originally between 1917 and 1948.

Covello, Leonard. *The Social Background of the Italo American School Child: A Study of the Southern Italian Mores and Their Effect on the School Situation in Italy and America.* Leiden: E. J. Brill, 1967. xxxii, 488 pp. Repr. Totowa, NJ: Rawman & Littlefield, 1972.

Diggins, John P. *Mussolini and Fascism: The View from America.* Princeton, NJ: Princeton University Press, 1972. 524 pp. Published in Italian as *L'America, Mussolini e il fascismo.* Bari: Laterza, 1972. 690 pp. Excellent on the Fascist movement in the United States and the activities of Italian Americans.

Ehrman, Herbert B. *The Case That Will Not Die: Commonwealth Versus Sacco and Vanzetti.* Boston: Little, Brown, 1969. An account of the Sacco and Vanzetti case written by the junior counsel for the defense during the last two years of the case; shows how political factors caused a temporary breakdown of the legal process.

Fenton, Edwin. *Immigrants and Unions, A Case Study: Italians and American Labor, 1870-1920.* New York: Arno Press, 1975, 630 pp. This Harvard dissertation of 1958 studies the transition made by southern Italian *contadini* in becoming factory workers and construction workers in America.

Fishman, Joshua A. *Language Loyalty in the United States: The Maintenance and Perpetuation of Non-English Mother Tongues by American Ethnic Groups.* The Hague: Mouton, 1976. 478 pp. Major work on language retention by Italian Americans.

Fucilla, Joseph G. *The Teaching of Italian in the United States: A Documentary History.* New Brunswick, NJ: Rutgers University Press/American Association of Teachers of Italian, 1967. 299 pp. Repr. New York: Arno Press, 1975. Comprehensive study from colonial times to the 1960s.

Gallo, Patrick J. *Ethnic Alienation: The Italian Americans.* Cranbury, NJ: Fairleigh Dickinson University Press, 1974. 254 pp. Examines the role of ethnicity in American political life through three generations of Italian Americans.

Ganz, Herbert J. *The Urban Villagers: Group and Class in the Life of Italian Americans.* New York: The Free Press, 1962. 367 pp. Italian American culture within a working-class context in Boston's North End.

Harney, Robert F., & J. Vincenza Scarpaci, eds. *Little Italies of North America.* Toronto: The Multicultural Society of Ontario, 1981. 210 pp. Nine papers on as many Little Italies—six in the United States and three in Canada.

Iorrizzo, Luciano, ed. *An Inquiry into Organized Crime.* New York: American Italian Historical Association, 1970. 87 pp. Proceedings of the Third Annual Conference.

Johnson, Colleen Leary. *Growing Up and Growing Old in Italian American Families.* New Brunswick, NJ: Rutgers University Press, 1985. 219 pp. How the Italian Americans view the cycle of life.

Matthews, Sister Mary Fabian. *The Role of the Public School in the Assimilation of the Italian Immigrant Child in New York City, 1900-1914.* Unpublished doctoral dissertation, Fordham University, 1966.

Meltzer, Milton. *Bread and Roses: The Struggle in American Labor, 1865-1915.* New York: Knopf, 1967. Repr. New York: New American Library, 1977. Studies the radical labor movement in the United States, with emphasis on the 1912 Lawrence, Massachusetts, textile strike and the role of Italians in that strike.

Nelli, Humbert S. *The Business of Crime: Italians and Syndicate Crime in the United States.* New York: Oxford University Press, 1976. xiii, 314 pp. Illus. Comprehensive history of involvement in crime in fourteen U.S. cities, based on primary source material; corrects widely believed myths and presents the subject in a historical and nationwide perspective.

Odencranz, Louise C. *Italian Women in Industry: A Study of Conditions in New York City.* New York: Russell Sage Foundation, 1919. 345 pp. Repr. Clifton, NJ: A. M. Kelley, 1974; New York: Arno Press, 1979.

Parenti, Michael J. *Ethnic and Political Attitudes: A Depth Study of Italian Americans.* New York: Arno Press, 1975. 354 pp. This 1962 Yale dissertation is based on interviews with eighteen Italian American males.

Pisani, Lawrence F. *The Italian in America: A Social Study and History.* New York: Exposition Press, 1957. 293 pp. The progressive view of a people with a dynamic heritage facing a melting-pot society.

Pozzetta, George E., ed. *Pane e Lavoro: The Italian American Working Class.* New York: American Italian Historical Association, 1980. 176 pp. Proceedings of the Eleventh Annual Conference.

Rolle, Andrew. *The Italian Americans: Troubled Roots.* New York: The Free Press, 1980. 222 pp. Repr. paperback ed. Norman, OK: University of Oklahoma Press, 1984. 240 pp. An essay on psychohistory studying the conflicts in the lives of Italian Americans.

Russell, Francis. *Tragedy in Dedham: The Story of the Sacco-Vanzetti Case.* New York: McGraw-Hill, 1962. xxiii, 480 pp. Repr. 1971.

Salvemini, Gaetano. *Italian Fascist Activities in the United States.* New York: Center for Migration Studies, 1977. 267 pp.

Sartorio, Enrico C. *Social and Religious Life of Italians in America.* Boston: Christopher, 1918. 149 pp. Repr. Clifton, NJ: A. M. Kelley, 1974. A scholarly contemporary insight into Italian American religious life up to the First World War by an immigrant who became a Protestant minister.

Schiavo, Giovanni E. *The Truth About the Mafia and Organized Crime in America.* New York: Vigo Press, 1962. 318 pp. Written to explode the myth of Italian American predominance in organized crime in America.

Shriver, William P. *Adventure in Missions. The Story of Presbyterian Work with Italians.* 5th ed. New York: Board of National Missions of the Presbyterian Church in the United States, Unit of City and Industrial Work, 1946. 93 pp.

Stella, Antonio. *Some Aspects of Italian Immigration to the United States: Statistical Data and General Consideration Based Chiefly Upon United States Censuses and Other Official Publications Showing Standard of Living, Behavior, and Progress Made by Italians in America.* New York: G. P. Putnam's Sons, 1924. xx, 124 pp. Repr. San Francisco: R & E Research Associates, 1970; New York: Arno Press, 1975.

Tait, Joseph W. *Some Aspects of the Effect of the Dominant American Culture upon Children of Italian-Born Parents.* New York: Columbia University Press, 1942. ix, 74 pp. Repr. New York: Arno Press, 1972.

Talese, Gay. *Honor Thy Father.* New York: World, 1971. xvi, 526 pp. Paperback ed. New York: Fawcett, 1972. Based on the life of Joseph Bonanno, with less emphasis on gangland crime and more on the private family life of an alleged Mafia leader.

Tomasi, Silvano M. *Piety and Power: The Role of Italian Parishes in the New York Metropolitan Area (1880-1930).* New York: Center for Migration Studies, 1975. xi, 201 pp. The role of the Catholic Church in relation to Italian immigrants and their adjustment to the new culture.

_____, ed. *The Religious Experience of Italian Americans.* New York: American Italian Historical Association. 1975. 133 pp. Proceedings of the Sixth Annual Conference.

_____, & M. H. Engel, eds. *The Italian Experience in the United States.* New York: Center for Migration Studies, 1970. x, 239 pp. Ten chapters by specialists representing current research on Italian immigration and assimilation, with a rich bibliography.

Ulin, Richard O. *The Italo American Student in the American Public School: A Description and Analysis of Differential Behavior.* New York: Arno Press, 1975. x, 201 pp. 1958 Harvard dissertation.

Watts, George B. *The Waldenses in the New World.* Durham, NC: Duke University Press, 1941. xi, 309 pp. Deals with the early migration of the Waldensians to North and South America. Excellent bibliography.

Whyte, William Foot. *Street Corner Society: The Social Structure of an Italian Slum.* Chicago: University of Chicago Press, 1943. Rev. ed. 1945; 3rd ed., rev. and enlarged, 1981. xx, 386 pp. Very good sociological study of acculturation problems.

4 CULTURAL HISTORIES

Davis, Ronald L. *A History of Opera in the American West.* Englewood Cliffs, NJ: Prentice-Hall, 1965. xii, 178 pp. Italian opera and performances by Italian artists in the western United States, including Chicago and New Orleans; covers all major opera companies outside of the East Coast.

Fairman, Charles. "Art of the Italian Artists in the United States Capitol." *Congressional Record,* January 29, 1930. The curator of art of the Capitol illustrates, in this and the following article cited, the work of Italian artists in the Capitol.

_____. "Our Debt to Italy." *Congressional Record,* January 28, 1925.

Fermi, Laura. *Illustrious Immigrants: The Intellectual Migration from Europe, 1930-1941.* Chicago: University of Chicago Press, 1968. xii, 440 pp. Illus. Rev ed. 1971. 431 pp. Among the scholars and scientists discussed in the book are forty-two Italians who remained in the United States and made valuable contributions in all fields, from the author's own husband, Enrico Fermi, to other Nobel Prize winners, Emilio Segrè (1959), Salvador Luria (1969), and Franco Modigliani (1975), as well as Arturo Toscanini, and many other outstanding United States citizens.

Greene, Rose Basile. *The Italian American Novel: Document of the Interaction of Two Cultures.* Rutherford, NJ: Fairleigh Dickinson University Press, 1974. 416 pp.

Grieb, Lyndal. *The Operas of Gian Carlo Menotti 1937-1972: A Selective Bibliography.* Metuchen, NJ: The Scarecrow Press, 1974.

Italian Influences on American Literature. An Address by C. Waller Barrett and a Catalogue of an Exhibition of Books, Manuscripts and Art Showing This Influence on American Literature and Art, Held at the Grolier Club, October 17 to December 10, 1961. New York: The Grolier Club, 1962. 131 pp.

La Piana, Angelina. *La cultura americana e l'Italia.* Turin: Einaudi, 1938. A history of the growth of a knowledge in America of Italy and Italian literature of the sixteenth century.

Musmanno, Michael A. *The Story of the Italians in America.* Garden City, NY: Doubleday, 1965. x, 300 pp. A wide-ranging appreciation of the Italian American contribution to the United States.

Pane, Remigio U., ed. *Italian Americans in the Professions.* New York: American Italian Historical Association, 1983. viii, 290 pp. Proceedings of the Twelfth Annual Conference.

Peragallo, Olga. *Italian American Authors and Their Contributions to American Literature.* New York: S. F. Vanni, 1949. xii, 242 pp. A valuable source providing a relatively complete list of fifty-nine Italian American authors and their contributions prior to 1949.

Schiavo, Giovanni E. *Italian American History. Vol I.* New York: Vigo Press, 1947. 604 pp. Illus. Repr. New York: Arno Press, 1975. Book I, *Italian Music and Musicians in America,* is a survey from colonial times to the 1930s; Book II, *Dictionary of Musical Biography,* covers conductors, composers, singers, musicians and musical entrepreneurs; Book III is a comprehensive survey of Italian American public officials in the United States from the earliest colonial times to the 1940s.

_____. *Italian American History, Vol. II: The Italian Contribution to the Catholic Church in America.* New York: Vigo Press, 1949. 1056 pp. Illustrated with over 400 pictures. A comprehensive history of Italian missionaries, priests, nuns and religious orders and friars who helped to explore, Christianize, and educate Indians and settlers and, later, immigrants in the United States, parts of Canada and Alaska, and earlier in the Spanish territories that became part of the United States. The second part of the work gives a history of every Italian parish in the United States, state by state, up to the 1940s.

USA Bicentennial—The Italian Contribution. Chicago: *La Parola del Popolo,* No. 134 (September-October, 1976). 352 pp. Special number dedicated to Italian immigrants' contributions to America from its discovery to the present.

United States Congress. *Art in the United States Capitol*. Washington, DC: U.S. Government Printing Office, 1978. xi, 455 pp. Illus. Includes over 100 reproductions of works of art done at the Capitol by twenty-six Italian artists brought to America for the purpose.

5 RELATIONS WITH OVERALL COMMUNITY

Alba, Richard D. *Italian Americans into the Twilight of Ethnicity*. Englewood Cliffs, NJ: Prentice-Hall, 1985. 240 pp. Illus. Increasing rate of intermarriage with other ethnic groups will lead to a loss of ethnic identity by the end of the century.

Angle, Paul M. *Bloody Williamson: A Chapter in American Lawlessness*. New York: Knopf, 1952. Describes Ku Klux Klan activities against Italian Americans.

Barton, Joseph J. *Peasants and Strangers: Italians, Rumanians, and Slovaks in an American City, 1890-1950*. Cambridge, MA: Harvard University Press, 1975. 217 pp. Compares and contrasts the American experience of Italians, Rumanians and Slovaks in Cleveland, Ohio.

Bayor, Ronald H. *Neighbors in Conflict: The Irish, Germans, Jews, and Italians of New York City, 1929-1941*. Baltimore, MD: Johns Hopkins University Press, 1978. 252 pp. Examines factors leading to intergroup conflicts, their manifestation and eventual solutions.

Bodnar, John, Roger Simon & Michael P. Weber. *Lives of Their Own: Blacks, Italians, and Poles in Pittsburgh, 1900-1960*. Champaign, IL: University of Illinois Press, 1981. 302 pp. Illus. Paperback ed. 1983.

Brace, Charles L. *The Dangerous Classes of New York, and Twenty Years' Work Among Them*. New York: Wynkoop & Hallenbeck, 1872. Reveals anti-Italian bias and prejudice among "native" Americans even before Italians arrived in large numbers.

Cordasco, Francesco, ed. *Assimilation of the Italian Immigrant*. New York: Arno Press, 1975. Reprints J. F. Carr's *Guide for the Italian Immigrant in the United States* (1911) and S. G. Pomeroy's *The Italians: A Study of the Countrymen of Columbus, Dante and Michelangelo* (1914). Both deal with problems faced by Italian immigrants.

Feldman, Herman. *Racial Factors in American Industry*. New York: Harper, 1931. Argues that Italians were the worst-treated among immigrant groups.

Femminella, Francis X., ed. *Italians and Irish in America*. New York: American Italian Historical Association, 1985. 308 pp. Proceedings of the Sixteenth Annual Conference.

Gabriel, Richard A. *The Irish and the Italians: Ethnics in City and Suburb*. New York: Arno Press, 1980. xix, 284 pp.

Glanz, Rudolf. *Jew and Italian: Historic Group Relations and the New Immigration, 1881-1924*. New York: KTAV Publishing Co., 1971. A comparison of Jewish and Italian immigrants in their quest for acculturation.

Glazer, Nathan, & Daniel P. Moynihan. *Beyond the Melting Pot: Negroes, Puerto Ricans, Jews, Italians and the Irish of New York City*. Cambridge, MA: Massachusetts Institute of Technology Press, 1963, xvii, 363 pp. 2nd rev. ed. 1970. The Italian chapter focuses on the development of New York's "Little Italies" and their generational conflicts.

Harvard Encyclopedia of American Ethnic Groups. Cambridge, MA: Harvard University Press, 1980. 1076 pp. The chapter on the Italians (pp. 545-560), written by Humbert S. Nelli, is a concise historical summary of Italians in America.

Higham, John R. *Strangers in the Land: Patterns of American Nativism, 1860-1925*. New Brunswick, NJ: Rutgers University Press, 1955. Corrected ed. New York: Atheneum, 1972. Studies the effects of nativism on all European immigrant groups and concludes that the Italians suffered the most hostility.

Kent, Maxwell. *A Comparative Analysis of the Italians & of the Jews: The Two People Who Contributed the Most to the Civilization of Mankind with Strange and Unexpected Conclusions*. Albuquerque, NM: American Classical College Press, 1977.

Kessner, Thomas. *The Golden Door: Italian and Jewish Immigrant Mobility in New York City, 1880-1915*. New York: Oxford University Press, 1977. xxvi, 224 pp.

LaGumina, Salvatore, ed. *Wop: A Documentary History of Anti-Italian Discrimination in the United States*. San Francisco: Straight Arrow, 1973. 319 pp.

Panunzio, Constantine M. *Immigration Crossroads*. New York: Macmillan, 1927. 307 pp. Repr. New York: Ozer, 1971. Studies U.S. immigration restriction laws and their failure to consider the plight of alien residents in the U.S.

Scarpaci, Jean, ed. *The Interaction of Italians and Jews in America*. New York: American Italian Historical Association, 1975. 117 pp. Proceedings of the Seventh Annual Conference.

Smith, Judith E. *Family Connections. A History of Italian and Jewish Immigrant Lives in Providence, Rhode Island, 1900-1940*. Ithaca, NY: SUNY Press, 1986.

Stack, John F., Jr. *International Conflict in an American City: Boston's Irish, Italians, and Jews, 1935-1944*. Westport, CT: Greenwood Press, 1979.

Suttles, Gerald D. *The Social Order of the Slum: Ethnicity and Territory in the Inner City*. Chicago: University of Chicago Press, 1968. xxii, 243 pp. Repr. *The Social Construction of Communities*. 1972. Comprehensive analysis of internal relations of various ethnic groups within a slum area.

Woods, Robert A., ed. *Americans in Process: A Settlement Study*. Boston: Houghton Mifflin, 1903. 389 pp. Repr. New York: Arno Press, 1975. Describes the deprived living and working conditions of Jewish and Italian communities in the North End of Boston at the end of the last century.

6 RELATIONS WITH ITALY

Amfitheatrof, Erik. *The Enchanted Ground: Americans in Italy, 1760-1980*. Boston: Little, Brown, 1980. 222 pp. Illus. The Italian experience of Americans who lived it, from colonial times to the present.

Belfiglio, Valentine J. *Alliances*. Lexington, MA: Ginn Press, 1986. 139 pp. Italian American relations from 1776 to the present.

Brooks, Van Wyck. *The Dream of Arcadia: American Writers and Artists in Italy, 1760-1915*. New York: Dutton, 1958. 272 pp.

Guidi, Angelo Flavio. *Relazioni culturali fra Italia e Stati Uniti d'America*. Padua: Cedam,

1940. Cultural relations between Italy and the United States.

Heiney, Donald W. *America in Modern Italian Literature*. New Brunswick, NJ: Rutgers University Press, 1964. 278 pp. Influence of America and its myth on Italian literature from the 1930s to the 1950s.

Italia e Stati Uniti dall'indipendenza americana ad oggi (1766-1978). Genoa: Tilgher, 1978. 390 pp. Proceedings of the First International Conference on American History, held May 26-29, 1976. Papers dealing with Italian American relations.

Italia e Stati Uniti nell'età del Risorgimento e della Guerra Civile. Florence: La Nuova Italia, 1969. 406 pp. Proceedings of the Second Symposium of American Studies, held in Florence, May 27-29, 1966. Papers by Italian and American scholars on Italian American relations during the Italian Risorgimento and the American Civil War.

The Italians and the Creation of America. Catalogue of an Exhibition at the John Carter Brown Library. Prepared by Samuel J. Hough. Providence, RI: The John Carter Brown Library, 1980. 83 pp. The significance of the interaction between Italians and America from its discovery to 1800 is illustrated by the 100 publications and 28 maps displayed at the exhibition and described and annotated in the catalogue.

Marraro, Howard R. *American Opinion on the Unification of Italy, 1846-1861*. New York: Columbia University Press, 1932. 345 pp. Repr. New York: AMS Press, 1969. Published in Italian as *L'unificazione italiana vista dai diplomatici statunitensi (1849-1861)*. 2 vols. Rome, 1963-1964.

_____. *Relazioni fra l'Italia e gli Stati Uniti*. Rome: Edizioni dell'Ateneo, 1954. Political and cultural relations between Italy and the United States.

Napolitano, Gaetano. *Italia e Stati Uniti. Correnti emigratorie e commerciali*. Roma: Tipografia, 1925. Emigration and commercial relations between Italy and the United States.

Nelli, Humbert S., ed. *The United States and Italy: The First Two Hundred Years*. New York: American Italian Historical Association, 1977. 242 pp. Proceedings of the Ninth Annual Conference. Papers by Italian and American scholars on historical and cultural relations.

Pace, Antonio. *Benjamin Franklin and Italy*. Philadelphia: American Philosophical Society, 1958.

Prezzolini, Giuseppe. *Come gli Americani scoprirono l'Italia (1750-1950)*. Milan: Treves, 1933. 305 pp. Repr. Bologna: Massimiliano Boni, 1973. Examines published records and diaries of Americans who traveled or studied in Italy from 1750 to 1950.

Soria, Regina. *Dictionary of Nineteenth-Century American Artists in Italy, 1760-1914*. East Brunswick, NJ: Fairleigh Dickinson University Press, 1982. 336 pp.

Spini, Giorgio, et al., eds. *Italia e America dal Settecento all'età dell'imperialismo*. Florence: Marsilio Editore, 1976. 472 pp.

_____. *Italia e America dalla Grande Guerra a oggi*. Florence: Marsilio Editore, 1976. 283 pp. Both volumes of Spini's deal with Italian-American relations from American independence to the present.

Trauth, Sister Mary Philip. *Italian-American Diplomatic Relations*. Washington, DC, 1958.

Villari, Luigi. *Gli Stati Uniti d'America e l'emigrazione italiana*. Milan: Treves, 1912. 314 pp. Repr. New York: Arno Press, 1975. The results of the Italian immigrants' contact with American life.

Wright, Natalia. *American Novelists in Italy. The Discoverers: Allston to James*. Philadelphia: University of Pennsylvania Press, 1965. 316 pp. Repr. paperback ed. 1974.

7 NEWSPAPERS & PERIODICALS

(a) Daily

Il Progresso Italo Americano, New York. Founded 1880. The only national Italian daily. Sunday ed. includes the weekly magazine *Due Mondi*.

(b) Weekly

L'Agenda. Brooklyn, NY. Founded 1970. Italian and English.

Italian Tribune. Newark, NJ. Founded 1931. English. A picture newspaper.

L'Italo Americano di Los Angeles. Founded 1908. Italian/English.

Sons of Italy Times. Philadelphia, PA. Founded 1936. English, one page Italian.

La Tribuna del Popolo/The Voice of the People. Detroit, MI. Founded 1909. Italian.

Unione per il Progresso degli Italiani in America. Pittsburgh, PA. Founded 1890. Italian/English.

(c) Monthly

Fra Noi. Chicago. Founded 1961. English.

OSIA News. National Publication of the Supreme Lodge Order Sons of Italy in America. Worcester, MA. Founded 1946. English/Italian.

Il Popolo Italiano. Atlantic City, NJ. Founded 1935. Italian/English.

Sons of Italy News. Boston. Founded 1928. English, with some Italian.

(d) Journals and Magazines

Attenzione. New York. Bimonthly. Founded 1979. English. Illustrated.

La Follia di New York. New York. Monthly. Founded 1893. Italian/English. Illustrated.

Forum Italicum. Quarterly. Founded 1967. Scholarly journal in English and Italian published now at SUNY at Stony Brook, NY.

Italian Americana. Semiannually. Founded 1974. SUNY at Buffalo.

Italian Quarterly. Founded 1957. Literary and cultural journal, since 1979 published at Rutgers University, New Brunswick, NJ. English and some Italian.

ITALICA. Quarterly journal of the American Association of Teachers of Italian. Founded 1924. University of Wisconsin, Madison, WI. English/Italian.

Italy, Italy. Monthly. Founded 1983. Rome, Italy. English. Cultural magazine lavishly illustrated in color, published expressly for Americans.

La Parola del Popolo. Founded in 1908 and published by Egidio Clemente in Chicago from 1951 as a monthly and later bimonthly; stopped publication with his death in 1983.

Unico National Magazine. Founded 1948. Monthly. Bloomfield, NJ. English.

8 ITALIAN AMERICAN LITERATURE

(a) Novels

Barolini, Helen, ed. *The Dream Book: An Anthology of Writings by Italian American Women.* New York: Schocken Books, 1985. xiv, 397 pp.

Benasutti, Marion. *No Steady Job for Papa.* New York: Vanguard, 1966. Nostalgic account of poor Italian Americans in Philadelphia.

Cautela, Giuseppe. *Moon Harvest.* New York: Dial Press, 1925. 253 pp. The acculturation of an immigrant schoolteacher and his family.

D'Agostino, Guido. *Olives in the Apple Tree.* Garden City, NY: Doubleday, 1940. Repr. New York: Arno Press, 1975. Marco struggles to understand and accept American society, while his immigrant friends reject assimilation.

De Capite, Raymond. *The Coming of Fabrizze.* New York: McKay, 1960. The story of an immigrant who works his way up the financial ladder in Cleveland's Italian colony, until the stock market crash destroys him.

Fante, John. *Dago Red.* New York: Viking Press, 1940. Thirteen short stories sketching Italian American life in the author's native Colorado.

Mangione, Jerre. *Mount Allegro.* New York: Columbia University Press, 1981. Originally published in 1942, this classic is the author's recollection of his childhood among the Sicilians of Rochester, New York.

Pagano, Jo. *Golden Wedding.* New York: Random House, 1943. Repr. New York: Arno Press, 1975. A retrospective of the American experience of the Simon family, culminating with the celebration of the parents' golden anniversary of their wedding.

Panetta, George. *We Ride a White Donkey.* New York: Harcourt, Brace, 1944. Hilarious sketches about a family living on the East Side of Manhattan.

Papaleo, Joseph. *Out of Place.* Boston: Little, Brown, 1970. Italian Americans have sacrificed their important heritage to assimilation and acculturation.

Pola, Antonia. *Who Can Buy The Stars?* New York, 1957. Italians in the coal-mining community of Union City, Indiana.

Puzo, Mario. *The Fortunate Pilgrim.* New York: Atheneum, 1964. The story of a very strong Italian immigrant woman as she struggles for her family's survival in New York's Hell's Kitchen in the 1930s.

Tomasi, Mari. *Like Lesser Gods.* Milwaukee, WI: Bruce, 1949. Italian granite cutters in Barre, Vermont, live and work in fear of tuberculosis.

(b) Poetry

Alfonsi, Ferdinando. *Poeti italoamericani, antologia bilingue.* Catanzaro: Antonio Carrello Editore, 1985. 434 pp. Bilingual anthology of poems by Italian American poets.

Ciardi, John. *The Achievement of John Ciardi. A Comprehensive Selection of His Poems.* Glenville, IL: Scott, Foresman, 1969.

Corso, Gregory Nunzio. *Long Live Man.* New York: New Directions, 1962.

Ferlinghetti, Lawrence. *Endless Life: Selected Poems.* New York: New Directions, 1981.

Giovannitti, Arturo. *The Collected Poems.* Chicago: Clemente, 1962. Repr. New York: Arno Press, 1975.

Greene, Rose Basile. *Primo Vino.* South Brunswick, NJ: A. S. Barnes, 1974. Seventy sonnets celebrating the accomplishments of Italian Americans in the United States.

Tusiani, Joseph. *Gente Mia and Other Poems.* Stone Park, IL: Italian Culture Center, 1978.

(c) Drama

Innaurato, Albert. *Bizarre Behavior: Six Plays.* New York: Avon, 1980.

Menotti, Gian Carlo. *The Saint of Bleecker Street.* New York: RCA, 1954.

(d) Autobiography

Arrighi, Antonio R. *The Story of Antonio, the Galley Slave: A Romance of Real Life in Three Parts.* New York: Revell, 1911. 266 pp.

Barzini, Luigi. *O America: When You and I Were Young.* New York: Harper & Row, 1977. 329 pp.

Capra, Frank. *The Name Above the Title.* New York: Bantam, 1972.

Cateura, Linda Brandi, ed. *Growing Up Italian.* New York: William Morrow, 1987. 268 pp. Illus. Essays written by twelve prominent Italian Americans.

Covello, Leonard, with Guido D'Agostino. *The Heart is the Teacher.* New York: McGraw-Hill, 1958. Repr. as *Teacher in the Urban Community.* Totowa, NJ: Littlefield, Adams, 1970.

Cuomo, Mario. *Diaries of Mario Cuomo.* New York: Random House, 1985. 2 vols.

D'Angelo, Pascal. *Pascal D'Angelo: Son of Italy.* New York: Macmillan, 1924. Repr. Detroit, MI: Gale Research, 1968; New York: Arno Press, 1975.

Da Ponte, Lorenzo. *Memoirs of Lorenzo Da Ponte.* Philadelphia: Lippincott, 1929. 512 pp.

Di Donato, Pietro. *Christ in Concrete.* Indianapolis, IN: Bobbs-Merrill, 1939. Repr. New York: Macmillan, 1985. Classic autobiographical novel of Italian Americans in the construction industry of New York–New Jersey.

Ets, Marie Hall. *Rosa—The Life of an Italian Immigrant.* Minneapolis, MN: University of Minnesota Press, 1970.

Ferraro, Geraldine, with Linda Bird Francke. *Ferraro, My Story.* New York: Bantam, 1985. 340 pp.

Gallenga, Antonio. *Episodes of My Second Life. American and English Experiences.* London: Chapman & Hall, 1884. 2 vols. Philadelphia: J. B. Lippincott, 1885.

Iacocca, Lee, with William Novak. *Iacocca: An Autobiography.* New York: Bantam, 1984. 352 pp.

La Guardia, Fiorello. *The Making of an Insurgent: An Autobiography. 1882-1919.* Philadelphia, 1948. Repr. New York: Capricorn, 1961.

Luria, Salvador, E. *Life: The Unfinished Experiment.* New York: Scribner's, 1974. Nobel Prize winner for Medicine, 1969.

Mazzei, Philip. *My Life & Wanderings.* Trans. by S. E. Scalia and ed. by M. Marchione. Morristown, NJ: Institute of Italian Studies, 1980. 437 pp.

Panunzio, Constantine. *The Soul of An Immigrant.* New York: Macmillan, 1921. Repr. 1924; 1934; New York: Arno Press, 1969.

Patri, Angelo. *A Schoolmaster of the Great City.* New York: Macmillan, 1917. 221 pp. Reprinted many times and translated into many foreign languages. Patri was an Italian-born schoolteacher and principal in New York and an outstanding school reformer.

Segale, Sister Blandina. *At the End of the Santa Fe Trail.* Milwaukee, WI: Bruce, 1948. 298 pp. The journals of an Italian-born missionary nun who pioneered in the Southwest from 1872 to 1892.

Vanzetti, Bartolomeo. *Autobiografia e lettere inedite.* Florence: Vallecchi, 1977. Autobiography and unpublished letters in Italian.

(e) Biography

Alfonsi, Ferdinando. *Incontri italoamericani di successo.* Catanzaro: Antonio Carrello Editore, 1983. 232 pp. Brief biographies of forty-four leading Italian Americans.

Auletta, Ken. "Profile: Governor [Mario Cuomo]." *The New Yorker*, April 9 and 16, 1984.

Bolton, Herbert E. *Rim of Christendom: A Biography of Eusebio Francisco Kino, Pacific Coast Pioneer.* New York: Macmillan, 1936. xvi, 644 pp.

Dana, Julian. *A. P. Giannini, Giant in the West.* New York: Prentice-Hall, 1947.

Di Donato, Pietro. *Immigrant Saint: The Life of Mother Cabrini.* New York: McGraw-Hill, 1960.

Evans, Mary E. *The Seed and the Glory: The Career of Samuel Charles Mazzuchelli, O.P., on the Mid-American Frontier.* New York: Macmillan, 1950. 200 pp.

Felici, Icilio. *Father to the Immigrants: The Life of John Baptist Scalabrini.* New York: Center for Migration Studies, 1965. 248 pp.

Fermi, Laura. *Atoms in the Family: My Life with Enrico Fermi.* Chicago: University of Chicago Press, 1954. Published in Italian as *Atomi in famiglia.* Milan: Mondadori, 1955.

Hallenbeck, Cleve, ed. *The Journey of Fray Marcos de Niza.* Dallas: Southern Methodist University Press, 1949. 115 pp.

Jackson, Stanley. *Caruso.* New York: Stein & Day, 1972.

Johnson, Robert K. *Francis Ford Coppola.* Boston: Twayne, 1978.

LaGumina, Salvatore. *Vito Marcantonio: The People's Politician.* Dubuque, IA: Kendall-Hunt, 1969. Illustrates the power of ethnicity in political life.

Marinacci, Barbara. *They Came from Italy: The Story of Famous Italian Americans.* New York: Dodd, Mead, 1967. Brief lives of seven famous Italian Americans for young readers.

McFadden, Elizabeth. *The Glitter and the Gold: A Spirited Account of the Metropolitan Museum of Art's First Director, the Audacious and High-Handed Luigi Palma di Cesnola.* New York: Dial, 1971.

Murdock, Myrtle Cheney. *Constantino Brumidi, Michelangelo of the United States Capitol.* Washington, DC: Monumental Press, 1950.

Murphy, Edmund R. *Henry De Tonty: Fur Trader of the Mississippi.* Baltimore, MD: Johns Hopkins University Press, 1941.

Petacco, Arrigo. *Joe Petrosino.* New York: Macmillan, 1924. Italian-born Lt. Joseph Petrosino of New York City's Police Department was head of its Italian Squad and went to Sicily to investigate the background of some New York criminals. He was killed in Palermo in 1909.

Rockwell, John. *Sinatra: An American Classic.* New York: Rolling Stone Press, 1984. 251 pp. Illus. with 157 photographs, 29 in color. A biography by the music critic of *The New York Times.*

Roselli, Bruno. *Vigo: A Forgotten Builder of the American Republic.* Boston: The Stratford Co., 1933. 280 pp. Italian-born Francesco Vigo, a fur trader in the Northwest at the time of the American Revolution, aided George Rogers Clark with money and information to defeat the British at Fort Vincennes, ending British influence in the Northwest.

Schiavo, Giovanni. *Antonio Meucci: Inventor of the Telephone.* New York: Vigo Press, 1985. 288 pp. Illus.

ACKNOWLEDGMENTS

A book such as this can hardly be considered the result of one individual's effort, because there are numerous people, each in his own way, who have made a considerable contribution to the final product. Although I am the author-editor-producer of this book, there are two people who were my prime collaborators, to whom I want to express my appreciation: A. Bartlett Giamatti and Remigio U. Pane.

A. Bartlett Giamatti prepared a brilliant and passionate commentary which served as the inspiration for my planning the visual organization of this book. Although his essay was based on my picture and text research, after reading it I realized that its style suggested the grand scale of an opera. Thus a filmic opera became the metaphor for the order and rhythm of the text, images and pagination.

Remigio U. Pane served as my sole consultant and prepared an exceptional bibliography, which has no equals. However, his contribution to the shape and content of this book far exceeds the bibliography. His encyclopedic knowledge of Italian American and Italian social and cultural history pervades every page. Beyond that, his endless energy and keen sensitivity to the appropriateness of ideas, images and words were always available to me.

Although he was never involved in the day-to-day preparation of this book, Dr. Alfred Rotondaro, Executive Director of The National Italian American Foundation, provided continuous guidance on matters of significance that shaped its final content. Though I had nurtured the idea of a book on Italian Americans for over ten years, it could not have become a reality if my editor, Robert Stewart (to whom I was introduced by my agent, Joseph Spieler), had not proposed doing such a book. As an editor, Robert Stewart provided me with the kind of freedom I find necessary.

This is a book of documentary text and images drawn from public archives and family collections in this country and in Italy. Though I did all the text research and some of the picture research myself, the visual quality of this book results from the assistance I obtained from the following people. Diane Hamilton, an expert on the picture collections in Washington, D.C., discovered remarkable images at The Library of Congress, the National Archives and the Smithsonian Institution. Shari Segel researched public and private sources in New York and was able to find some treasures in the special collections of The New York Public Library. Robert Tuggle, Archivist of the Metropolitan Opera, was extremely helpful in making available unusual material from his archives. Charles Sachs of the Staten Island Historical Society and A. Mae Seeley of the Garibaldi Meucci Museum were also helpful in making material from their collections available. I was able to benefit from Alan Teller's experienced eye and intimate knowledge of Chicago's social and cultural history. San Francisco is well-represented throughout the book because of four individuals: Karen Larsen's knowledge of picture sources in San Francisco was invaluable and led me to some exceptional photographs. Richard Monaco was extremely helpful and generous in making photographs by his grandfather, J. B. Monaco (an outstanding and yet-to-be-heralded photographer), available to me. I would like to pay tribute to the remarkable collection of San Francisco Italian historical photographs assembled by Alessandro Baccari and to thank him for his willingness to share these treasures with me. Frank Spadarella was equally generous with the excellent photographs that he collected for an exhibition at the San Mateo County Historical Society. In Philadelphia, I want to thank Gail Stern, Museum Director, and David Sutton, Archivist, of the Balch Institute for Ethnic Studies, for their assistance, and Grace

Russoniello, who organized the Balch Institute's exhibition about Italian Americans in the greater Philadelphia area, from which I benefited greatly. David Nasby of The Seagram Museum in Waterloo, Ontario, and Brian St. Pierre of The Wine Institute in San Francisco were helpful in my search for documentation of the wine industry. Joelen Mulvaney of the Aldrich Public Library in Barre, Vermont, gathered some exceptional photographs from local families, and these were made available to me.

In addition to utilizing private and public archives, I was able to obtain other material from friends. Ray Contrucci has preserved a remarkable group of family records and photographs which have contributed a great deal to this book. Susan Sichel made her photographs and those of the Panella family available. Giocondo Jacuzzi assembled a considerable amount of material documenting his family's history, from which I was able to make my selection. Al Striano and Rick Troiano provided me with their family photographs, which added to the highly personal quality of this book.

In Italy, I was assisted by a number of people. In Rome, Father Gian Fausto Rosoli, Director of the Centro Studi Emigrazione, was helpful, putting the resources of his exceptional study center at my disposal and locating other materials. Maria Teresa Contini facilitated my obtaining photographs from the collections of the Gabinetto Fotografico Nazionale of the Instituto Centrale per il Catalogo e la Documentazione. In particular I want to thank Maria Vitale for her tireless efforts in coordinating and expediting the procurement of photographs from a variety of sources in Rome. In Florence, George Tatge of Archivi Alinari made it possible for me to utilize this remarkable resource and introduced me to a number of other people who were of considerable assistance. Also in Florence, I want to thank Ferruccio Malandrini for letting me see and use some of the treasures of his exceptional private collection of photographs. In Milan, I am grateful to Iva Bergamini, Director of Communications Services, IBM Italia, for having suggested that I contact Cesare Colombo, in whom I discovered a person with an exceptional knowledge of the history of photography in Italy and someone more than willing to share information and resources. Roberto Spampinato, Director of Fototeca 3M in Milan, has created a remarkable photographic archive and was generous in allowing me to use it. Also in Milan, the staff of the Fototeca Touring Club Italiano was very helpful. Jimmy Fox of Magnum Photos in Paris provided me with a number of valuable suggestions, and Elizabeth Gallin of Magnum Photos in New York assisted me in my search through the archives. At Archive Pictures, Ann Schneider was very helpful.

For text research, my starting point was the library of the Center for Migration Studies, Staten Island, New York, the leading study and research center for Italian American subjects. I want to thank CMS librarian Diane Zimmerman for her assistance. The New York Public Library, The Library of Congress and Dartmouth College Library were other sources for my text research.

In one way or another, many other individuals made contributions that I would like to acknowledge. Dr. Ennio Troili, Deputy Director of the Istituto Italiano di Cultura in New York, wrote letters of introduction to archives and libraries in Italy. Anna Lomax Chairetakis provided a number of valuable suggestions. Marjorie Hunt of the Smithsonian Institution's Folklife Program was helpful. Both Steve Zeitlin and Susan Slyomovics of City Lore made their outstanding photographic collection available to me. Martha Cooper, who has devoted the last six years to photographing ethnic traditions in New York, has created hundreds of marvelous images, a few of which appear in this book. Martha was

aided in locating and identifying subjects for her photographs by Joseph Sciorra, an accomplished folklorist who provided me with the detailed caption information for her photographs. Ethel Wolvovitz has dedicated herself to documenting Italian American life in the New York metropolitan area and supplied some of her remarkable photographs for this book.

Marcia Lesser was helpful with editorial consultation and Mary Lou Risley was of great assistance to A. Bartlett Giamatti in typing his manuscript. Nancy Vickers, associate professor of Italian and French at Dartmouth College, produced readable translations of the Italian texts, and Alvino Fantini of the Experiment for International Living assisted with correspondence. Gene Garthwaite, professor of history at Dartmouth College, provided Arabic transliterations used in Mr. Giamatti's essay. Sister Margherita Marchione made available the color transparency of a miniature portrait of Philip Mazzei and text from her edited works of Mazzei.

I also wish to thank Martin Moskof and his staff for the graphic design of this book and for their dedicated attention to its many complex details. Ken Coburn of Interprint has guided its printing through many difficulties. And I want to thank my wife, Mary, who has taken time from her own work to assist me in numerous ways throughout the entire history of this project.

—Allon Schoener

PICTURE SOURCES

The following abbreviations have been used:

Alinari	Archivi Alinari, Florence, Italy
Archive	Archive Pictures, New York, NY
Autorino	Anthony Michael Autorino, Lambertville, NJ
Baccari	Alessandro Baccari, San Francisco, CA
Balch	Balch Institute for Ethnic Studies, Philadelphia, PA
Bancroft	The Bancroft Library, University of California, Berkeley, CA
Barre	Aldrich Public Library, Barre, VT
Bettmann	The Bettmann Archive, New York, NY
Biblioteca	Biblioteca di Storia Moderna e Contemporanea, Rome, Italy
BL	The British Library, London, England
BOA	Bank of America, San Francisco, CA
Boiardi	Mrs. Hector Boiardi, Cleveland, OH
Bostonian	Bostonian Society, Boston, MA
CHS	California Historical Society, San Francisco, CA
City Lore	City Lore, New York, NY
Colony	Italian Swiss Colony Winery, Asti, CA
Contrucci	Ray Contrucci, Rochester, MI
Cribari	Cribari Family, Modesto, CA
CSI	Centro Studi Emigrazione, Rome, Italy
DC Library	District of Columbia Library, Washington, DC
Eureka	Eureka Savings and Loan, North Beach Museum, San Francisco, CA
FD	Frank Driggs Collection, Brooklyn, NY
Fototeca 3M	Fototeca 3M, 3M Italia, Milan, Italy
Gabinetto	Gabinetto Fotografico Nazionale, Istituto Centrale per il Catalogo e la Documentazione, Rome, Italy
Gamma-Liaison	Gamma-Liaison Agency, New York, NY
Harvard	Harvard University Archives, Cambridge, MA
ILGWU	International Ladies Garment Workers Union, New York, NY
Jacuzzi	Giocondo Jacuzzi, Fort Lee, NJ
LC	The Library of Congress, Washington, DC
Magnum	Magnum Photos, New York, NY
Malandrini	Ferruccio Malandrini, Florence, Italy
MCNY	Museum of the City of New York, New York, NY
Metropolitan Archives	Metropolitan Opera Archives, New York, NY
MMA	The Metropolitan Museum of Art, New York, NY
Monaco	J. R. Monaco, San Francisco, CA
NA	National Archives, Washington, DC
NYPL	The New York Public Library, New York, NY
NYPL Dance	The New York Public Library, Dance Collection, New York, NY
NYPL Music	The New York Public Library, Music Collection, New York, NY
Peabody	Peabody Museum, Salem, MA
Philadelphia	Philadelphia Orchestra, Philadelphia, PA
PML	The Pierpont Morgan Library, New York, NY
Primoli	Fondazione Primoli, Rome, Italy
PRO	Public Record Office, London, England
Seagram	The Seagram Museum, Waterloo, Ontario, Canada
Sforzesco	Archivio Fotografico, Castello Sforzesco, Milan, Italy
SFPL	San Francisco Public Library, San Francisco, CA
SHSW	State Historical Society of Wisconsin, Madison, WI
Sichel	Susan Sichel, Marlboro, VT
SIHS	Staten Island Historical Society, Staten Island, NY
SMCHS	San Mateo County Historical Society, San Mateo, CA
Smithsonian	Smithsonian Institution, Washington, DC
Striano	Al Striano, New York, NY
Time	Time Magazine, New York, NY
Sygma	Sygma, New York, NY
TCI	Fototeca Touring Club Italiano, Milan, Italy
UIC	Italian American Collection, Special Collections, The University Library, University of Illinois at Chicago, Chicago, IL
UV	Library, University of Virginia, Charlottesville, VA
Valentine	Valentine Museum, Richmond, VA

TEXT SOURCES

Chapter One
Italian Culture in America / 1492–1880

"Discovery of the New World," Christopher Columbus. From *The Four Voyages of Christopher Columbus*, edited and translated by J. M. Cohen. Baltimore: Penguin Books, 1969, pp. 37–39, 51–56.

"An Appraisal of Columbus's Discovery," Girolamo Benzoni. From *History of the New World* by Girolamo Benzoni. London: The Hakuylt Society, 1857, pp. 17–21.

"'On the Principles of the American Revolution,'" Philip Mazzei. From *Philip Mazzei: Selected Writings and Correspondence, Volume 1. 1765–1788*, edited by Margherita Marchione. Prato: Cassa di Risparmio e Deposito di Prato, 1983, pp. 68–70.

"The Introduction of Italian Opera," Lorenzo Da Ponte. From *Memoirs of Lorenzo Da Ponte*, edited by Elisabeth Abbott, 1959. New York: Dover Publications, 1967, pp. 31–33.

"Garibaldi on Staten Island." From *Autobiography of Giuseppe Garibaldi, Volume 2. 1849–1872*, translated by A. Werner. New York: Howard Fertig, 1971, pp. 54–57.

"Controversy About Brumidi's Frescoes in the Capitol." From *The New York Daily Tribune*, May 31, 1858.

Chapter Two
The Old Country / Turn-of-the-Century Italy

"'Everybody works. There is poverty,'" Pascal D'Angelo. From *Son of Italy*, by Pascal D'Angelo. New York: Macmillan, 1924, pp. 13, 21–22, 46–49.

"The Italian Attitude Toward Emigration," Antonio Mangano. From *Charities*, April 4, 1908.

"Against the Supposed Concern of the Bourgeoisie for the Emigrants." From *La Plebe*, no. 18, October 9, 1876, appearing in *L'emigrazione nella storia d'Italia, 1868–1975* by Zeffiro Ciuffoletti and Maurizio degl' Innocenti. Florence: Vallecchi, 1978.

"Letter from *Contadini* in Northern Italy to the Minister of the Interior." From *La Plebe*, no. 24, November 25, 1876, appearing in *L'emigrazione nella storia d'Italia, 1868–1975* by Zeffiro Ciuffoletti and Maurizio degl' Innocenti. Florence: Vallecchi, 1978.

"Serious Riots in the Streets of Milan." From *Corriere della Sera*, May 8–9, 1898.

Chapter Three
New Lives in the New World / 1881–1914

"The Trauma of Departing from a Sicilian Village," Angelo Mosso. From *Vita moderna degli Italiani* by Angelo Mosso. Milan: Fratelli Treves, 1896, pp. 11–15.

"The Emigrants' Lament in Song." From *Canti dell'emigrazione*. Milan: Garzanti, pp. 56–57, 80–82.

"Conditions Endured by Emigrants Aboard Ship," Edmondo De Amicis. From *On Blue Water* by Edmondo De Amicis, translated by Jacob B. Brown. New York: G. P. Putnam's Sons, 1907, pp. 1–11.

"The Italians of New York," Jacob Riis. From *How the Other Half Lives* by Jacob Riis. New York: Charles Scribner's Sons, 1890, pp. 43–47.

"Arriving in Boston," Constantine Panunzio. From *The Soul of an Immigrant* by Constantine Panunzio. New York: Macmillan, 1921, pp. 227–230.

"A Son Writes to His Parents in Siena," G. Battista Turchi. From the collection of Ferrucio Malandrini, Florence.

"Miserable Working Conditions." From *Forum*, April 1893.

"The Italians of California," Marius J. Spinello. From *Sunset*, January 1905.

Chapter Four
Success and Disappointments / 1915–1929

"Emigrating in the 1920s," Luigi Barzini. From *O America: When You and I Were Young* by Luigi Barzini. New York: Harper & Row, 1977, pp. 78–81, 171–173.

"Returning Home," Constantine Panunzio. From *The Soul of an Immigrant* by Constantine Panunzio. New York: Macmillan, 1921, pp. 303–307.

"The Giannini Success Story." From *The New York Times*, October 30, 1927.

"Caruso's Silver Jubilee," From *The World*, March 28, 1919.

"The Last Statement of Bartolomeo Vanzetti." From *The Sacco-Vanzetti Case*, vol. 5. Mamaroneck, NY: Paul P. Appel, 1969, pp. 4896–4900.

Chapter Five
Immigrants and Their Children / 1930–1945

"A Second-Generation View," Angelo P. Bertocci. From "Memoir of My Mother" by Angelo P. Bertocci. *Harper's Magazine*, vol. 175, June 1937, pp. 8–19.

"'Breaking Away,'" Jerre Mangione. From *Mount Allegro: A Memoir of Italian American Life* by Jerre Mangione. New York: Columbia University Press, 1981, pp. 207–209, 223–224.

"Emigrating in 1939," Riccardo Massoni. From *American Mosaic: The Immigrant Experience in the Words of Those Who Lived It* by Joan Morrison and Charlotte Fox Zabusky. New York: E. P. Dutton, 1980, pp. 174–181.

"Italian Americans, Fascism and the War," Constantine Panunzio. From *The Yale Review*, vol. 31, 1941–1942, pp. 771–782.

"600,000 Italians No Longer Regarded as Enemy Aliens," Carlo Sforza and Gaetano Salvemini. From *The Nation*, vol. 155, November 7, 1942.

Chapter Six
From Little Italy to Front Page / Since 1945

"Second-Generation Teenagers," Francis A. J. Ianni. From *The Annals of The American Academy of Political and Social Science*, vol. 338, November 1961, pp. 74–78.

"'I Am Another Italian Success Story,'" Mario Puzo. From *The Immigrant Experience*, edited by Thomas G. Wheeler. New York: Dial Press, 1971, pp. 35–39, 48–49.

"A Recent Immigrant," Mario Lucci. From *American Mosaic: The Immigrant Experience in the Words of Those Who Lived It* by Joan Morrison and Charlotte Fox Zabusky. New York: E. P. Dutton, 1980, pp. 361–364.

"Mafia Myths and Mafia Facts." From "The Big Lie About Organized Crime: An *Attenzione* Magazine Symposium, *Attenzione*, vol. 2, no. 2, February 1980, pp. 50–59.

"Coming Into Their Own," Stephen S. Hall. From *The New York Times Sunday Magazine*, May 15, 1983.

INDEX

A

Abbott, Berenice, *180*
Abruzzi, Italy, 41
  dialect of, 17
  Popoli, *116*
Acculturation. *See* Assimilation
Adolescence. *See* Teenagers
Aeneid, The (Virgil), *12–13*
Agnese, Battista, *10–11*
Agriculture
  machinery in, *46–47*
  pump company, *155*
  seasonal workers in, *175–176*
  vineyards, 112–113, *176–177*
Albanese, Lucia, *206*
Albemarle County, Virginia, *14*, 31
Alberghetti, Anna Maria, *206*
Al Capone (movie), *211*
Alda, Alan, *211*
Alfonso V, king of Portugal, 28
Alitalia Airlines, 216
Allen, Ethan, *174*
Alto Adige, *13*, 44
America, Spanish expeditions in, 25–30
  See also specific areas, cities
America (de Bry), *28*
America in Search of Itself (White), 229
Americanization. *See* Assimilation
American Revolution, *14*, 188
American Sociological Association, 232
Andretti, Mario, *210*
Annin Flag Company, Verona, New Jersey, *166*
Antonini, Luigi, *174*
Apollo Fife and Drum Corps, Chicago, *130*
Arcaro, Eddie, *204*
Argentina, 191
Artists, Italian American, 37, 229. *See also* specific artists
Art of Dancing, The (Ferrero), *36*
Arthur, Jean, *187*
Asolo, Italy, *131*
Assimilation, 16, 22, *143–145*
  Americanization schools and, *80–81*, 148
  suburbs and, *169–170*
  See also Immigrants
Assisi, Italy, 168
Associations for immigrants, 18
  in Boston, 71
  mutual aid, 77, *159*, 188, *197–198*
Asti, California, 112
Atlantic City, New Jersey, gambling in, 225–226
Atlantic Macaroni Company, Long Island City, New York, *180*
Attività Italiane in California, *157*
Austen, Alice, *73*
Avis Corporation, *196*

B

Baccari, Edith Fantozzi, *125*, *153*
Bacigalupi, James, 155
Bacigalupi, M. S., haberdashery, San Francisco, *156*
Balbo, Italo, 189
Ballet, *36*
Baltimore-Washington 250-mile race (1925), *163*
Bancitaly Corporation, *154–155*
Bancroft, Anne, *200*

Bank(s)
  foreign, 71
  Italian American, *104–105*, 154–155
  See also specific banks
Bank of America. *See* Bank of Italy, U.S.
Bank of Italy, U.S., *104–105*, 154–155
Bankitaly Company, 154–155
Barber of Seville, The, *32–33*
Barbershop, Chicago, *156*
Bari, Italy, 150–151
Barre, Vermont, *103*, *118–119*, 122
Barzini, Ettore, 144
Barzini, Luigi, 16, *143–144*
Baseball, *83*, 143, *204–205*, *209–210*, 216
Bassetti, Augusto, 18, *76–77*
Batta, Frank, *151*
Battaglia, Salvatore, 20
Battistesa, Domenico, and sons, *124*
Bava-Beccaris, General, 55
Bavasi, Buzzi, *210*
Bazan, Ernesto, *217–218*, 222
Beck, James M., 158
Beltrami, J. C., *30*
Benedetti, Francesca (Mrs. Francesco Contrucci), *47*
Benediction of animals, *51*
Benedict, Michael, 229
Benzoni, Girolamo, *28*
Berkeley, California, *155*
Bernardin, Joseph Cardinal, *196*, 229
Berra, Yogi, *204*
Biblioteca delle tradizioni popolari siciliane (Pitrè), 19
Biddle, Attorney General, 190
Bigotry, 21–23
  Mafia and, 18–19, *224–227*
  See also Discrimination
Billy the Kid, 21
Biltmore Hotel, New York City, 144
Blacks, Italian Americans and, *84*
Blessed Mother Incoronata, street procession, Chicago, *181*
Blood of My Blood (Gambino), 224
Bocce, *51*, *162*, 197, *236*
Boiardi, Hector, *186*
Bonanno family, 226
Bonfanti, Marietta, *36*
Bonfanti Ballet Troupe, *36*
Bonnet, Georges, 191
Books for immigrants, *76–77*, 79. *See also* by title
Bootblacks, *73*
Borgnine, Ernest, *211*
Boris Godunov, *206*
Boston
  Boston University, 167
  Copp's Hill, 70
  Faneuil Hall, 70
  immigration to, 70–74
  North End, *70–71*
  Old North Church, 70, *129*
  Olympic Theatre, *36*
  Tea Party, 71
  See also Little Italy, Boston
Bozeman, Montana, *171*
Brady, Mathew, *36*
Braintree, Massachusetts, 165
"Bread and Roses" festival, ILGWU Italian Local No. 89, *174*
Brianza, Italy, 60

Bridgeton, New Jersey, *175–176*
Brignoli, Pasquale, 158
Briscola, 169
Bronx, The, New York, *218–219*
Brooklyn, New York, *217–218*
  Academy of Music, 158
  Bensonhurst, 220, 232
  bocce in, *236*
  Carroll Gardens, *234*
  Dyker Heights, *223*
  housing in, 222
  Williamsburg, *234–235*, 242
  yard shrines, *234–235*
Brumidi, Constantino, 9, *15*, *37–38*
Bruno, D. A. (Tony), *157*
Buon Gusto Sausage Factory, San Francisco, *156*
Burlington County, New Jersey, *176*

C

Cabot, John, *30*
Cabot, Sebastian, *30*
Caboto, Giovanni. *See* John Cabot
Cabrini, Mother Frances, *128*
Cádiz, Spain, 29
Calabria, Italy, 46
Calamecca, Italy, 46
Califano, Joseph, *230*
California, Italians of, 112–115, 122–124. *See also* specific cities
California Promotion Committee, 114
Campania, Italy, 229
Campanini, Italo, 158
Campobasso, Italy, 77
Canada, British claim to, *30*
Canary Islands, 25, 29
Cangelosi, Mary (Mrs. T. J. Lampson), *161*
Canova, Antonio, 37
Capone, Al, 188, *211*
Capra, Frank, *187*
Carlino, Rose (Mrs. Dominick Justave), *160*
Carnegie Hall, *206*
Carpanetto, Francesco, 35
Carrara, Italy, *43*
Carter, Jimmy, *230*
Cartographers, *10–11*
Caruana, Lillian, 235
Caruso, Enrico, *133*, *136–139*, 158
Carvers, stone, 37, *100–101*, 152
Casale, Tony ("Bologna"), *98*
Casinos, 225–226
Castellano, Paul, 227
Castellucci, Antonio, *183*
Castellucci, Maria Fanella (Mrs. Antonio), *183*
Castiglione, Baldassare, 19
Castillo, president of Argentina, 191
Castrofilippo, Italy, 58
Cataldi shoe store, San Francisco, *107*
Catholic Church. *See* Roman Catholic Church
Catholic Youth Organization, 197
Cavalli, Giorgio, *79*
CBS, 225–226
Centennial of the Statue of Liberty, *244*
Central America, Garibaldi's trip to, 35
Cepaglia, Philip, *151*
Chamberlain, Neville, 191
Champagne, *113*
Charles, Ezzard, *204*

Charles I, king of England, 54
Charlestown, Massachusetts, 165
Chef Boy-ar-dee foods, *186*
Chiarugi Brothers store, Chicago, *156*
Chicago
  All Saints Church, *182*
  barbershop, *156*
  Bratta family, *171*
  Chicago Fair, 189
  Chicago Heights, *162*
  Chicago National Gas-Pipe Company, 91
  Damante Band, *163*
  40 East 115th Street, *156*
  ghettos in, 15–16
  street scene, *159*
  string quintet, *162*
Chrysler Corporation, *196*, 229
Churches, immigrant. *See* Roman Catholic Church; specific cities
Churchill, Winston, 190
Cigar companies, *157*
Cimino, Michael, *212*
Cincinnatus, 38
Citizenship, U.S., *61*, 189
  Americanization schools, *80–81*, 148
  classes, *148*, *172*
City of Palermo, 145
Civil authority, distrust of, 12, 19–21, 72
Civiletti, Benjamin R., 232
Civil War, U.S., 18, 21, 35
Clark, Ramsey, 227
Clothing factories, *106*, 152
Coal mines, Pennsylvania, *47*
Code of secrecy, 19–20. *See also* Mafia
Colchester, Connecticut, 168
Collins, Marjorie, *166*, *170*, *172*, *178*, *180*, *192*, *193*
Colony restaurant, New York City, 144
Columbia College, 32
Columbia Journalism Review, 226
Columbus, Bartholomew, *28–29*
Columbus, Christopher, 24–25
  logbook of, 25
  New World, discovery by, *25–27*
Columbus Day celebrations, *148*, 190, 228
Communist Party, 226
Community reading room, New York City, 77
Congregation of the Missionary Sisters of the Sacred Heart, 128
Congress, House Committee investigating un-American activities, 189
Congressional Medal of Honor, *194*
Conscription, Italian, 54, 74
Construction workers, *91*, *153*
Contadini. *See* Peasants
Contarini, Matteo, 26
Conte Verde, 145
Conte Rosso, 147
Contractors, *90–91*. *See also* Middlemen
Contrucci, family, *146–147*
Contrucci, Francesco (Frank), *61*, *146–147*
Coolidge, Calvin, *157*
Cooper, Martha, *232*, *234–237*, *240*, *242*
Coppola, Francis Ford, *212*, 229
Cornwallis Sues for Cessation of Hostilities Under the Flag of Truce, *39*
Corriere della Sera, 226
Cosa Nostra. *See* Mafia
Così Fan Tutte, 32
Courtier, The (Castiglione), 19

Covello, Leonard, *82*
Cowboys, 21, *171*
Crane operators, *153*
Cribari, Angelo, *176*
Crime, 19–20, 224–227. *See also* Mafia
Crime Confederation (Salerno), 224
Cromwell, Oliver, 54
Cuba, 172
Cuomo, Andrea, 229
Cuomo, Mario M., *196*, 229, *231*
Cuomo family, *231*

D

Dagioli's New Method of Singing, 36
Damante Band, *163*
D'Amato, Alfonse M., *196*
Damone, Vic, *203*
Dancers, *36*
D'Angelo, Pascal, 15, 41
Dante, 9, 17
Da Ponte, Lorenzo, 32
D'Archia, Luisa (Mrs. Peter Striano), *127*
Davis, Dixie, 227
De Amicis, Edmondo, 62–65
DeBartolo, Edward J., Sr., 229
De Bernardinas, Pietro, *150*
de Bry, T., *28*
Debs, Eugene, 165
Dedham, Massachusetts, *165*
Deer Hunter, The, *212*
de Las Casas, Bartolomé, 25
Della Croce, Agnello, 227
Dello Joio, Norman, *187*
del Piombo, Sebastiano, *24*
De Martino's fish market, New York City, *180*
Democracy, representative, 32
De Niro, Robert, Sr., *215*
De Niro, Robert, Jr., *212*
de Paolo, Peter, *163*
De Reszke, Jean, 158
Detroit, *47*
Dialects, 17
Diamond Jubilee Preakness, *204*
Di Constanza restaurant, New York City, *179*
DiMaggio, Joe, *186*, *205*, *209*, 229
Di Pietro, V., *107*
Discrimination, 12
Immigration Acts (1921, 1924), 188
lynching and, *84–85*
prejudice, 21–22
Di Suvero, Mark, *215*
Ditchdiggers, 144
Dizionario siciliano-italiano, 19–20
Dolce, Louis C., *150*
Domenici, Pete V., *196*
Don Giovanni, 32–33
Dreamgirls, 229
Dulbecco, Renato, *230*
Dump settlements, 69
Durante, Jimmy, *202*
Duse, Eleanora, *131*

E

Earthquakes, *140–141*, 154
East River National Bank, 154–155
Eastwood, Clint, 21
Education
college, 167
distinctions, 17
Italian American studies, 224
Italian Americans in, 229
religious, 199
versus work values, 23, 167
See also Public schools
Elizabeth I, queen of England, 32
Ellis Island, New York, 12, *64*, 229, 245
detention cell at, *67*
1905, *160*
1926, *143*
processing immigrants, *66*
Emigrants
aboard ship, *56*, 62–65
economic rationale of, 14, 41–56
Italian bourgeoisie concern about, 46, 53–54
language barriers for, 16–18
1920s, 143–145
1939, 172–173
northern Italian, 14–16
return to Italy of, 47
rights of, 53
Sicilian, 14–15

trauma of, 53, 57–61
England
American Revolution against, 31–32
Columbus and, 28–29
Mazzei's critique of, 32
English language
classes in, *149*, *172*, 216
difficulty of mastering, 16–17, 69
manual for, *76–77*
pronunciation of, 18
See also Public schools
Equality, political, 13
Erie Canal, *91*
Ethiopian war, 189
Ethnicity
ethnic succession, 226
self-esteem and, 232
Ethnic colony. *See* Little Italy
Ettor, Joseph, *103*
Evans, Walker, *183*
Ewen Breaker, Pennsylvania Coal Company, *94–95*
Extortion, 224

F

Fall River, Massachusetts, *125*
Families
acculturative experience, 199
community and, 229
as extension of self, 12
importance of, 9, 19, 23
income of, 232
loyalty to, 22
Mafia and, 224–227
patriarchal, 23, 197
peasant, 197
separation of, 41, 57
sibling businesses, *116–117*
Farm workers, 41–45, 112, 175–177
Fascism
Attorney General Biddle's speech about, 190
Italian Americans and, 188–189
Fatalism, in Italians, 12–14
Faust, 132
Federal Bureau of Investigation, 224
Cosa Nostra file, 225
Tables of Organization of Crime Families, 19
Federal Bureau of Narcotics, 225
Ferdinand, king of Spain, 26, 29
Fermi, Enrico, *186*
Ferraguti, Arnaldo, 62–63
Ferraro, Geraldine A., *196*
Ferrero, Edward, 36
Ferretti, Fred, 224–227
Festivals and ceremonies, *51*, *148*, *174*, *181*, 190, *198*, *228*, *234–237*, *242–243*
Fior d'Italia Restaurant, San Francisco, *111*
Florence, Italy, 9, *14*, 168
Flynn, James, 225
Foggia, Italy, 150–151
Folklore, Italian, 19
Folk songs, 60, *195*
Ford Motor Company, *47*
Franklin, Benjamin, *14*, 31
Fraternal organizations, 18. *See also* Immigrants, associations of
Freed, Leonard, *196*, *198–199*
Free Italian Legion, 190–191
Freeman, Bishop James, *152*
French Revolution, 188
Fresco paintings, 15, 37–39
Fresno, California, 112

G

Gaeta, Italy, 168
Gajani, Guglielmo, 37
Galante, Carmine, 226
Galileo, 62–65
Gallup poll, 188
Gambino, Richard, 224–227
Gambino family, 227
Gambling, 224–226
Garfield, John, 207
Garibaldi, Giuseppe, 9, *14*, 34, 188–189
Garibaldi Guard, *35*
Garment industry, *103*, 208
Gatti-Casazza, Giulio, *133–134*, 158, *184*
Gazzara, Ben, *211*
General Electric, *193*

Genoa, Italy, 232
emigration from, *59*, 63–67
fishermen, *115*
railroad station, *47*
Genovese, Vito, 227
Germany. *See* World War II
Giaimo, Grace (Mrs. Emilio Panella), *160*
Giamatti, A. Bartlett, *196*, 229
Giannini, A. H., *155*
Giannini, A. P., 16, 154–155
Giannini, Claire, *159*
Giannini, L. M., *159*
Giannini, Lloyd, *159*
Giannini, Virgil, *159*
Giglio festival, *242–243*
Giovannitti, Arturo, *103*
Girl of the Golden West, The, *133*, *136–137*
Giuliani, Rudolph, 224
Gloucester, Massachusetts, *170*
Gobineau doctrines, 188
Godfather, The, *18*
Godfather, Part II, The, *207*, 226
Godparenthood, 198
Gold Rush, 112
Gomera Island, 29
Gottlieb, William, *203*
Gounod, Charles, *132*
Granacci, Francesco, 37
Grande dizionario della lingua italiana, 20
Grandi, Italian foreign minister, 189
Grand Trunk Railroad, Chicago, *153*
Greco, José, *206*
Green Bay Packers, *210*
Grido della Stirpe, 189
Grillo, Nick, *171*
Grucci fireworks, *244*
Guadalcanal, *194*
Guanahani, 25
Giulio Cesare, *145*
Gulf of Taranto, *47*
Gustozo family, *160*

H

Habits and Customs, Beliefs and Prejudices of the Sicilian People (Pitré), 19
Hall, Stephen S., 229, 232
Hamilton, Alexander, 15
Hannibal, 12
Harper's Weekly, *85*
Hartford, Connecticut, 98
Harvard University, *190*
Hennessy, David C., *85*, 224
Henry VII, king of England, 28, *30*
Hine, Lewis, *64*, *67*, *72*, *88*, *91–92*, *96–99*, *102*, *108–109*, *125*, *143*, *152*, *160*, *174*
History of the New World (Benzoni), 28
Hitler, Adolf, 189
Hoboken, New Jersey, *127*
Hollywood, California, *187*, 207
Honor system, U.S., 143
Hoover, Herbert, 189
Hoover, J. Edgar, 225
Horatio Greenough in His Studio in Florence, 33
Horst, *184*
Hotel workers, 144
Housing, 15–16
high urban, 199
residential, 197
suburban life, 169
Hubard, William James, 33
Hudson River, *27*

I

Iacocca, Lido A. (Lee), *196*, *228*, 229, *244*
Ianniello, Dominick, *241*
Ianni, Francis A. J., *197–199*
Illiteracy, 144, 207
I Mafiusi di' li Vicaria (Rizzotto), 20
"I'm Leaving for America," 60
Immigrants
acculturation of, 143–145
Americanization classes, *80–81*, *148*
associations of, 18, *77*, *159*, 188, *197–198*
caricature of, *65*
children of, 12, 167–195
distribution of, 88
distrust of authority, 12
ethnic succession theory, 226
exploitation of, 68–69, 88–92

generalizations about, 15
housing for, 15–16, 169, 197, 199
illiteracy, 207
language barriers, 16–17
lynching of, *84–85*
1930–1945, 167–195
occupational mobility of, 197
radicals, 165, 188
recent, 216
restriction movement, 172, 188, 225
return to Italy by, 150–151, 167
shipboard, *142*, *145*. *See also* specific ships
Spanish-speaking, 198
spiritual care of, *128*
typical female, 167
working conditions, 88–92, *93–103*
See also Emigrants; Italian Americans
Immigration Acts (1921, 1924), 172, 188, 225
Income tax, 54
Indians, 26
Indies, discovery of, 25–29
Innocenta, Oliva (Mrs. Francesco Contrucci), *46*
Intermarriage, 22
International Ladies Garment Workers Union (ILGWU), *102*, 174
International Workers of the World (IWW), *103*
Introdacqua, Italy, 41
Iron worker, *125*
Isabella, queen of Spain, 26, 29, *148*
Isola delle Femmine, Sicily, *115*
Italglish, 18
Italian Americans
ambivalence of, 12, 18
Californians, 112–115, 122–124
defined, 9, 12
described as born gamblers, 69
family values of, 9, 19, 23, 232
1492–1880, 25–39
gangsters, 18, 224–227
GIs, 22
homesickness of, 167
identity of, 21–22, 232
liberalized attitude toward, 190
lynching of, 84
rejection of ethnicity, 198
second-generation teenagers, 197–199
shared assumptions of, 12
social acceptance of, 199
social classes, 199
spectacular rise of, 228
white-collar workers, 232
Italian Chamber of Commerce, New York City, 154
Italian Fasci Abroad, 189
Italian language, 17–18
dialects, 17
opera and, 33
U.S. evolution of, 17, 32
Italian National Committee, 190–191
Italian School Young Men's Association, 77
"Italian Society of Victor Emanuel 3rd," Waukesha, Wisconsin, *120–121*
Italian Swiss Colony Vineyard, *112–113*
Italy
army of, 47
civil stability of, 9, 11, 188
country villas, 53
emigrants' return to, 150–151, 167
fascism and, 188–190
Golden Age of, 167
Hitler's descent into, 189
Montevideo Conference, 190
poverty in, 41
revolution of 1848, 20
tenant farmers in, 41–42
territorial divisions of, 88
turn-of-the-century, 41–56
urban teenagers, 199
Virgilian sentiment and, 13
See also specific persons, towns, regions
Iwo Jima, *194*

J

Jacuzzi Giovanni, *124*
Jacuzzi, Rachel, *155*
Jacuzzi, Teresa, *124*
Jacuzzi family, *201*
Jefferson, Thomas, *14–15*, 31, *33*
Jersey City, New Jersey, 229
Jesuit University of Santa Clara, California, 15

Jews
  bigotry toward, 21
  German, 172
  in ILGWU, *102*
  immigrant life of, 16, 172
  Italian, 22
  Sephardic, 16
Jokes, Italian, 21
Juilliard, A. D., 158
Justave, Dominick, *67, 160*
Justave family, *160*
Justice Department, 224–226

K

Kahn, Otto H., 158
Kennedy, Robert, 224–225
Kennedy Justice (Navasky), 224
Kingdom of the Two Sicilies, 14
Knights of Columbus, Chicago, *181*
Kotzebue, August Friedrich, 38
Krug Winery, *177*
Kwitny, Jonathan, 224

L

Laborers
  day, *175–176*
  exploitation of, 144
  home workshops, *93, 96–97*
  migrant, *97*
  occupational mobility of, 197
  railroad, 208
  sons of, 167
  tradition and, 88
  See also specific jobs
La Guardia, Fiorello H., *164, 186, 229*
Lake Garda region, immigrants from, *149*
Lake Maggiore, 144
Lampson (Lamposona), T. J., *161*
Land, emigration and, 15. *See also* Agriculture
Landowners, Italian
  absentee, 21
  cheap labor and, 53
Lange, Dorothea, *175*
Language. *See* specific language
Lanza, Mario, *203*
La Pizzo, Anna, *103*
La Place, Joe, *153*
La Plebe, 53, 54
LaSorda, Tommy, *229*
La Scala, *135, 214*
La Spezia, Italy, *63*
Latin America, Italians of, 191
Lawrence, Massachusetts, *99, 103*
Law enforcement agencies, organized crime and, 224–227
Lee, Russell, *176–177*
L'Elisir d'Amore, 158
Leoncavallo, Ruggiero, *138*
Leone, Sergio, 21
Le Prophète, 158
Library of Sicilian Popular Traditions (Pitré), 19
Library of the Traditions of the Ordinary Life of the Sicilian People (Pitré), 19
Libreria Italiana, San Francisco, *79*
Libro, Secondino, *99*
Liguria, Italy, 190
L'Illustrazione Italiana, 51, 53, 55, 60
Lippincott's Magazine, 19
Lippmann, Walter, 25
L'Italia, 130
L'Italo-Americano, 89
Literacy of immigrants, 16–17
Little Italy, Boston, *70–71*
Little Italy, New York City, *68–69, 75, 82, 179, 198–199, 217*
  choir boys in, *197*
  movement from, 198
  restaurants of, *241*
  See also New York City
Little Italy, Norristown, Pennsylvania, 197
Little Italy, San Francisco, *79. See also* San Francisco
Loansharking, 224
Logansport, Indiana, 91
Lombardi, Vince, *210*
Lombardo, Guy, *203*
Lombardy, Italy, 17, 88
Los Angeles, 112
  Dodgers, *210*
  Hollywood, *211–213*

LoSchiavo, John, 229
Luria, Salvador E., *196*
Lynchings, *84–85*

M

Maas, Peter, 225
Machiavelli, Niccolò, 19
McClellan Senate Subcommittee, 224, 227
McFadden Act, 154
McHale's Navy, 211
Madison, Wisconsin, State Historical Society Building, *100*
Maffia, Daniel, *196*
Mafia, 18
  myths about, 224–227
  national perception of, 224
  news reports of, 225–226
  Night of the Long Knives, 227
  origins of the word, 19–21
  pastoral theory of, 21
  Sicilian, 227
Mafia Mystique, The (Smith), 224
Magellan, Ferdinand, *10–11*
Malaria, 42
"Mama, Give Me a Hundred Lire," 60
Mangano, Antonio, 46
Mangione, Jerre, 169–170
Manhattan. *See* New York City
Manteo, Mike ("Papa"), 232
Maps, world, *10–11, 26*
Marble, *43*
Marca Petri cigars, *157*
Marca-Relli, Corrado, *215*
Marchioness of Montferrat, 33
Marciano, Rocky, *204*
Mario, Giovanni, 158
Marionette theater, *232*
Marriage of Figaro, The, 32
Marsala, Italy, 190
Marsella Band, Philadelphia, *131*
Martin, Billy (Alfred Manuel Pesano), *209, 229*
Martinelli, Mr., *123*
M*A*S*H, *211*
Massoni, Riccardo, 172
Mazzei, Philip, 9, *14,* 31–32
Mazzini, Giuseppe, 9, 20, 188
Mazzini Society, 189
Melrose Park, Illinois, *181*
Menotti, Gian-Carlo, *202*
Messina, Italy, *195*
Metropolitan Museum of Art, *38–39*
Metropolitan Opera, *134–139*
  Caruso's Silver Jubilee, 158
  directors of, 158
  Emergency Fund, 158
  opening night, *133*
  Toscanini at, *184*
Meucci, Antonio, *14,* 34
Mezzojuso, Italy, *194*
Michelangelo, *37,* 168
Middlemen, 16, 18
  exploitation by, 69, 90–91
  food, 209
Migrant laborers, *97, 175–176*
Milan, 168
  factories in, 55
  La Scala, *214*
  Piazza del Duomo, *55*
  railroad station, *57*
  riots in, 54–55
  street merchants, *49–50*
Military, Italian, *54–55. See also* World War I; World War II
Milling taxes, 54
Mr. Smith Goes to Washington, 187
Molfetta, Italy, 70, *150–151*
Molise, Italy, 46
Monaco, Dante, *140*
Monaco, J. B., *79, 123–124, 128, 131, 140*
Monaco, Katherine, *140*
Monaco, Louis, *81*
Monaco, Nina, *81*
Mondavi, Michael, *177*
Mount Allegro (Mangione), 169
Monte Majella, *41*
Montevideo, Uruguay, 35, 190
Montpelier, Vermont, *174*
Morlacchi, Giuseppina, *36*
Morra, 186
Mosso, Angelo, *57–59*
Mott Street Industrial School, New York City, *78*

Movie stars, as ideals, 170, 207
Moving business, *116*
Mozart, Wolfgang Amadeus, 32–33
Murder, Inc. (Turkis and Feder), 227
Music, opera, 32–33, 133–139, 158, *184*
Musicians' union, *202*
Mussolini, Benito, 173, 188, 190–191
Muti, Riccardo, *214*
Mutual aid societies, 77, *159,* 188, 197–198

N

Names, evolution of, *17*
Namuth, Hans, *215*
Napa, California, 112
Naples, Italy, 88, 150
  emigrants from, *60, 62, 69, 147*
  Ottaviano, *141*
  sidewalk vendor, *48*
  Street of Steps, *43*
  street scenes in, *50, 52*
  urban poor of, *41*
Napoleon, 37
Nation, The, 190, 224
National Cathedral, Washington, D.C., *152*
National Opinion Research Center, 232
National Organization of Italian-American Women, 232
National Organization for Women (NOW), 22, 229
Naturalization, 189
Navasky, Victor, 224–227
Nazism, 173, 189
NBC, 226
NBC Symphony Orchestra, *184–185*
Neighborhoods, Italian, 14, 198. *See also* Little Italy; specific cities
Neighborhood House, Madison, Wisconsin, *148*
Nelli, Umberto, 227
Newburgh, New York, *223*
Newfoundland, *10–11, 30*
New Haven, Connecticut, 114
New Mexico, 196
New Orleans
  Hennessy murder, 224
  L'Italo-Americano, 89
  lynching in, 85
Newspapers, 89
  Italian-language, 76
  New York, 143
  organized crime and, *226–227*
  See also specific newspapers
New World, pictorial images of, *26, 28–29*
New York Central Railroad, *207–208*
New York City, 64
  Benjamin Franklin High School, *82*
  Bleecker Street, *92, 180*
  Broadway, 173
  Broome Street, *102*
  cabinet maker in, *114*
  citizenship class, *172*
  Church of St. Vincent Ferrer, *131*
  City Hall Park, *73*
  Columbus Day parade, *228*
  East Harlem, *82*
  East 187th Street, *218*
  First Avenue, *180, 192*
  Fulton Fish Market, *238–239*
  Garibaldi in, *14,* 34–35
  Greenwich Avenue, *102*
  Greenwich Village, *179*
  harbor, *27*
  Hell's Kitchen, 207
  Italian American businesses, *105*
  Italian butcher shop, *192*
  Italian grocery, *108–109, 178*
  Jersey Street, *16, 79, 87*
  Leonard Street Public School, *77*
  Lower East Side, 68
  Macdougal Street, *179*
  Mulberry Street, *68–69, 75, 90, 143, 179, 198–199*
  opera in, 32–33, 158
  police department, 224
  restaurants, *110, 144, 179, 241*
  Roosevelt Street, *86*
  shoemaker, *167*
  Sixth Avenue Elevated, *88*
  Statue of Liberty, *244*
  tenement sweatshops in, *97–99*
  213 East 111th Street, *96*
  Union Square, *103*

Verrazzano's journey to, *10–11*
Yankees, *209*
  See also Little Italy, New York City; specific boroughs
New York Daily News, 143
New York Daily Tribune, The, 37, 68
New York Philharmonic, *184*
New York State Barge Canal, *91*
New York Symphony, *184*
New York Times, The, 143, 224, 226–227
New York Times Magazine, The, 196
Night of the Long Knives, 227
Niña, 25
Nixon, Richard, 224
Nobel Prize
  Medicine, *196,* 230
  Physics, 186
Norristown, Pennsylvania, 197
North American coast, map of, *26*
Nova Scotia, 30
Nuns, 197, *198*
Nuovo vocabolario (Traina), 19

O

Oakland, California, *201*
Omertà, 20
"On the Principles of the American Revolution" (Mazzei), 31–32
Opera. *See* Music, opera; specific operas
Orchards, *112–113. See also* Vineyards
Organ grinder, *73*
Organized crime, 18, 224–227. *See also* Mafia
Organized Crime Strike Force, 224
Ottaviano, Italy, *141*
Ovid, 41

P

Pacciardi, Randolfo, 190
Pacino, Al, 226
Padrone. See Middlemen
Pagliacci, 138, 158
Palermo, Italy, 88, *115,* 232
  Borgo, 19
  Mezzojuso, *194*
  prison, 20
Palisades, New Jersey, 208
Pallavelini, Mr., *123*
Palma di Cesnola, Louis, 38
Pan-American Conference of Free Italians, 190
Panella, Emilio, *160*
Panunzio, Constantine, 18, 70, *150–151,* 188
Paper box factory, *96*
Parente, Mark, *238–239*
Parini, Piero, 189
Paris, 172
Parks, Gordon, *170, 180*
Parma, Italy, *184*
Parochial schools, 197
Passport office, Italian, *61, 63*
Passport, U.S., Contrucci family, *146*
Pasta labels, *108*
Paterno, Joe, 229
Patrizi, Ettore, *130*
Patti, Adelina, *36*
Paul III, Pope, 38
Paulinus, St., *242*
Pavarotti, Luciano, *214*
Peasants
  governmental abuses and, 54
  immigration of, 41–56
  See also Emigrants
Pellagra, 54
Pennsylvania Railroad, *193*
Perugia, Italy, 168
Petri company, San Francisco, *157*
Petrillo, James C., *202*
Philadelphia
  Academy of Music, *36*
  Athletics, 205
  clothing factory, *106*
  day-laborer farms, *175*
  Di Marco family, *125*
  V. Di Pietro store, *107*
  Italian American businesses, *105*
  Leone family, *201*
  opera distance, 158
  Orchestra, *214*
  Shibe Park, *205*
Philanthropy, tradition of, 23

Piano factory, 74
Piedmont, Italy, 17, 88, 190
Pilgrimage in Europe and America, A
    (Beltrami), 30
Pinta, 25
Pinza, Ezio, 206
Pinzón, Martin Alonzo, 25
Piperini, Father Raffaele, 128
Pitcairn, Pennsylvania, 193
Pitré, Giuseppe, 19–21
Plachy, Sylvia, 213
Plymouth, Massachusetts, 165
Poker, 169
Politics, Italian Americans in, 229
Polo, Marco, 154
Pompeii, Italy, 38, 168
Porticello, Sicily, 115
Portugal, 28
Postcards, 74
Poverty, urban, 209
Pozzilli, Italy, 195
Prejudice, 112. See also Discrimination
President's Commission on Law
    Enforcement and Administration of
    Justice (1967), 224–225, 227
Priests, Italian, 197
Prima, Louis, 203
Primoli, Giuseppe, 43–45, 51–52, 55, 57
Prince, The (Machiavelli), 19
Principessa Mafalda, 142
Propaganda, fascist, 189
Public schools, 71, 77–81, 143, 197. See
    also Education
Puccini, Giacomo, 133
Puccio, Thomas, 224
Puglia, Italy, 150–151
Pulsano, Italy, 47
Putnam, General Israel, 38
Puzo, Mario, 207–209
Pyrospectaculars, 244

Q
Quakers, 37
Queens, New York, 222
    Jackson Heights, 195
    Queens College, 224

R
Racalmuto, Italy, 58
Racism, 21
Radical individualism, 20
Railroads, Italian, 150–151
Raphael, 37, 168
Reader's Digest, 225
Reconstruction, post–Civil War, 18
Red Star Line, 59
Religious festivals. See Festivals and
    ceremonies
Restaurant workers, 144
Restriction movement. See Immigration
    Acts
Revolutionary War, 70–71
Riccadonna restaurant, New York City, 110
Ricci, Corrado, 158
Ricigliamo, Italy, 181
Riis, Jacob, 16–17, 68, 78–79, 86–87, 102
River Plate, 24
Rizzotto, Giuseppe, 20
Rochester, New York, 152
Rodino, Peter, 208
Romagna, Italy, political exiles, 88
Roman Catholic Church
    American, 22
    Irish, 199
    nuclear arms and, 229
    religious processions, 181–182
    social groups, 129, 197
Roman Republic, 9, 32, 38
Rome
    Ariccia, 51
    Basilica of St. Paul, 38
    fresco painters of, 38
    Genzano, 44
    Pantheon, 33
    peasants in, 52
    Piazza Campo de' Fiori, 49
    Piazza Santa Croce in Gerusalemme, 55
    republican government of, 9, 32, 38
    Sistine Chapel, 37
    Via Veneto, 173
Ronzani Ballet Troupe, 36
Roosevelt, Franklin D., 173

Roosevelt, Theodore, 157
Rossini, 32–33
Rothstein, Arthur, 170–171, 176
Rotterdam, emigration from, 172
Rozelle, Pete, 210
Russian Ballet of Monte Carlo, 172
Rutgers University, 224, 247
Rutland, Vermont, 67, 174

S
Sacco, Nicola, 165
Sacco and Vanzetti trial, 22
St. Joseph's Day procession, Chicago, 182
St. Regis Hotel, New York City, 74
Salerno, Ralph, 224–227
Salesian associations, San Francisco, 83, 148
Salvemini, Gaetano, 189–191
Samnites, 41
San Francisco
    Bank of Italy in, 154–155
    blessing the fleet, 182
    Broadway, 111
    Columbus Avenue, 156
    construction workers in, 153
    Fisherman's Wharf, 114–115, 169
    Golden Gate Park, 130
    Grant Avenue, 106
    immigrants in, 112–115, 122–124
    Leavenworth Street, 140
    Montgomery Street, 104
    1906 earthquake, 140, 154
    North Beach, 79, 107, 156
    Presentation Convent School, 83
    restaurants of, 110–111
    Russian Hill, 140
    St. Mary's Park, 153
    Saints Peter and Paul Church, 80–81,
        83, 128, 161
    Telegraph Hill–Montgomery Street
        Baseball Team, 83
San Francisco Panama Pacific International
    Exhibition, 157
San Mateo County, California, 112, 122
Sansone-Pacelli, Carmela, 232
Santa Clara Valley, California, 112,
    154, 175
Santa Flavia, Italy, 115
Sant'Elia, Sicily, 115
Santini, Pasquale, 116
Santini, Pietro, 116
Sarazen, Gene, 164
Sardinian government, 35
Scalia, Antonin, 231
Scarpa, Mario, 153
Schultz, Dutch, 227
Scorsese, Martin, 196, 213, 229
Scranton, Pennsylvania, 67
    Justave wedding, 160
    mutual aid society, 159
Scribner's, 85
Seaford, Delaware, 97
Secret organizations. See Mafia
Seligsberg, Alfred E., 158
Sensano, Italy, 44
Sephardic Jews, 16
Seragnoli, Mr., 123
Seven Santini Brothers, 116
Sforza, Carlo, 189–190
Shepherds, 43
Sherman, Augustus Francis, 67
Shipboard life, 62–63, 64–67
Shoemaker, 102
Shoe-shine stand, 102
Shrine of Our Lady of Mt. Carmel, 235
Sicilian Vespers, 20, 227
Sicily, 40
    Arab domination of, 20
    dialects of, 17, 19–20
    emigration from, 14–15, 57, 85
    fishermen, 115
    illiteracy in, 144
    Kingdom of the Two Sicilies, 14
    Mafia and, 19
    primitive life of, 21
    theater of, 20, 232
    See also specific cities and towns
Siena, Italy, 74
Sierras, California, 112
Sinatra, Frank, 202, 209, 229
Sirey, Aileen Riotto, 232
Sistine Chapel, 37
Slums, 68, 86–87, 93, 96–97

Smeal, Eleanor Curti, 196, 229
Smith, Dwight, 224–227
Social mobility, 197
Social service houses, 71
Socialism, 188
    Italian, 188
    May Day parade, 55
Societies, fraternal, 18. See also
    Immigrants, associations of
Solari's Restaurant, San Francisco, 111
Sonoma County, California, 176–177
South American coast, map of, 26
Southington, Connecticut, 171
South Pittston, Pennsylvania, 94–95
Spaghetti westerns, 21
Spain
    Columbus and, 26, 28–29
    route to America, 10–11
Spinello, Marius J., 112–114
Sports, Italian Americans in, 229. See also
    specific athletes
Stafford, Texas, 161
Stallone, Sylvester, 213
Staten Island, New York, 14
    Bitetti's Grove, 127
    Garibaldi in, 34
    Rosebank, 235
    yard shrines, 235
Statue of Liberty, 13
Statue of Liberty–Ellis Island Foundation,
    244
Staying Alive, 213
Steinway & Sons, 132
Stella, Frank, 215
Stewart, Jimmy, 187
Stockton, California, 112
Stone carvers, 100–101, 152
Straw weavers, 44
Striano, Peter, 127
Stucco workshop, 101
Sulmona, Italy, 41
Supreme Court, U.S., 22, 231
Sweatshops, 97–99
Syndicalism, 188

T
Tallulah, Louisiana, 84
Tangier, 35
Taormina, Italy, 40
Tardieu Pierre-Alexandre, 14
Taxes, Italian, 54
Teenagers
    immigrants, 216
    second-generation, 197–199
Telephone, invention of, 14, 34
Tella, Alfred J., 232
Tenement sweatshops, 97–98
Teresa and Mimmo's restaurant, New York
    City, 241
Tetrazzini, Luisa, 135
Textile mills, 99, 103
Theft of a Nation (Cressey), 227
Thorwaldsen, Bertel, 38
Tojetti, Domenico, 131
Torlonia, Prince, 38
Tortolano, Angelina, 156
Tortolano, Antonio, 156
Toscanini, Arturo, 133, 184–185
Traviata, 206
Travolta, John, 213
Trinchieri, Father Oreste, 128
Trombetta, Domenico, 189, 191
Tulare, California, 112
Turchi, G. Battista, 74
Tuscany, Italy, 44–45, 116
    regional speech, 17
    political exiles, 88
    See also specific towns

U
Unemployment, immigrant, 74
University Club, Boston, 165
University of California, 112, 188
University of Florence, 190
University of Kentucky, 227
University of San Francisco, 229
University of Vermont, 232
University of Virginia, 33
Urban areas
    culture of, 197, 199
    pastoral visions and, 21
    poverty in, 68

See also specific cities
*Usi e costumi, credenze e pregiudizi del
    popolo siciliano* (Pitré), 19

V
Vais, Mario Nunes, 44, 47, 49, 59, 131, 133
Valachi, Joe, 225
Valachi Papers, The (Maas), 225
Valentino, Rudolph, 164
Valvano, Jim, 229
Vanzetti, Bartolomeo, 165
Vendetta (Gambino), 224
Venturi, Robert, 189, 196, 229
Venus de' Medici, 38
Verdi Day Memorial, 130
Verona, New Jersey, 166, 193
Vespucci, Amerigo, 25
Vestris, Ronzi, 36
Vesuvius, 141
Vicious Circles (Kwitny), 224
Victor Talking Machine Company, 139, 15
Village Voice, The, 226
Vineyards, 112–113, 176–177
Virgil, 9, 12–13
Virginia, experimental agricultural colony,
    14, 31
Vittoria, Joseph V., 196, 232

W
Wages, 88, 90
Wall Street Journal, The, 224
Washington, D.C.
    D. A. (Tony) Bruno's workshop, 157
    Library of Congress, 101
    U.S. Capitol frescoes, 15, 37, 38
Washington, George, 15, 31
Waukesha, Wisconsin, 120–121
Webster, William, 224
Weitz, Hugo, 83
Welles, Sumner, 191
Westville, Connecticut, 173
White, Theodore H., 229
Williams, Ted, 204
Wilson, Woodrow, 157
Wine growers, 112–113, 176–177
Wolcott, Marjorie Post, 175–176
Wolvovitz, Ethel, 218–220, 223
Women
    home workshops, 93, 96–97
    immigrant laborers, 16
    left behind in Italy, 53, 57
    marriage as career for, 23
    National Organization of Italian-
        American Women, 232
    National Organization for Women, 22,
        229
    parish group, Boston, 129
    See also Families
"Wop," 20
Work
    education versus, 23, 167
    freedom to, 13–14
    inevitability of, 12
World War I
    Distinguished Service Cross, 150-151
    German surrender, 74
    heroes, 190
    Italians in, 46, 147, 150
World War II, 172
    air-raid warden, 192
    Allies, 190–191
    conscription for, 74
    Italian Americans and, 188–191,
        192–194, 198
    standard Italian language and, 17
    women workers during, 193
World maps, 10–11, 26

Y
Yale University, 196, 229, 232
Yard shrines, 234–235
YMCA, France, 150
Young Men's Lincoln Club, New York, 82

Z
Zabaldano, Adele, 80–81
Zappa, Frank, 211
Zembelli International, 244
Zocchi, G., 27
Zoetrope Studios, 212